THE
HISTORY OF
CONGO

THE HISTORY OF CONGO

Ch. Didier Gondola

The Greenwood Histories of the Modern Nations
Frank W. Thackeray and John E. Findling, Series Editors

Greenwood Press
Westport, Connecticut • London

Library of Congress Cataloging-in-Publication Data

Gondola, Ch. Didier.
  The history of Congo / Ch. Didier Gondola.
      p. cm.—(Greenwood histories of the modern nations, ISSN 1096-2905)
  Includes bibliographical references and index.
  ISBN 0-313-31696-1 (alk. paper)
  1. Congo (Democratic Republic)--History. I. Title. II. Series.

  DT652 .G66 2002
  967.51—dc21   2002075316

British Library Cataloguing-in-Publication Data is available.

Library of Congress Catalog Card Number: 2002075316
ISBN: 0-313-31696-1
ISSN: 1096-2905

First published in 2002

Greenwood Press, 88 Post Road West, Westport, CT 06881
An imprint of Greenwood Publishing Group, Inc.
www.greenwood.com

Printed in the United States of America

The paper used in this book complies with the
Permanent Paper Standard issued by the National
Information Standards Organization (Z39.48-1984).

10 9 8 7 6 5 4 3 2 1

For Shelumiel and Timothy

Contents

Series Foreword

he Greenwood Histories of the Modern Nations series is intended to provide
*u*dents and interested laypeople with up-to-date, concise, and analyti-
l histories of many of the nations of the contemporary world. Not since
e 1960s has there been a systematic attempt to publish a series of
*a*tional histories, and, as editors, we believe that this series will prove to
e a valuable contribution to our understanding of other countries in our
*creasingly interdependent world.

Over thirty years ago, at the end of the 1960s, the Cold War was an
*c*cepted reality of global politics, the process of decolonization was still
*progress, the idea of a unified Europe with a single currency was
*heard of, the United States was mired in a war in Vietnam, and the eco-
*mic boom of Asia was still years in the future. Richard Nixon was pres-
*ent of the United States, Mao Tse-tung (not yet Mao Zedong) ruled
*h*ina, Leonid Brezhnev guided the Soviet Union, and Harold Wilson was
*ime minister of the United Kingdom. Authoritarian dictators still ruled
*ost of Latin America, the Middle East was reeling in the wake of the Six-
*ay War, and Shah Reza Pahlavi was at the height of his power in Iran.
*learly, the past thirty years have been witness to a great deal of histori-
*l change, and it is to this change that this series is primarily addressed.

With the help of a distinguished advisory board, we have selecte nations whose political, economic, and social affairs mark them as amor the most important in the waning years of the twentieth century, and fo each nation we have found an author who is recognized as a specialist i the history of that nation. These authors have worked most cooperativ ly with us and with Greenwood Press to produce volumes that refle current research on their nation and that are interesting and informativ to their prospective readers.

The importance of a series such as this cannot be underestimated. A a superpower whose influence is felt all over the world, the Unite States can claim a "special" relationship with almost every other natio Yet many Americans know very little about the histories of the natio with which the United States relates. How did they get to be the wa they are? What kind of political systems have evolved there? What kin of influence do they have in their own region? What are the dominar political, religious, and cultural forces that move their leaders? Thes and many other questions are answered in the volumes of this series.

The authors who have contributed to this series have written con prehensive histories of their nations, dating back to prehistoric times i some cases. Each of them, however, has devoted a significant portion o the book to events of the past thirty years, because the modern era ha contributed the most to contemporary issues that have an impact on U. policy. Authors have made an effort to be as up-to-date as possible s that readers can benefit from the most recent scholarship and a narrativ that includes very recent events.

In addition to the historical narrative, each volume in this series co tains an introductory overview of the country's geography, political inst tutions, economic structure, and cultural attributes. This is designed give readers a picture of the nation as it exists in the contemporary worl Each volume also contains additional chapters that add interesting ar useful detail to the historical narrative. One chapter is a thorough chronc ogy of important historical events, making it easy for readers to follo the flow of a particular nation's history. Another chapter features bio, raphical sketches of the nation's most important figures in order humanize some of the individuals who have contributed to the historic development of their nation. Each volume also contains a comprehei sive bibliography, so that those readers whose interest has been sparke may find out more about the nation and its history. Finally, there is a cai fully prepared topic and person index.

Readers of these volumes will find them fascinating to read and useful in understanding the contemporary world and the nations that comprise it. As series editors, it is our hope that this series will contribute to a heightened sense of global understanding as we embark on a new century.

Frank W. Thackeray and John E. Findling
Indiana University Southeast

Preface and Acknowledgments

The dearth of historical surveys of African countries is striking, given that they have played and continue to play such a key role on the international scene and that they have contributed to a large extent to the capitalistic accumulation that defines today's global economy. This shortage is puzzling all the more because numerous general histories of the African continent exist, for the general public as well as for the scholar, and monographs dealing with a specific theme or issue in a given country are now abundant. There is certainly a gap to be filled.

This book attempts to fill this gap by providing a detailed historical account of one of Africa's most complex and paradoxical countries, the Democratic Republic of Congo. Complex, because Congo is a vast country, endowed with a diversity of cultures and peoples that came together within the same boundaries in a matter of a few years as a result of foreign intervention. Paradoxical, because this is a rich country, arguably one of the richest countries in the world in terms of its natural resources—a rich country where, sadly, the majority of people starve. This book has been written with these two elements in mind. Here, I seek to explore how this complex cultural and social texture and these economic paradoxes have beset Congo's political developments from the time the country fell under colonial rule to the present political imbroglio.

I would like to thank Frank W. Thackeray and John E. Findling, editors of *The Greenwood Histories of the Modern Nations*, for giving me the opportunity to embark upon this project. They, along with Greenwood's senior editors Barbara A. Rader and Kevin Ohe, did their best to see this manuscript through to completion. Argosy Publishing's project manager Morgan Halstead offered invaluable assistance in the final stages of the project. I thank them all for helping clear so many logistical hurdles in the process of producing this book. The history department at Indiana University–Purdue University at Indianapolis has provided a uniquely thriving environment that made possible the undertaking of such a project, and I most heartily thank my colleagues for their camaraderie.

My primary debt is to Crawford Young, Thomas Turner, Michael Schatzberg, Mutamba Makombo, René Lemarchand, Adam Hochschild, and other specialists of Congolese studies upon whose work I have drawn. I owe thanks particularly to John Clark, Kisangani Emizet, and François Ngolet for making available to me their publications and for pointing my attention to other bibliographical sources, which proved invaluable. When I asked them on short notice to read some segments of this book, each of them kindly obliged, offering forthright critiques and many improvements. To Charles Tshimanga I am especially grateful for his continuing friendship and assistance at crucial stages. He particularly helped with bibliographic citations by providing hard-to-find facts about a number of Congolese public figures. I have also benefited from conversations with many of my fellow countrymen that have broadened my understanding of current political and social developments in Congo. Congolese are particularly passionate about their history, and those who are not trained as professional historians still profess to have a grassroots vantage point that most scholars lack. I am particularly grateful to Faustin Ntala and Francis Didier, who kindly perused several chapters of this work and made some insightful critiques. In the early stages, the manuscript passed into the hands of Tracy Luedke, who readily sifted through the text and provided invaluable editing. I am deeply grateful for her patience and diligence. I would also like to express my gratitude to Kenny Streett, who worked tirelessly to design the maps and never lost his patience and sense of humor under pressure.

My wife Nina deserves much credit for this book as for many a project that I have been fortunate to complete in my academic career. Her unflinching optimism alleviated much of the anxiety that befell me, as it oes most authors, in writing this book. She has devoted much of her me, enthusiasm, and especially love to this particular project, and I ondly thank her. My hope is that this book will be an eye-opener to both cademics and laypeople alike who seek to understand the predicament of one of Africa's fallen giants.

Ch. Didier Gondola

Acronyms

ABAKO	Association des Bakongo (Association of Bakongo)
ABIR	Anglo-Belgian India Rubber and Exploration Company
AFDL	Alliance des Forces Démocratiques pour la Libération du Congo-Zaïre (Alliance of Democratic Forces for the Liberation of Congo-Zaire)
ANC	Armée Nationale Congolaise (Congolese National Army)
BCK	Compagnie du Chemin de Fer du Bas-Congo (Bas-Congo Railroad Company)
BMS	British Missionary Society
CELZA	Cultures Et Elevages du Zaïre (Agriculture and Animal Husbandry of Zaïre)
CIA	Central Intelligence Agency
CNL	Conseil National de Libération (National Liberation Council)
CNS	Conférence Nationale Souveraine (Sovereign National Conference)
DRC	Democratic Republic of Congo

DSP	Division Spéciale Présidentielle (Special Presidential Division)
EIC	État Indépendant du Congo (Congo Free State)
EJCSK	Église de Jésus-Christ sur Terre par le Prophète Simon Kimbangu (The Church of Jesus Christ on Earth through the Prophet Simon Kimbangu)
FAZ	Forces Armées Zaïroises (Zairean Armed Forces)
FEA	French Equatorial Africa
GDP	gross domestic product
HCB	Huileries du Congo Belge (Belgian Congo Palm Oil Company)
HCR	Haut Conseil de la République (High Council of the Republic)
IMF	International Monetary Fund
MLC	Mouvement pour la Libération du Congo (Movement for the Liberation of Congo)
MNC	Mouvement National Congolais (Congolese National Movement)
MNC/L	Mouvement National Congolais, Aile Lumumba (Congolese National Movement, Lumumba wing)
MNL	Mouvement National Lumumbiste (National Lumumbist Movement)
MONUC	Mission des Nations Unies au Congo (United Nations Mission in Congo)
MPR	Mouvement Populaire de la Révolution (Popular Movement of the Revolution)
NGO	Nongovernmental Organization
OAU	Organization of African Unity
OCA	Office des Cités Africaines (Office of African Townships)
RCD	Rassemblement Congolais pour la Démocratie (Congolese Democratic Rally)

RCD/ML	Rassemblement Congolais pour la Démocratie/ Mouvement de Libération (Congolese Rally for Democracy/Liberation Movement)
RPA	Rwandan Patriotic Army
RPF	Rwandan Patriotic Front
SAB	Société Anonyme Belge pour le Commerce du Haut Congo (Belgian Trading Company of Upper Congo)
SADC	Southern African Development Community
UDPS	Union pour la Démocratie et le Progrès Social (Union for Democracy and Social Progress)
UGEC	Union Générale des Étudiants Congolais (General Union of Congolese Students)
UMHK	Union Minière du Haut-Katanga (Mining Union of Upper Katanga)
UN	United Nations
UNAZA	Université Nationale du Zaïre (National University of Zaire)
UNITA	União Nacional para a Independêcia Total de Angola (National Union for the Total Independence of Angola)
UPDF	Ugandan People's Defence Forces
USO	Union Sacrée de l'Opposition (Opposition Sacred Union)

CURRENT AND FORMER NAMES OF PLACES

Former	Current
Alberta	Ebonda
Albertville	Kalemie
Bakwanga	Mbuji-Mayi
Banningville	Bandundu
Banzyville	Mobaye

Baudoinville	Moba
Belgian Congo	Congo
Brabanta	Mapangu
Charlesville	Djokopunda
Coquilhatville	Mbandaka
Costermanville	Bukavu
Crystal (Mountains)	Mayumbe (Mountains)
Dendale (District)	Kasavubu (District)
Elisabetha	Lukutu
Elisabethville	Lubumbashi
Jadotville	Likasi
Kalina (District)	Gombe (District)
Katanga	Shaba
Kindu-Port-Empain	Kindu
Leopold II (Lake)	Maindombe (Lake)
Leopoldville	Kinshasa
Leverville	Lusanga
Luluabourg	Kananga
Nouvelle-Anvers	Mankanza
Paulis	Isiro
Ponthierville	Ubundu
Port-Franqui	Ilebo
Renkin (District)	Matonge
Saint-Jean (District)	Lingwala (District)
Stanley (Mount)	Ngaliema (Mount)
Stanley Pool	Malebo Pool
Stanleyville	Kisangani
Thysville	Mbanza-Ngungu

Timeline of Historical Events

Ca. 2000 B.C.	The First Bantu, also called proto-Bantu, settle in the Bas-Congo and Uele regions. They arrive from the Benue area in Nigeria.
000 B.C.	Bantu-speaking peoples settle en masse in the Congo Basin as a result of a long series of migrations.
00 A.D.	The Kuba people are unified under the leadership of a mythical king known as Woot.
20–845	The Luba people are unified.
00–800	Iron and copper come into use in the Congo Basin. Archeological excavations around Lake Kissale point to the widespread use of copper and iron-smelting techniques.
275	The Kongo Kingdom emerges. It is founded by Nimi-a-Lukenie, also known as Mani Kongo (king) Ntinu Wene.
482	Portuguese explorer Diogo Cão reaches the mouth of the Congo River, initiating a long-term relationship between Europe and the Kongo Kingdom.

1491	The first Catholic missionaries arrive in the Kongo Kingdom and inaugurate a long period of evangelization that will transform Kongo into a Christian kingdom.
1500s	Nilotic peoples, including the Zande and Mangbetu, move in successive migratory waves into north and central Congo and create powerful chiefdoms. Legendary figures Kongolo and Ilunga Kalala create the Luba kingdoms. Patrilineal farming villages, governed by a divine king (*mulopwe*), constitute the nuclei of the Luba state. The Lunda Kingdom, founded by Luba chief Tshibinda Ilunga, emerges.
1506–1543	Mani Kongo Mvemba Nzinga Afonso I reigns. Under his leadership Kongo Kingdom reaches its apogee and strengthens diplomatic and economic relationships with Portugal and the Vatican.
1518	Kinu Mvemba Dom Henrique, the son of Afonso I, is consecrated bishop in Rome by Pope Leo X and becomes the first African bishop in the Catholic Church.
1600	Under the reign of Mani Kongo Alvaro II (1587–1614), maize, cassava, and other varieties of New World cereals and crops find their way into central Africa.
1600–1630	During his time in power, Nyimi (king) Shyam a Mbul a Ngwoong, a legendary Kuba figure, reorganizes the Kuba Kingdom and brings it to the height of its influence. Nyimi Shyam introduces crucial innovations such as the culture of maize and tobacco, raffia weaving, and sophisticated woodcarving techniques.
1816	British explorer Captain James Kingston Tuckey leads an expedition up to the mouth of the Congo River in the Bas-Congo region and inaugurates the era of "scientific explorations" in the central Congo Basin.
1867–1871	Dr. David Livingstone, Scottish missionary and explorer, ventures into the central Congo River Basin and reaches Lakes Mweru and Bangwelu, then Lake Tanganyika in 1869.

1871–1877   Henry Morton Stanley, a Welsh journalist commissioned to search for Livingstone, sets off on a long expedition in central Africa and meets with Livingstone at Ujiji (in present-day Tanzania) on October 27, 1871. He then continues Livingstone's exploratory expeditions with backing from the *New York Herald* and the *Daily Telegraph*. His African explorations bring him an international fame that prompts Belgium's king Leopold II to hire him with the mission of establishing trading posts and signing protectorate treaties with local chiefs along the Congo River in the name of the International Association of the Congo.

1884–1885   German Chancellor Bismarck convenes a conference of European imperialist powers in Berlin from November 15, 1884 to February 26, 1885 to settle colonial disputes. The *Berlin Act on the Congo,* signed at the conclusion of the conference, recognizes Leopold's claims to the International Association of the Congo, which soon becomes Congo Free State.

1890s   Exploitation of Congo's wealth in ivory, rubber, and other commodities begins, using mostly forced labor. In order to export these various commodities to Europe, a transportation system network is constructed.

1895   Congolese soldiers of the Force Publique stationed at Luluabourg mutiny against their European commanders. The mutiny transforms into a full-scale rebellion that spreads into central and southeast Congo and lasts until 1908.

1903–1905   Several reports made by missionaries, activists, and diplomats reveal to the international community the horrors that presided over Leopoldian Congo. Gruesome stories of mutilations, floggings, ruthless repression, and slave trading prompt an international campaign against Leopold's rule in Congo.

1908   Leopold II transfers sovereignty over the Congo Free State to Belgium. Congo Free State becomes Belgian Congo.

1921   Simon Kimbangu leads a Christian revival movement in the Bas-Congo region. Colonial repression

	decapitates the movement, which goes under-ground until 1959.
1941–1945	As a result of the Allied loss of Southeast Asia to Japan during the course of World War II, Belgian Congo becomes a principal purveyor of strategic resources to the war effort and increases its production of gold, copper, copal, tin, rubber, and palm oil to feed the Allied war machine.
1950	Bakongo urban elite found the ABAKO (led by Joseph Kasavubu), an organization dedicated to the promotion of Bakongo language and culture, which later becomes the first Congolese political party.
1956	Belgian colonial authorities agree to provide Africans with some political rights, including the right to elect mayors and mobilize within political parties. A group of Congolese elite, known as *évolués*, issues a manifesto (*le Manifeste de Conscience Africaine*) demanding a progressive transfer of power to the Africans. ABAKO rejects the manifesto and calls instead for immediate independence.
1958	Patrice Lumumba founds the Congolese National Movement (Mouvement National Congolais—MNC), which stands out as a pan-territorial nationalist party, and declares the objective of his party to achieve total independence from Belgium.
1959	In January, political demonstration in favor of independence gives way to violent riots in Leopoldville. An angry mob attacks European residents and destroys churches, schools, and hospitals. The police and the army are called in and brutally repress the rioters, killing at least one hundred Congolese and wounding more than two hundred. Not a single European is killed during the riots.
1960	As a result of the Independence Roundtable convened in Brussels, Congo becomes independent on June 30. Joseph Kasavubu and Patrice Lumumba form a coalition government and hold the post of president and prime minister, respectively.
1960–1965	Independence in the Democratic Republic of Congo is marred by civil unrest and the secession, fueled

by Belgium, of the two key provinces of Katanga and South Kasai. Belgium sends in paratroopers to occupy a number of cities. In retaliation, the Congolese government appeals to the United Nations for military and administrative assistance. In the midst of political turmoil, Kasavubu and Lumumba, who hold each other in distrust, vie to control the situation, and on July 11, Kasavubu dismisses and jails Lumumba.

961   Kept prisoner in Leopoldville, then transferred to Thysville and later to Elisabethville, Patrice Lumumba is brutally tortured and murdered on January 17 along with two of his cabinet members, Maurice M'Polo and Joseph Okito.

965   General Joseph-Désiré Mobutu stages a successful coup on November 24 and proclaims the Second Republic, with Léonard Mulamba as prime minister.

966   Mobutu dismisses Mulamba and assumes the entire control of the government. Cities with European names are conferred African names in a process that will be known in later years as *authenticité* (authenticity). The capital city, Leopoldville, becomes Kinshasa.

967   Mobutu takes up dictatorial powers and rules by decrees. He bans all political parties and creates the Popular Movement of Revolution (Mouvement Populaire de la Révolution—MPR) as Congo's sole legal party. A new constitution is promulgated that institutes the presidential regime.

970   Presidential elections are held in Congo, and Mobutu, the sole candidate, is elected. Congo also holds its first national demographic census, which shows a steady growth to 21,637,876 inhabitants.

971   Mobutu coins the concept of *authenticité*. Following this concept, he changes the name of the country from the Democratic Republic of Congo to Zaire. Zairean men are forbidden to wear Western suits and ties, and women to wear pants. Colonial or Christian names are dropped and all Zairean *citoyens* (citizens) are required to adopt an "authentic" name. Accordingly, Mobutu renames himself Mobutu Sese Seko Kuku Ngbendu wa za Banga.

1973   Under a new policy touted as Zaireanization, for-
                eign-owned businesses and properties are expropri-
                ated and turned over to Mobutu's cronies, resulting
                in economic chaos.

1975–1983   A period of economic crisis with unprecedented
                inflation follows a fall in the price of copper, whose
                imports account for 70 percent of Zaire's revenue.

1976   Zaireanization is reversed and most expropriated
                properties are returned to their foreign owners.

1977   First War of Shaba (Shaba I) occurs between March
                8 and May 28. The National Front for the
                Liberation of Congo (Front National de Libération
                du Congo—FNLC) invades from Angola the
                southeastern mineral region of Shaba with the
                objective of sparking a general uprising in the
                country. The rebellion is only defeated with the
                backing of Moroccan troops and French logistical
                support.

1978   The Second War of Shaba (Shaba II) occurs between
                May 11 and May 31. In it, the FNLC launches an
                attack from Zambia and occupies the strategic min-
                ing town of Kolwezi. The government sends armed
                forces backed by French and Belgian troops and
                recaptures the city after two weeks of intensive
                fighting.

1982   Opponents of Mobutu's one-party rule form the
                Union for Democracy and Social Progress (Union
                pour la Démocratie et le Progrès Social—UDPS),
                whose leaders are harassed and imprisoned through-
                out the 1980s. Following timid democratic reforms,
                opposition candidates participate for the first time in
                legislative elections and unseat a few incumbents.
                Thirteen representatives, including Étienne
                Tshisekedi (leader of the UDPS), attempt to form a
                dissident party and are immediately arrested.

1983–1985   Economic reforms attempt to reduce inflation and
                liberalize the economy. Foreign donors reschedule
                Zaire's debt by ten years.

1984   Mobutu is elected to a third term without
                opposition.

1986	Due to IMF austerity programs combined with growing inflation, mounting national debt, and a slump in the prices of copper, the country enters a long period of intractable economic deterioration.
1990	The U.S. Congress decides to cut direct military and economic aid to Zaire because of alleged corruption and human rights abuses by Mobutu's regime. The U.S. has backed Mobutu's regime since 1965 and supplied it with hundreds of millions of dollars in aid. In a historical speech to the nation, Mobutu promises national multiparty elections the following year and political reforms designed to restore democracy. The Third Republic is declared.
1990	The Sovereign National Conference (Conférence Nationale Souveraine—CNS) is held with the mandate of drafting a new constitution to set the stage for new democratic elections. Opposition leader Étienne Tshisekedi is named prime minister only to be fired a week later by Mobutu, spurring foreign donors to suspend aid to Zaire. Violent demonstrations erupt throughout the country.
1992	Mobutu's repeated attempts at undermining the work of the national conference are challenged by its members, who declare the conference to have sovereign powers to draw up a new constitution and legislate a multiparty system. In an act of defiance, the Sovereign National Conference elects Mobutu's longtime political foe Étienne Tshisekedi prime minister of a new transitional government.
1993	Several of Mobutu's traditional allies, including France and the United States, urge him to step down. A defiant Mobutu decides, instead, to dismiss Tshisekedi.
1994	In the aftermath of the Rwandan genocide, some 1.5 million Hutus flee Rwanda's civil war and pour across Congo's borders into refugee camps. Among them are many of the Hutu militants responsible for Rwanda's genocidal killings.
1996	Ethnic Tutsis living in eastern Zaire are deprived of Zairean citizenship and threatened with expulsion.

A growing revolt among them gives way to a full-fledged anti-Mobutu rebellion led by veteran warlord Laurent Kabila with the support of several neighboring countries. Hundreds of thousands of Hutu refugees return to Rwanda. Mobutu remains at his villa in France, undergoing treatment for prostate cancer.

1997	Under pressure from Tshisekedi's UDPS and threatened by advancing troops of Kabila's AFDL, Mobutu, already ravaged by prostate cancer, relinquishes power and flees the country. Kabila declares himself head of state and changes the country's name back to the Democratic Republic of Congo. On September 7, Mobutu dies in exile in Morocco.
1998–2000	Kabila's rule proves to be marred with uncertainty. Poverty, debt, and corruption remain rampant while the prospects of peace and democracy continue to be elusive and illusory.
2001	On January 16, President Laurent Kabila is gunned down in the presidential palace by one of his bodyguards. Later that month his son Joseph is sworn into office in replacement of his father.
2002	The Nyiragongo volcano erupts in eastern Congo on January 18, leaving dozens dead. Tongues of red, hot lava fork down to Lake Kivu, destroying in their paths several towns and the city of Goma. Hundreds of thousands of residents cross the border to seek refuge in neighboring Rwanda.

After several months of negotiations during the inter-Congolese dialogue held in Sun City, South Africa, the new government signs a peace deal with most rebel factions in April. Under the terms of the agreement, the government wins nominal control over 70 percent of the country in exchange for some forms of power sharing.

1

Introduction

As is the case for most African countries, the Democratic Republic of Congo (DRC) is a fairly recent creation. It dates from the late nineteenth century, when European nations carved up and claimed most of Africa. The fates of African societies were determined at the Berlin Conference of 1884–1885. At this conference, an ambitious King Leopold II of Belgium worked behind the scenes and grabbed for himself a territory eighty times larger than Belgium. The territory was first called Congo Free State. It was later renamed Belgian Congo, when in 1908 the king finally relinquished his personal sovereignty over the colony. Belgian rule in Congo lasted until 1960, when the country became independent and adopted the name Democratic Republic of Congo. During Mobutu's rule (1965–1997), Congo was renamed Zaire. Since independence, the country has suffered the crippling effects of its colonial legacy, despite the fact that it is regarded as one of the wealthiest countries in Africa in terms of its natural resources.

GEOGRAPHY

The Democratic Republic of Congo, formerly Zaire, is located at the center of Africa. It encompasses the entire Congo River Basin, which is the potential source of 13 percent of the world's hydroelectric power. The

Congo River Basin also contains one-third of Africa's rainforests and is home to countless species of trees (including ebony, mahogany, and teak) and more than 10,000 species of flowering plants. This vegetation plays a vital part in the Earth's hydrologic cycle and acts as a natural climate control system. A small portion of Congo's extensive tropical forests is commercially exploited, despite the difficulties caused by the lack of a transport network and facilities. Increased productivity, however, would entail considerable risk, as the development of transport facilities would present many hazards to the environment.

Congo River is the second largest river in the world in terms of volume of flowing water, exceeded only by the Amazon River of South America. Its tributaries cover an immense area, as large as the United States east of the Mississippi River. This is Africa's most extensive network of navigable waterways and a source of hundreds of different species of fish. To the north and south of the Congo River Basin lie higher plains and hills covered with a mixture of savanna grasslands and woodlands. The eastern portion of Congo is a region of highlands, bounded on the east by the Great Rift Valley, with average altitudes of 10,000–12,000 feet and some mountains as high as 16,000 feet. A constellation of lakes, Lake Albert, Lake Edward, Lake Kivu, Lake Tanganyika, and Lake Mweru, forms the eastern borders with Uganda, Rwanda, Burundi, Tanzania, and Zambia. In the west, a narrow coastline of approximately twenty-three miles provides Congo with a precious opening to the Atlantic Ocean (see Map 1).

Congo's tropical climates include several variations. There is a long rainy season in the Congo River Basin, which receives the highest rates of rainfall in the world. The southern uplands experience alternating wet and dry seasons. In the eastern part of the country, there are tropical highlands. Temperatures average 25°C on the western coast and between 23°C and 25°C in the northern portion of the Basin, including northern Katanga, Kasai, the Kinshasa area, and Lower Congo. In the elevated and mountainous areas of the east, average temperatures fall below 20°C due to altitude. In general, the highest temperatures are recorded in most parts of the country in March and April, while July is the coolest month. Katanga, in the south, records the most dramatic variation in temperatures with an average of 24°C in October and 17°C in July. Average annual rainfall varies between 1200 millimeters and 2200 millimeters. The highest rainfall is recorded in the central Basin and the lowest in the highlands of Katanga and Kivu.

The country's fauna and flora are some of the richest and most varied in the world. Some species, however, are on their way to extinction due environmental degradation, deforestation, human encroachment, and poaching, especially in the eastern part of the country. In some areas, the natural habitat is shrinking at a rapid pace. Some endangered species now find themselves in fragile environments adjoining dense human settlements. Because some species are only found in Congo, efforts have been made recently to protect some of them. One animal found only in Congo is the okapi, which, in the early 1900s, was one of the last mammals to be discovered by the scientific community and today is one of the world's rarest animals in captivity. Other animals commonly found in Congo include lions, leopards, elephants, giraffes, rhinoceros, mountain gorillas and other primates, exotic birds of all sorts, and many types of reptiles and insects.

Map 1. Congo: Topography

Congo is potentially one of the richest mining countries in Afri. Huge deposits of diamonds, copper, and cobalt account for a major p(tion of the country's GDP. Although these mining industries have t potential to be the largest in Africa, they have been hindered in th development by various factors such as the unstable political clima corruption, smuggling, and a shortage of capital. The country is s Africa's biggest diamond producer by volume, producing 24 metric to in 1998. But copper, cobalt, and zinc production have plummeted sir the mid-1980s, totaling in 1998 only 35,000 tons, 4,000 tons, and 1,2 tons, respectively, compared with 437,000, 12,000, and 55,100 tons in 19.

Congo has an estimated population of 46 million people, growing an annual rate of 3.4 percent. It is less populous than its eastern neighbo of the Great Lakes region (Rwanda, Burundi, and Uganda) but has higher population density when compared to neighboring Republic Congo (Congo-Brazzaville), Gabon, and Central African Republic. least one-third of the country's population lives in major cities, and least half of this urban population resides in the capital.

GOVERNMENT AND POLITICS

During Belgian rule in Congo, the state represented a powerful instr ment of foreign hegemony. The colony was ruled from Belgium, a important political decisions were made in the royal palace and colon offices in Brussels rather than in Congo. In the colony itself, a network bureaucrats, administrators, soldiers, missionaries, and company ager enforced a political system known as *Bula Matari*.[1] This political syst(was reminiscent of the apartheid regime implemented by white settl in South Africa. Congolese were deprived of political rights, and m(decisions concerning their welfare were made in a paternalistic way wi out their participation or consent.

Postcolonial political history in Congo has witnessed the successi of three constitutional regimes: the First Republic (1960–1965), (Second Republic (1965–1990), a democratization period known as (Transition (1990–1997), and the Third Republic (since 1997). After inc pendence, the country experienced a civil war (1960–1965) marked the disintegration of the administrative system and the collapse of (state. In 1965, General Mobutu took control of the failing governm(and embarked on a long reign of dictatorship. He set a pattern of au(cratic rule not only in Congo but in the rest of sub-Saharan Africa well. In order to secure his grip over the people of Congo, Mobutu us the juridical and institutional system left in place by the colonizers, and he attempted to replicate the attributes of the *Bula Matari* state. He ran the government single-handedly as a personal fiefdom, using the national treasury as his checkbook. He promoted cronyism, nepotism, and corruption in all sectors of society. Mobutu introduced the one-party system into Congolese politics when he created the Popular Revolutionary Movement (Mouvement Populaire de la Révolution—MPR) shortly after achieving power. The MPR was the sole legal political party that all Congolese were coerced into joining, and it was fused with the administrative structure and the state itself. This system would last until 1990, when a beleaguered Mobutu announced a move toward multiparty democracy. In the aftermath of Mobutu's announcement, numerous opposition as well as pro-government political parties sprang up and promoted a seemingly democratic system. But in 1997, Laurent-Désiré Kabila, a former warlord, toppled Mobutu's longtime regime, abolished the constitution, and reestablished an anachronistic one-party system. Congo today is once again in the political situation that prevailed during its first years of independence. The central government is maintained by only a semblance of authority and legitimacy and is besieged by various rebel factions that hold sway over most of the northern and eastern provinces (see Map 2).

ECONOMY

It has been said that "Congo is a rich country where people starve." This has been true for the country since the late 1970s and is even more the case in recent years. The country is rich in natural resources, including vast mineral deposits of gold, copper, and cobalt. It also possesses arable land in abundance and enjoys a climatic and hydrographic environment suitable for a thriving agricultural sector. However, it counts today among the poorest countries in the world. The majority of the population lives in poverty and finds it hard to satisfy the basic needs of their everyday lives. Since colonial times, the country's economy has relied heavily on the export of a number of commodities, including diamonds, cobalt, copper, rubber, and coffee. This emphasis on the export of raw materials has exposed Congo's economy to the fluctuations of the international market. In 1975, for instance, Congo experienced a major crisis when the price of copper, which had steadily increased in the international market since 1967, suddenly collapsed. This left the country in a catastrophic financial situation. Copper had accounted for 70 percent of state income, and the collapse of the copper market dramatically affected the state's ability to repay its national debt and fund various programs. It also affected the access of average Congolese to food, consumer goods, and health care and other services. In 1980 and 1981, the price of copper recovered briefly but then plummeted again the following year. This vulnerability is the defining characteristic of the Congolese economy and accounts for the continuous instability of Congo's economic situation. Another negative consequence of the emphasis on exports is the neglect of the agricultural sector. Instead of producing its own goods, Congo relies on imported foodstuffs and consumer commodities, which are in high demand in the growing urban centers, especially in the capital, Kinshasa. In the early 1990s, the economic situation worsened and Congo's economy, in spite of its important mineral output, verged on collapse. As a result, the population became increasingly dependent on the informal sector, which is estimated to be at least three times the size of the official economy.

Congo's GDP (gross domestic product) is a significant indicator of its economic decline, as are other indicators such as national debt and rate of inflation. The GDP's growth has been negative since the 1970s, dropping 3.5 percent per year since 1975. When Mobutu's long reign ended in 1997, the GDP per capita was estimated at 65 percent less than that of 1960, the year the country became independent. Inflation has grown to unprecedented heights since the late 1970s, reaching 265 percent in 1990. External debt was estimated at $15 million in 1997, ten times the value of Congo's total exports. Congolese households are affected by continually rising consumer prices, which skyrocketed by 4,687 percent between 1972 and 1991.

When the new government of Laurent-Désiré Kabila came to power, most Congolese were hoping for substantial reforms that would target key economic sectors. Kabila's government instituted a tight fiscal policy that initially curbed inflation and currency depreciation. However, these small gains were not significant enough to jump-start a stagnant economy, and they were quickly reversed when rebellion in the eastern part of the country began in August 1998. The war has considerably crippled the government by reducing its revenues, which came from regions now under the control of rebel factions. As a consequence there has been an increase in external debt and a decrease in foreign business investment in the country. Congo seems to have gone back to the darkest years of Mobutu's regime. Inflation is on the rise, corruption is rampant, and all administrative and economic structures suffer from a lack of resources.

The absence of a stable government, shortage of financial resources, and lack of transparency in government economic policy continue to inhibit economic recovery and growth.

Map 2. Congo: Political Subdivisions

SOCIAL AND CULTURAL CONTEXT

With more than 220 different languages identified within its borders, Congo is one of the most ethnically diverse countries in Africa. Major languages spoken by large sections of the population include Kikongo, Tshiluba, Swahili, and Lingala. Kikongo is spoken in the Lower Congo as well as in most of the southern part of neighboring Congo-Brazzaville and the northern part of Angola. Tshiluba is the language of the Luba people, who make up most of the population of both Kasai regions and are also found in Katanga. Tshiluba has also made some inroads in Kinshasa, the capital of the country, with the recent migration of Luba groups. Swahili, a language widely used in the Great Lakes region of East Africa, in countries such as Kenya, Uganda, and Tanzania, is the lingua franca in eastern Congo. Lingala provides a common cultural ground to the growing urban population of Kinshasa, where the language is universally spoken.

Although important in the way people identify themselves, traditional ethnicity no longer plays a dominant role in the lives of Congolese. This is largely because of the social and political disturbances most people have experienced since the Mobutu era. Prolonged periods of oppression and poverty have been the lot of most Congolese since independence. These experiences and the survival strategies that have evolved out of them have forged new identities and coalesced into new allegiances that often supersede ethnicity. However, there are other social categories that sharply divide Congolese society today. These divisions are one of the most significant aspects of Mobutu's legacy. During more than three decades of autocratic rule, Mobutu created an artificial elite class that derived its wealth from presidential largesse and gave its unconditional support to his regime. This group of people used the state, with Mobutu's approval, to advance their personal economic interests rather than to create a thriving business sector or a civil society. This co-opting of the state for the interests of a few left the majority of Congolese, who were landless peasants, workers, low-ranking civil servants, and the mass of unemployed, to rely on the informal sector for survival. Toward the end of Mobutu's regime, the social gap between the former group and the latter widened to such an extent that it burst into open conflict. There were riots in 1991 and 1993 when Kinshasa's poor went on a looting rampage, targeting elite properties.

Congolese society is also divided between a pauperized urban mass and a poor rural population. Seven out of ten Congolese live in the countryside, most without electricity, roads, transportation, or running water. Their livelihoods derive from intensive agriculture on lands that surround the villages where they reside. Although a few urban centers existed prior to Belgian colonial rule, urbanization in Congo came with colonization. In precolonial times, Kinshasa, today the nation's capital and the largest city, consisted of clusters of large villages inhabited by an estimated 30,000 residents at its peak. This number increased more than tenfold by the 1950s. Today, Kinshasa is inhabited by nearly 8 million people, and it is one of the largest metropolises south of the Sahara Desert. Kinshasa was by no means the only urban center to grow after the 1930s. Between 1940 and 1970, the populations of all urban centers (including Lubumbashi, Kananga, Mbuji-Mayi, and Kisangani) increased by a factor of ten. Growth has steadily continued since then, with annual growth rates of 4 to 5 percent in the 1980s. Today, 40 percent of the population is classified as urban, up from 30 percent in 1970 and 34 percent in 1980. More than one-third of all city dwellers live in Kinshasa alone.

This demographic change is the result of many factors, including the concentration of resources in the urban areas, the civil war following independence in 1960, and, more recently, the decline of standards of living. This decline has more sharply affected rural inhabitants than city dwellers and has attracted scores of rural inhabitants to the city.

The family remains an important social structure in Congo, and recent economic chaos has solidified family networks. Most Congolese belong to a patriarchal family within an extended kin group. It is not uncommon for members of the extended family to live under the same roof. Congolese continue to view family as a large and interdependent network of close and distant relatives that serves various social, cultural, and economic functions. Heads of household and breadwinners are expected to take care of the needs not only of members of their nuclear families but also of distant family members, some of whom may live in a remote village or in another city. Young Congolese who reside abroad, particularly in Europe or North America, are among the migrant populations with the highest rates of remittance. In fact, cash remittances from Europe and North America to Congo account for a large portion of the daily subsistence of many families who otherwise would not be able to make ends meet. However, family life in Congo has changed. Many families have had to adjust to modern urban life and the deterioration of social conditions in cities. Before the 1980s, polygamy (which continues in some rural areas) was a common practice in the urban milieu. The polygamous husband lived with his first wife, also called the senior wife, but would frequently visit his additional wife or wives and children. Polygamy in Congolese cities was practiced by a majority of men regardless of their social status; that is, it was not exclusive to the urban bourgeoisie. The decreased standard of living and the progress of AIDS awareness programs have caused many urbanites to distance themselves from this practice. City dwellers have embraced monogamy as an economic arrangement better suited to worsening economic and social conditions.

The majority of Congolese adhere to the Christian faith. Nearly half of the population is affiliated with the Catholic Church. Another 25 percent belong to Protestant denominations, and as many as 16 percent are Kimbanguists. Muslims and followers of traditional African religions are the minority in a country with a long history of Christian missionary activity. As with ethnicity, affiliation to religious organizations is situational. Many Congolese may seek concurrently the assistance of traditional healers, modern medicine, and Christian prayer groups when faced with illness. A store owner who patronizes the Catholic Church may resort to both Catholic and African traditional rituals to ensure success and ward off potential thieves.

Religious life has experienced a recent revival, which has had political consequences. The various churches that have been competing to attract followers since the late 1980s have encouraged the emergence of civil society in Congo. Indeed, Christian independent churches were among the most vocal and active in opposing Mobutu's dictatorship in the 1990s. In early 1992, Mobutu decided to disband the Sovereign National Conference (Conférence Nationale Souveraine—CNS), an assembly whose main task was to create a new constitution and organize democratic elections. In response to this decision, strong opposition mounted among Kinshasa's independent churches. On February 16, 1992, thousands of church members took their grievances to the streets of the capital in what was dubbed by its organizers as the "March of Hope" (Marche de l'Espoir). Marchers held banners demanding the reopening of the CNS, and they chanted songs against violence and dictatorship. The peaceful march ended in a bloodbath when the army intervened and gunned down dozens of demonstrators. The March of Hope has since been held up as a major turning point in the relations between church and state. It was also an event that precipitated the end of Mobutu's regime. Starting in the late 1980s, political support from Christian organizations had played a crucial role in helping Mobutu's regime to maintain its popularity among some sections of the population. The Catholic Church especially had turned a blind eye to human rights abuses and had collaborated with the regime. In return, Mobutu had offered political and financial support and had banned all other independent churches that could have competed with the Catholic Church. The Kimbanguist Church, an African Christian church with a history of resistance against colonialism and a stronghold of the Bakongo people, also capitulated to Mobutu's regime and helped Mobutu garner the support of the Bakongo people. But after events such as the March of Hope, the church began to distance itself from the government.

Many of the newer Congolese cultural forms are a blend of both traditional and modern styles. Congolese popular music offers a good example of this blending. Originating in the urban context of colonial Kinshasa, Congolese popular music combines Western musical instruments such as the accordion and the electric guitar with traditional instruments, such as the *likembe* (a small keyboard played with the thumbs) and the *tam tam*. This genre owes much to various musical styles, including West African highlife, brought to Kinshasa by Nigerians, Ghanaians, Liberians, and Dahomeans who held clerical positions in some of the largest companies; Cuban rumba, which found its way to Kinshasa in the 1930s; *biguines* of the French Antilles, a style introduced by soldiers from Martinique who arrived in nearby Brazzaville, then the capital of De Gaulle's France Libre; French *guinguettes* and love songs of the 1930s and 1940s; religious choirs; scout songs; military parades; and traditional African rhythms.

Two generations of musicians contributed to the emergence of what is commonly called Congolese rumba. Antoine Wendo gave his name to the first generation of musicians, who are known as musicians of *tango ya ba Wendo*, "the era of the Wendos." They composed and performed as early as 1942 and reached the height of their fame during the early 1950s, thanks to the establishment of recording studios in Kinshasa. The era of the second generation of musicians is considered the golden age of Congolese music, whose influence spread beyond Congo and Africa. The formation of the band African Jazz by Joseph Kabasele in 1951 and the emergence a few years later of its rival, Ok Jazz (set up by a group of young Congolese musicians from Kinshasa and Brazzaville, including François Luambo, also known as "Franco"), marked the beginning of this *siècle d'or*. This period continued until 1970, when the Congolese musician Pascal Tabu (Rochereau) performed at Olympia Theater in Paris. Today, a host of talented artists bring Congolese rumba to the international music scene. Many of these musicians have moved outside of the country to seek fame and recognition. Kinshasa is no longer the center of musical production it once was, but it has remained a breeding ground for lesser-known talents. The most famous musicians, such as Papa Wemba and Kofi Olomide, pursue their musical activities in Europe and increasingly cater to a diasporic audience rather than the Congolese market at home.

Among the sports that attract youth, soccer remains the most popular. Soccer has always generated extraordinary enthusiasm among Congolese since its introduction at the beginning of the colonial period. This popularity also reflects the absence of equipment and amenities needed to practice other sports. Teams of young people play soccer barefoot with homemade balls and goalie posts on street corners throughout Congolese cities. Soccer is so popular in Congo that when the national team clinches a slot in the World Cup or in the African Cup, the government makes it a state affair.

In recent years there has been a growing production of literary works in Congo. It is now possible to enjoy novels and plays from Congolese authors published in the country. Dance clubs are the main entertainment venues for nightlife in Congolese cities. Imported television shows and programs offer Congolese a window on Western culture. Satellite dishes are a common feature of the urban landscape, and Congolese watch news from CNN or French and Belgian channels and tune in to the latest episodes of American soap operas and TV shows.

Western cultures and values influence a growing portion of the population. However, people remain attached to traditional cultural norms regarding solidarity, respect for elders, extended family loyalty, and gender roles. Despite women's gains in status through education and commerce, Congolese society remains very patriarchal and women are still subjected to male dominance. They are generally more affected by the economic recession than men and have less access to formal economic instruments such as banks and credit. For these reasons, the informal sector in Congo is largely female. Women organize informal lending institutions (known as *likelemba* in Lingala) in order to get credit and accumulate savings, rather than seeking the assistance of formal institutions. *Likelemba* has helped some women to rise to comfortable financial positions and become the main breadwinners in their extended families. Women's social and economic success has yet to extend to the sphere of politics, in which they still constitute only a small fraction of the players.

HEALTH AND EDUCATION

One of the most critical consequences of the country's economic chaos is the collapse of the state-run health care system. The most potent symbol of this failure is the country's public hospitals, where patients have to bring in their own medicines and, in some instances, to share beds and sheets with other patients. This has created a situation in which access to health care is reserved for the wealthier members of the population, who can afford the expensive private health care system. AIDS, malaria, trypanosomiasis (sleeping sickness), and recurrent epidemics of cholera threaten the ability of a population already weakened by malnutrition and poor standards of living to stay alive and healthy. As a result, destitute patients increasingly enlist the help of traditional healers and prayer groups. AIDS, besides causing loss of life and decline in life expectancy (estimated at forty-seven years in 1994), has had a profound impact on the general well-being of the economy and the society.

From the early days of the colonial era, education in Congo has been imbued with Western values and principles. During the colonial era, education remained in the hands of the powerful Catholic Church, which sought above all to transform Congolese into faithful Catholics and obedient subjects. The Belgian colonial system was paternalistic and attempted to deprive natives of not only their land but also their culture. Colonial educational policy was geared to systematically suppressing the kinds of educational experiences out of which independent thinking might grow. Accordingly, academic training provided Congolese with nothing more than a veneer of moral education based on Catholic principles and the technical skills necessary to create a lower middle class. In line with this policy, in 1954 Belgian colonizers established the first university in Congo, University of Lovanium, located in the hills of Kimuenza, fifteen miles outside of Kinshasa. The Catholic administrators, backed by the colonial government, argued that Congolese were not yet ready for higher education. They barred the few qualified Congolese from studying law, forcing them to take one or two years of pre-university study. After independence, education remained centered on Western values and pedagogy. In spite of Mobutu's policy of "authenticity" (that is, the return to African values), French continued to be emphasized as the language of education at the expense of African languages, and Catholic schools are still predominant to this day. Since independence, the number of schools has increased, although enrollment remains relatively low: 78 percent for primary schools and 23 percent for secondary schools in 1990. The adult literacy rate (ability to read and write French) was estimated at 72 percent in 1992. During Mobutu's long reign, university students were amongst the most vocal opponents of his regime, and Mobutu repeatedly tried to muffle their grievances by means of his strong-arm policies. Universities were regularly closed, sometimes for more than a whole academic year, and dissent by students as well as professors was violently suppressed. Confrontation between Mobutu's regime and Lovanium students climaxed on June 4, 1969, when a peaceful student march ended in a bloodbath after the army intervened. The following year, students held a demonstration to commemorate the first anniversary of this massacre. The military once again intervened to disperse the crowd. In the aftermath of these demonstrations, Mobutu closed down the university and had most students rounded up and enrolled in forced military service for a year. Mobutu was notorious for using various Machiavellian means to stifle opposition from students and professors.

HISTORY

The precolonial history of Congo includes a diversity of social entities. These include segmentary, small-scale groups of hunters and gatherers in the northeast of the country, centralized chiefdoms of the savannas, powerful Luba and Lunda empires on the Kasai plateau, and the Kongo Kingdom on the Atlantic coast. Even among the so-called stateless societies, there was some form of political organization. Not all groups organized highly complex polities; some were based upon a single family. But they all indicate the development of political hierarchies in order to solve the problems that every community encounters. Archaeological excavations point to the development of political organization as early as the beginning of the ninth century A.D. Based on copper and wooden artifacts found in northern Katanga, archaeologists have conjectured that several groups in ancient Congo developed centralized political units around the end of the first millennium A.D.

Political organization in the savanna grasslands was based on chiefdoms, as low demographic densities in these areas prevented the organization of a more centralized political entity. The chiefdom was composed of several villages, with the elder of all village chiefs assuming the role of *primus inter pares*. The creation of a political structure above the village level was motivated in many cases by disputes over land between rival villages. A chief could act in arbitration to prevent such conflicts from occurring and to cultivate a sense of belonging to a community. Once a chief was chosen by all the villages, his clan automatically became noble. The chosen clan retained the chiefship unless provision was made to rotate among the villages. The chief had to command respect and display the wisdom of maturity. He also had to demonstrate the ability to judge equitably and ensure the cohesion of the community of villages. All the villages located within the jurisdiction of the chiefdom were subject to paying an annual tribute to confirm their allegiance. Generally, tribute consisted of game, crops, and other foodstuffs. Sometimes villages would bring a more noble tribute, such as elephant tusks or tails, leopard teeth or skin, ostrich feathers, or slaves, all symbols of prestige and power.

The chiefdom was the most common political structure before the emergence of kingdoms and empires. When they occurred, kingdoms did not obliterate chiefdoms, which continued to exist independently or as tributary provinces within a more centralized kingdom or empire. These later and more elaborate state formations differed from the chiefdoms in many respects. Kingdoms were more ambitious in their territorial expansion and more explicit in their political centralization. In addition, they always encompassed various ethnic groups, as opposed to the chiefdoms, which in most cases were ethnically homogenous. Kingdoms were less the political embodiment of ethnic identities than the manifestation of a political project that transcended ethnicity. This was the case for the Kongo Kingdom, which in addition to Kongo people also incorporated Mbundu and Besi-Ngombe people. It was also the case for the Kuba Kingdom, known for uniting within its borders Kuba, Luba, Kete, Mongo, and members of other ethnic groups. Rather than ethnic homogeneity, it was ethnic diversity that provided the demographic and cultural dynamics that helped some chiefdoms to expand into full-fledged kingdoms.

Another difference between chiefdoms and kingdoms lay in the nature of the power held by the rulers. The precolonial king was vested with far more power over the lives of his subjects. Not only did he represent absolute power as supreme judge and legislator, but he also embodied the spirit of the people. Royal ideology endowed the kingship with supernatural or magical attributes. The king was the link between the visible and the invisible worlds, between the community of the living and the supernatural sphere of the supreme creator and spirits, including the spirits of ancestors who were believed to bequeath protection to the community. By virtue of his divine attributes, he was far above common humanity and commanded respect and even reverence. Unlike the chief in the segmentary societies of the rainforest zone, the king maintained his power and ensured the loyalty of subordinate chiefs through a well-organized administrative network. Typically, power radiated from the capital, the seat of royal authority, to the outer provinces. This was accomplished by means of an efficient hierarchical system. Provincial chiefs and local clan heads assumed the role of governors and exercised authority on behalf of the king. In addition to the administrative system, the king could always count on the loyalty of a large military force, which acted to maintain peace, suppress internal plots when they occurred, acquire new territories by conquest, and safeguard the integrity of the borders. This theocratic system, sometimes referred to as divine kingship, provided order, stability, and economic prosperity in most areas where it arose. With the exception of the Kongo Kingdom, most of these kingdoms rarely developed economic and political relations with long-distance partners. Instead their economies were based on agriculture, crafts, local trade, and a tributary system.

By the late 1800s, the power of these political entities was being gradually undermined and would soon be totally obliterated by the intrusion of new actors, "Arabs" in the east and Europeans in the west. For over three centuries, Europeans (mostly Portuguese) had been slave trading on the Atlantic coast. They interfered with the internal affairs of coastal kingdoms (Kongo and Loango) and fueled internecine wars in order to ensure the continual flow of captives to the coast. By the late 1700s, Europe's view of the transatlantic slave trade had changed along with its new industrial economy. Africa was no longer viewed as a bottomless reservoir of slaves for the plantations of the New World. Instead, Africa was viewed as an untapped source of raw materials for European industries and the target of Europeans' God-given mission to spread the gospel of civilization. But while the slave trade was slowly dying down on the Atlantic coast, it intensified on the Indian Ocean coast in the hands of the "Arabs" who controlled the three main routes that conveyed captives from the interior to the coast. The first route, in the south, connected the area around Lake Nyassa to Kilwa. The second linked Lake Tanganyika to Bagamoyo. A third route cut across the hills of the Lake Victoria area to reach Mombassa. "Arab" traders had revived these three routes in the 1820s to meet the growing demand for African captives triggered by European slave traders. The British had posted numerous navy patrols along the Atlantic coast to enforce the abolition of the trade. Therefore, many European slave traders ventured into the waters of the Indian Ocean to purchase captives from "Arabs," most of whom were Swahili-speaking Africans from the east coast of Africa who used Arab-style dress and practiced Islam.

Ironically, one of the driving motivations behind Belgian king Leopold II's increasing interest in the Congo Basin was a purported desire to put an end to what colonial propaganda depicted as the "practices of dreadful Arab slave-traders." The Indian Ocean slave trade had indeed carved a wide swath of terror and misery through the eastern half of the Congo Basin. But King Leopold II's attitude toward this trade was clearly predicated more on his growing desire to acquire territories in the region than on concerns for its inhabitants. Toward this end, he hired and dispatched to Congo the most famous European "explorer" of the time, the Welsh-born journalist John Rowlands, known worldwide as Henry Morton Stanley. In 1871, Stanley had made a name for himself by trekking for more than eight months into the interior of central Africa to find Dr. David Livingstone. Livingstone was the famed British physician and missionary who traveled across Africa for three decades starting in the 1840s, becoming the first white man to cross the continent from coast to coast. Many in Europe had given Livingstone up for dead by the time Stanley went looking for him. Finding Livingstone well and alive in "darkest Africa" earned Stanley instant fame in Europe. In the early 1880s, he ventured to Congo under the auspices of Leopold's International Association of the Congo. He was sent to make treaties with local chiefs, who granted Leopold huge territories within the Congo Basin. African chiefs signed their land over to Leopold, some for almost nothing, others, according to Stanley's account, in exchange for "an ample supply of fine clothes, flunkey coats, and tinsel-braided uniforms, with a rich assortment of divers marketable wares . . . not omitting a couple of bottles of gin." Most chiefs had not seen the written word before marking an X on the French document that Stanley put before their eyes. Many thought they were agreeing to nothing more than a pact of friendship. Needless to say, none of them intended to give up freely and of their own accord, for themselves and their heirs and successors forever, "the sovereignty and all sovereign and governing rights to all their territories,"[2] including the exclusive rights to collecting tolls, hunting game, fishing, and mining, to a king they had never heard of. Nevertheless, by the time Stanley returned from his African mission in June 1884, he had secured for his royal employer the entire Congo Basin and staked out one of the largest and wealthiest African territories.

At the Berlin Conference of 1884–1885, European greed for African land took on gargantuan proportions. King Leopold was already in a strong position to bargain with his European rivals and was determined to claim and defend his legal rights to the Congo Basin. The conference ended in February 1885 with Leopold's representatives winning for him the right to create and own his personal domain in the heart of Africa. Congo Free State (État Indépendant du Congo—EIC) was born.

Congo under the harrowing reign of Leopold II has been aptly described, following Maurice Hennessy, as the "devil's paradise." During his twenty years of reign as the supreme legislative and executive authority in Congo Free State, Leopold never set foot in his tropical kingdom. Nevertheless, his presence haunted even the remotest villages and claimed the lives of millions of Congolese. Often his decisions regarding his colony were driven by an insatiable lust for wealth and grandeur. Leopold's rule over Congo was so brutal that it prompted the other European colonial powers to orchestrate an international campaign to end his reign of terror. Under Leopold, Congolese were deprived of any legal rights and subjected to the will of abusive colonial officials and companies acting on behalf of the Belgian king. Leopold wanted Congo's wealth at all costs, even if it meant reducing the population to virtual slavery. His system of exploitation was based on forced labor and taxation: Villagers were forced to work in order to pay taxes to Leopold's tax collectors. For the most part, this forced labor was managed by large concessionary companies, which were given ample leeway to administer justice and police the population. Their activities in the early years of Congo Free State involved the collection of wild rubber and ivory. These activities took Congolese villagers away from farm work and created an endemic state of famine during much of the Leopoldian period. Flogging by local officers was customary, as was hand and foot mutilation for those who failed to comply with the colonists' demands. Whole villages, including women and children, were wiped out because the inhabitants had failed to supply their quota of rubber or had fought back against the regime. Barbarism and tyranny were the rule, not the exception. Although it is difficult to assess the exact toll of this often forgotten genocide, Leopold's reign in Congo was responsible for millions of deaths and for a demographic crisis that plagued the country during most of the colonial period. During his reign in Congo, Leopold contracted from both Belgian private institutions and the state loans that he never repaid.

The Belgian parliament finally voted to annex Congo out of embarrassment. Belgium also hoped that annexation would allay international indignation at the mounting evidence of mass murders in Congo. Thus, in 1908, Congo changed hands, officially becoming a colony of Belgium and not the private property of one monarch. Belgian rule in Congo departed somewhat from Leopold's vicious methods. However, to use Adam Hochschild's image, Leopold's ghost lingered over the colony for many years after its acquisition by Belgium.

For fifty years, undisturbed by international opinion, Belgium followed a path of economic development and social prosperity based on isolating Congo from the outside world. "Benevolent paternalism" was the expression used to justify Belgian exploitation of this rich colony, which was eighty times the size of Belgium. Belgium pursued both a capitalistic and a philanthropic project: to profit from Congo and to bring civilization and progress to its inhabitants. To accomplish this, the Belgian state, the companies, and the church, what can be termed the "colonial trilogy," worked unabatedly and in perfect unison. Propaganda helped to spread the colonial gospel, especially in the years after World War II when Belgian paternalism came under sharp criticism by many observers. Hence, Governor General Ryckmans could write in his memoirs, "Rule in order to serve. . . . This is the sole excuse for colonial conquest; it is also its complete justification. To serve Africa—that means to civilize her."[3]

Congolese under Belgian colonialism were probably well off when compared to other colonial subjects in other territories. They received many benefits in terms of housing conditions, wages, health services and more generally access to Western material culture. The welfare state and the benevolent colonial companies ensured, with the support of the Catholic missions, the well-being and moral health of each Congolese. They provided him with free health care from the moment he was born until his death and subsidized his housing or provided generous loans for house building. However, the largesse of the state did not come without a price, and many Congolese resented the restrictions that were placed upon them. They were forbidden to consume wine and other local alcoholic beverages such as palm wine. They could not move from one province to another without authorization. A curfew was imposed upon them every night in their African quarters, where no white was allowed after sunset. Worst of all, the Congolese elite, carefully groomed and coached by Belgian missionaries and educators, was cut off from the rest of the world thanks to colonial propaganda and censorship. Political rights, freedom of expression, and freedom of the press were out of the question, and Congolese were carefully advised against exercising them. As a result, the Congolese elite developed a certain loyalty to the Belgian colonizers and adhered, with few exceptions, to the colonial gospel until it was shattered by the events that led to independence.

Belgium ignored Congolese desires for reforms and held steadfastly onto its colony. In January 1960, however, the Belgians were forced to retreat and to implement a timetable that would eventually lead to independence. At the time the Belgians made this decision, they were fully aware that not a single Congolese had been trained as an administrator, lawyer, judge, or medical doctor. They had ruled their colony with the firm conviction that it would remain under their control forever. When it was compelled to relinquish power, Belgium could barely accept the loss of such a profitable territory. Therefore, the move to independence was marked by unpreparedness and insincerity.

The years that followed Independence Day (June 30, 1960) can be best described as the rebirth of *Bula Matari* from its ashes. The newly independent country was immediately engulfed by a civil war that lasted until 1965, when Colonel Joseph-Désiré Mobutu came to power by means of a CIA-backed coup. Congo then began a descent into chaos under Mobutu's protracted rule between 1965 and 1997. The first years of his regime were marked by a drive for personal ascendancy over the state, which was achieved through nepotism. He appointed his cronies to key positions in order to control the entire power structure, while suppressing opposition and dissenting opinions. Once his autocratic rule was secured and all opposition stifled, Mobutu endeavored to siphon off state revenues. His Western backers turned a blind eye to the plight of the Congolese people. Through corruption, personal ambition, and deliberate mismanagement, he accumulated a personal fortune that was estimated at its peak to be twice as much as Congo's external debt.

Mobutu's regime ended in 1997. As the troops of Laurent-Désiré Kabila's Alliance of Democratic Forces for the Liberation of Congo-Zaire (Alliance des Forces Démocratiques pour la Libération du Congo-Zaïre—AFDL) were closing in on the capital, Mobutu found himself abandoned by his Western allies when he needed them most. He chose to flee the country. His era finally came to a close on September 7, 1997 when he died of prostate cancer in Morocco, where his long-time friend King Hassan II had granted him political asylum. The news of Mobutu's death was greeted in Congo with indifference as people were striving to size up the new regime that had ousted him.

CIVIL WAR AND POLITICAL UNREST

Mobutu's downfall led to what some observers have dubbed "Africa's First World War." As in the 1960s, the failure to bring multiparty democracy to Congo fueled a widespread conflict and the partition of the country among different rival military factions. Soon after taking over, President Kabila no longer controlled the entire country. Most of the western and northeastern areas fell into the hands of rebel groups whose declared objective was to overthrow his failing and beleaguered government. In fact, except for a few cosmetic changes, such as issuing a new currency and changing the name of the country from Zaire to Congo, Kabila's government was not able to fulfill the expectations of large sections of the population. After Mobutu's demise, most Congolese were hoping that the new government would focus on jump-starting the economy and reviving the fledgling democratic process that Mobutu had stalled. Kabila did neither of these things but instead continued to squander the country's resources. In a move designed to allow his government to rule without opposition, he banned all other political parties, including those, such as Étienne Tshisekedi's Union for Democracy and Social Progress (Union pour la Démocratie et le Progrès Social—UDPS), which had vigorously fought Mobutu's regime since the early 1980s.

Taking advantage of Congo's internal troubles, neighboring African countries rushed in, taking sides with either the "legal" government or with rebel groups. As a result, Congo is now one of the biggest battlefields in Africa's postcolonial history. There are six outside states (Rwanda, Burundi, Angola, Uganda, Zimbabwe, and Namibia) fighting inside the country. The various groups involved are battling for a bewildering number of reasons, including the lure of Congo's mineral resources, hegemonic motives, and the desire to create buffer zones in Congo. Kabila's military and political victory in 1997 had only been possible with the assistance of Rwandan troops. In the aftermath of the 1994 genocide in Rwanda, these troops were determined to topple Mobutu's regime and install a friendly government in Kinshasa. Rwanda's bold move was facilitated by Mobutu's crumbling army, which chose to retreat in disarray instead of containing rebels' westward advances from eastern Congo to Kinshasa. It was also facilitated by the United States' decision to dispose of Mobutu, who by the time of the rebels' invasion was crippled by prostate cancer and no longer needed by Washington as a puppet.

After only a year in power, however, Kabila broke up his alliance with the Tutsi-led government of Rwanda. This turned Rwanda and Uganda against his regime. These two nations, which had helped to catapult Kabila from obscurity to the leadership of the largest country in central Africa, now fought as fiercely to oust him from power. They now backed three Congolese rebel factions with the objective of installing yet another leader in lieu of Kabila. On the other side, Angola, Zimbabwe, and Namibia came to Kabila's rescue when civil war flared up anew in August 1998. They provided Kabila with much-needed troops and military equipment. In addition, tens of thousands of Hutu militiamen, who were responsible for the Rwandan genocide and who have sought and obtained refuge in the Congo, were also involved in the conflict. The involvement of these nations and groups has created a much larger zone of political and military instability that stretches across Congo's borders into Zambia, Burundi,

Tanzania, and Sudan. There is no doubt that a peaceful resolution of the conflict in Congo no longer rests solely on the willingness of Congolese factions to sit at the negotiation table. Instead, resolution will likely be settled on a regional or international level. Once more, the fate of this African giant will be decided in the interest of foreign powers and not by its own people.

NOTES

1. This Kikongo term means literally "he who breaks rocks." It was first applied to Henry Morton Stanley, King Leopold's agent in the Congo, as his large caravan attempted to find its way around the rapids of the lower Congo River by blowing up rocks barring the way. By metaphorical extension, the expression came to be used to represent the repressive and abusive Belgian colonial system.
   2. Quoted in Hochschild (1998: 72).
   3. Quoted in Slade (1961: 2).

2

The Congo Basin in Ancient and Precolonial Times

EARLIEST HISTORY

By the beginning of the first millennium B.C., regional exchange of commodities, people, and ideas in the Congo Basin had spread common modes of production and cultural practices among the various groups that populated the area. Archaeologists credit many cultural developments in the region to Bantu-speaking peoples. These people came from the Benue River area of present-day Nigeria, passing through the dense equatorial rainforest to settle throughout the Congo Basin. Their migration spanned several centuries, starting around 1000 B.C. and lasting well into the middle of the first millennium A.D. Congo's ancient history was marked by several of these migratory waves, which provided the country with its ethnic diversity and complexity. First came the Bantu-speaking migrants, who settled in the rainforests and southern savannas. Their arrival relegated the non-Bantu-speaking population, mostly "pygmies," to the grasslands north of the rainforest, along the Ubangi and the Uele rivers. But Bantu-speaking peoples were not the only nonindigenous groups that penetrated the Congo Basin. Sudanic people coming from the Darfur and Kordofan regions, in the north, blended with the Bantu peoples to create a complex ethnic mosaic and produced such diverse groups as the Gbandi, Ngbaka, Zande, and Mangbetu (see Map 3). To further the ethnic diversity, Nilotic cattle herders from East Africa migrated upstream along the Nile River Valley and settled in the Great Lakes region in eastern Congo. These successive migrations resulted in the blending of various groups, as the newcomers freely mixed with the groups that preceded them as well as with the indigenous populations. This created a fusion of languages, lifestyles, and religious beliefs.

The Bantu-speaking groups contributed more than any other group to shaping Congo's remarkable cultural heritage. Archaeological evidence suggests that the Bantu-speaking migrants brought with them two important social and economic innovations: intensive agriculture and metallurgy. These innovations influenced the social development of the areas where they finally settled. The agricultural activity of the Bantu speakers was based on yam and palm oil, which they had cultivated in the fertile regions of present-day Nigeria. The Congo Basin offered varied soils and climates suitable for the development of these agricultural techniques. The development of agriculture and the introduction of new food crops allowed for higher density populations in some areas, notably the savannas, and triggered the expansion of trade based on food surpluses.

Agricultural improvements were accompanied by iron technology. This technique allowed for the production of more sophisticated iron tools and further fueled agricultural output. Before the arrival of the Bantu-speaking peoples, it is likely that cultivation of indigenous food crops, such as millet, sorghum, palm trees, and a great variety of vegetables, sustained significant population densities in the grassland areas. Without iron tools, however, agriculture was limited in scope and did not generate enough food surpluses to spark trade. Iron smelting techniques were already widespread in West Africa as early as the third millennium B.C. Along with the abundance of fertile lands and the presence of various crops, these techniques contributed to the higher population densities characteristic of West Africa. The presence of these technologies in central Africa in the first millennium B.C. is directly connected to the settlement of Bantu-speaking groups. In the 1970s and 1980s, archaeologists excavated several sites in Katanga and Lower Congo. They unearthed a wide range of iron tools and artifacts, some dating from as early as the beginning of the first millennium A.D. This confirmed previously held beliefs that iron smelting was brought to the Congo Basin with the migration of Bantu-speaking peoples rather than invented by indigenous groups. Iron smelting techniques would further influence new food patterns when

migrant groups from East Africa brought in cereal cultivation and introduced new crops, including banana and taro, which probably originated
in southern Asia and made their way into East Africa in the early centuries A.D. before spreading across central Africa.

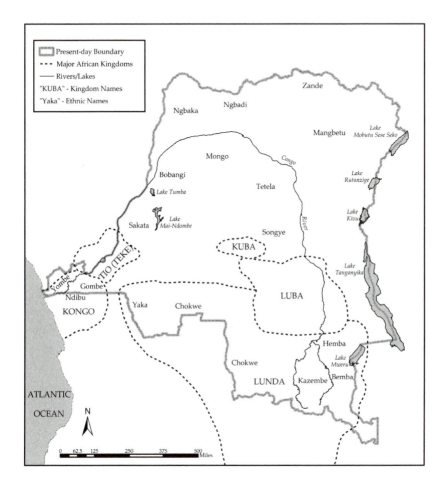

Map 3. Congo's Major Precolonial Polities and Ethnic Groups

Agriculture and hunting intensified through the use of metal tools. This
promoted the trading of food surpluses and other items such as pottery,
game, and tools. Social and political organization shifted from village-
based to more complex units. These new social formations were organized
around ethnicity or common language rather than village or kinship. This

important transformation led to the rise of several states in the grasslands while further strengthening stateless communities of the rainforest.

KINGDOMS AND EMPIRES

Kongo

Kongo was one of the most sophisticated and best known kingdoms in central Africa. Accounts of this Bantu kingdom come from Kongo oral tradition, from written records left by Portuguese missionaries, traders, and officials who visited and sometimes resided there, and from accounts written by literate Kongo themselves. In the early 1500s, King Afonso I (1506–1543) had secretaries record his decisions, including matters of internal politics and declarations of war. Afonso also wrote dozens of letters to the king of Portugal. In these letters, he expressed concerns about the presence of Portuguese, most of whom were slave trading within the jurisdiction of the kingdom. These letters are evidence of Kongo's unique position as the only precolonial sub-Saharan African state to have had political relations with Europe. Indeed, Portugal's influence was responsible for major economic developments in Kongo in the sixteenth century as well as the subsequent downfall of Kongo's political structures.

Today, the Kongo people are found in three different countries: DRC, Congo-Brazzaville, and Angola. Kikongo language (including its many variations and dialects) continues to be spoken in this region. Kongo people also utilize the languages, cultures, and religions of the respective European countries that colonized them starting in the late 1800s. European colonization of Congo, as elsewhere in Africa, obliterated pre-existing African political and cultural boundaries and replaced them with new ones. The Kongo people and polity were artificially divided by the borders of three European colonies, belonging to the Belgians, the French, and the Portuguese. The borders of modern African states, which are based on these colonial divisions, reflect the political endeavors of European colonists and not the boundaries of precolonial African polities or culture groups.

Kongo Kingdom was located south of the Congo River and east of the Kasai River. It encompassed only a part of the whole Kongo cultural region, which extended to the Kwilu and Niari rivers in the present Republic of Congo to the north, and to Malebo Pool and the Kwango River to the east. At the height of Kongo's expansion and regional influence, communities of Kikongo-speaking people could be found as far south as the Dande River, just north of present-day Luanda, Angola. Before serious research became available in the 1960s, it was assumed by some European authors that Kongo was a creation of the Portuguese, who first made contact with the coast of equatorial Africa around the 1480s. But recent studies and oral tradition show that this is not true. Most colonial researchers were prejudiced regarding African history. Because the kingdom was so well organized, these researchers quickly dismissed the possibility that indigenous initiative might have played a role in Kongo's development. But Kongo emerged as the major state in equatorial Africa at least two centuries before the arrival of the Portuguese. Various factors account for the kingdom's rise. Chief among these factors is the kingdom's location, which provided a wide range of resources, including fertile soil, water, minerals, and abundant and varied flora and fauna. Agriculture and copper smelting seem to have played an important role in the demographic expansion that occurred south of the mouth of the Congo River around the fourteenth century. There is an absence of written records or serious archaeological excavations that might answer questions about Kongo's development. One is left to conjecture, based on evidence provided by oral traditions, that agricultural innovations coincided with the rise of Kongo.

By the time the Portuguese settled in Kongo, the kingdom had achieved impressive proportions through its strong political institutions. As in many other African precolonial states, the basic unit of the political structure was the village, which in turn was made up of tightly knit extended matrilineal families known as *kanda*. At the organizational level above the village, there were districts headed by officials appointed by the king. District heads in turn were subordinate to the governor of the province of which they were a part. The *kanda*, or clan, consisted of the descendants of a common ancestor connected to each other by blood and as such sharing common interests. Women of free status were the pillars of the Kongo family, and by virtue of their social status only they could confer membership in the *kanda*. Under this matrilineal system, mother and son were of the same *kanda*, while the father remained an outsider even if he could be considered the head of the household. His wife's brothers (maternal uncles) had legal authority over his own children, leaving the father with a mere guardianship. This was an important feature of Kongo social organization and one that sparked much curiosity in Western visitors. One such visitor noted with astonishment that "The children do not inherit from their fathers, but only from their mothers and their maternal relatives. The father's property passes to the children of his uterine sisters."[1] Often, a *kanda* would incorporate individuals from other lineages. These individuals included clients who chose to place themselves in a state of dependence, people who were given away by their own *kanda* as payment for a debt, and slaves who were acquired by the *kanda* as domestic servants and ended up as full-fledged members of the *kanda*.

Within each *kanda*, power, wealth, and privilege were based on seniority and were usually passed by the male head of the *kanda* to his nephews, the sons of his sisters. In the sixteenth and seventeenth centuries it was also common for women to be heads of *kanda*. The head of an affluent *kanda* would usually fill the hereditary position of chief of the village. This matrilineal system of passing inheritance from maternal uncle to nephew applied not only to material wealth but also to social status and rank. Accordingly, princes and kings were always born within a royal *kanda*, inheriting their rank through their mothers.

Before the intrusion of the Portuguese in the late fifteenth century, the economy of the Kongo Kingdom had already reached some degree of prosperity, and Kongo's boundaries extended across a relatively large area. At this point, the kingdom included at least 3 million subjects and was divided into six principal provinces: Mpemba, Soyo, Mbamba, Mbata, Nsundi, and Mpangu. The first three of these were the wealthiest and most vital for the political unity of the state. Each province was headed by a governor, who commanded broad military, fiscal, and administrative powers conferred by the king. In times of war, the governors accompanied the king into battle, each at the head of his respective provincial army. At the end of the fifteenth century, the king of Kongo could field a powerful army of 80,000 men thanks to the loyalty of his provincial governors. The governors also collected tribute from subject groups, a large portion of which was delivered to the king's palace. As the king's provincial administrators, the governors' duties ranged from dispensing justice to providing a court of appeal for the king's subjects to maintaining the roads. The king (*Mani Kongo*) was the supreme ruler over the kingdom. In all his decisions he was aided by a council of elders. In the sixteenth and seventeenth centuries this council lost some of its influence as the *Mani Kongo* came to rely increasingly on Portuguese officials for advice on the affairs of the kingdom.

As in many precolonial African kingships, the king was both a civil and spiritual leader, commanding respect and even reverence. He was the highest priest within the kingdom, mediating between the living and the ancestors, between the world of the living (*nza ya yi*) and the land of the dead (*nzi ya bafwa*). He dispensed justice and created and enforced laws. He controlled the rains and the crops, regulated the sowing and harvesting, and maintained a privileged relationship with the various spirits that pervaded Kongo's religious world. His power, in fact, was founded upon a duality that corresponded to the cosmology of the people of Kongo. This cosmology viewed the spiritual and material worlds not as two separate worlds but as two components of the same universe, fully harmonious and perpetually interacting. The king was thus invested with a sacred aura that allowed him to straddle the two spheres. As such, he acted as priest, guardian of legitimacy, and guarantor of good relations between the living and the ancestors.

The *Mani Kongo*, along with members of affluent aristocratic *kandas*, resided in Mbanza Kongo (later renamed São Salvador). Mbanza Kongo was promoted long before the arrival of the Portuguese to the role of capital city. The city enjoyed one of the best geographical positions in the kingdom. It was situated on a wide mountainous plateau dominating its surroundings from some 2,000 feet above sea level. Today, Mbanza Kongo is a modest town in northern Angola that remains a symbolic center of Kongo culture. In its heyday, Mbanza Kongo was a place of important political as well as religious significance. As the kingdom grew wealthier and expanded its influence over a wider area, so did Mbanza Kongo. It surpassed most other towns such that Portuguese visitors marveled at the complexity of its layout and architecture. In 1491, a Portuguese traveler compared Mbanza Kongo to the Portuguese city of Evora and noted that its houses were better than most found in the rest of the continent. Mbanza Kongo's architecture expressed the strong sense of nature's sacredness held by the Kongo people. Builders made use of natural construction materials such as wood, woven and thatched grass, cob (a mixture of unburned clay and straw), and bark textiles. It was not until the arrival of the Portuguese that stone was used as a building material, first for churches and then for sections of the king's palace and elite houses. The size of houses and their elaborate architecture, location, and furniture were markers of social status. This was especially true after the introduction of objects manufactured in Europe. To indicate their superior social status, the elite of the town furnished their homes with luxurious items imported from Europe, including chests and trunks, tables, upholstered armchairs, tapestries, and rugs. The king's residence was the political as well as the symbolic center that dictated the design of the whole city. Around the king's palace, there was a sacred wood encircled by a complex enclosure made of stakes tied together with vines. This was where dead kings lay, and where the king dispensed justice, received homage from his subjects, and displayed his military power. The royal enclosure was divided into two sections, organized around a masculine pole (the king's quarters) and a feminine pole (the queen's quarters). Immediately next to the royal cluster were the houses of nobility, arranged according to affinities and clan hierarchies. The closer one was to the royal residence, the more important his or her *kanda* and the higher his or her individual social status.

The *Mani Kongo* derived most of his income from tribute acquired from peripheral dependencies. These dependencies escaped direct control by the capital and its taxes, tolls, and judiciary fines, but they still had to pay tribute. Tribute was paid using raffia cloth, ivory, hides, slaves, and foodstuffs, as well as with currency in the form of *nzimbu* (cowry) shells. The king tightly controlled this currency, which gradually depreciated as slaves became the most sought-after trading commodity during the Portuguese era. The royal fishery, located on the Atlantic coast on the shores of the island of Luanda, yielded these shells for the king and his royal treasury at Mbanza Kongo. During the various stages of producing and accumulating *nzimbu* shells, from collection at the coast to inspection and storage at the capital, royal officers closely monitored this precious currency, which could even buy gold and silver. Some of the officers were dispatched throughout the kingdom to supervise the collection of tribute. The king used this tribute to grant gifts to titleholders at his court and to territorial rulers. Royal gifts seem to have played an important role as a resource of the royal government that the *Mani Kongo* might use to assert his authority. Since most servants were not granted a regular salary, the king used gifts to retain as well as reward a sizable retinue of officials, soldiers, musicians, pages, and advisers at his court.

The economy of the kingdom was based on the division between the towns (*mbanza*), which produced a large surplus of foodstuffs and other commodities, and the villages (*lubata*). Mbanza Kongo, the largest and most prestigious of all towns, was by far the largest producer and consumer of the goods that circulated within the kingdom. In the villages, there was a sexual division of labor. Women worked in the fields and raised crops, which provided the bulk of food for the household. Men specialized in arboriculture, which yielded not only palm wine, but cloth, utensils, medicines, and building materials. The household, in villages as in the bustling towns, was the site of production in Kongo, for subsistence as well as for trade.

The first Portuguese caravan trekked across the coastal plain to reach Mbanza Kongo in 1482. By this time, Kongo's society had achieved a high degree of development by the standards of the day. The leader of this first European expedition to the mouth of the Congo River was Diogo Cão, a Portuguese seaman who reveled at the idea of spreading the "gospel of human progress" to what Europeans considered the "dark continent." The Portuguese also hoped that a missionary venture might yield profitable trade for Portugal. In 1491, eight years after initial contact, King João II of Portugal sent a missionary expedition to Kongo. The expedition included Franciscan and Dominican priests, armed soldiers, peasants, artisans of various crafts (especially masons and carpenters), and a few women. For the next two centuries, there followed what Georges Balandier has referred to as a "false marriage." The Portuguese enticed the Kongo aristocracy into embracing Catholicism. In doing so, they created a relation of dependence that sparked dynastic conflicts and civil war and led eventually to the collapse of the kingdom. The conversion of the nobility of Kongo to Catholicism was conducted in haste as a ploy of the Portuguese to win over the whole population to the new faith. But far from trickling down to the commoners, these conversions created a gulf between the nobility and the rest of Kongo society, which remained attached to traditional rituals and beliefs. In May 1491, the king, Nzinga a Nkuwu, was baptized along with a few notables. He adopted the name of João I in deference to the Portuguese sovereign. The next month it was the queen's turn to participate in the ritual of the new faith. She adopted as her baptismal name that of the queen of Portugal, Eleanor. During that same ceremony, which took place on June 4, 1491 at the capital, Nzinga Mbemba, the governor of the province of Nsundi, also received baptism. He was to become, under the name of Afonso I, the most famous and capable Catholic king of Kongo.

When João died in 1506, Afonso sought the support of the Portuguese to seize the throne. Under the leadership of Afonso I (1506–1543) Kongo was to experience some of the most critical events of its history. One of the most important developments was the establishment of diplomatic relations with Portugal. Afonso opened up Kongo to the activities of Portuguese merchants and missionaries. He established Catholicism as the state religion under the direction of his son Henrique, who had studied theology in Rome and had been consecrated as a bishop by the pope. He also sent other students to Portugal, one of whom became a schoolmaster in Lisbon. In addition, he maintained missionary schools that catered to the Kongo elite at Mbanza Kongo and the provincial capitals. Pupils were taught basic literacy, Christian doctrine, and Latin.

Afonso first traded with the Portuguese via the island of São Tomé, off the coast of present-day Gabon. The Portuguese had "discovered" this island in the late fifteenth century and were on the verge of colonizing it. In addition, he welcomed and traded with individual Portuguese traders who flocked to Mbanza Kongo. In exchange for palm cloth, skins, honey, copper, and ivory, the *Mani Kongo* received from the Portuguese canons, guns, ammunition, and luxury goods including fabrics, mirrors, brass hairpins, and parasols. Gradually, a new foreign market was created in Kongo, one based on wealth that was stable and convertible outside of Kongo's economic domain. Afonso responded to the demands of the Portuguese, even as they eventually sought to transform his kingdom into a slave warehouse. Before the Portuguese arrived, the buying and selling of slaves was customary in Kongo. Slaves were mostly a product of war, as evidenced by the fact that the same Kikongo word meant both "slave" and "war captive." Slaves were captured in war or bought. They served their masters as status symbols and also as additional kin-group members, domestic servants, courtiers, and advisers to powerful Kongo aristocrats. But the intervention of the Portuguese slave traders affected the economic and social role of slaves profoundly. Slaves became the staple of an international commerce that first linked Kongo to São Tomé and Europe, and then to the New World, once the Portuguese had moved their sugar plantations from São Tomé to Brazil.

The Portuguese transformed what had been an economy based on service to the state and the elite into a mercantile economy based on chattel slavery and spurred by ruthless greed. At the height of the trade, once the Portuguese had settled in Brazil, nearly ten thousand captives were exported each year from Kongo. Chief among those involved in the slave trade were the Catholic clergy, who openly participated in the slave system. Portuguese missionaries were sent to Kongo to gain souls for Christ. But they soon realized that transforming their own flocks of followers into slaves allowed them to reap huge profits. The missionaries created enormous agricultural projects whereby they cultivated vegetable gardens, fruit trees, marketable plants (some, including tobacco, imported from the New World), and sugarcane, and tended sheep and goats. This work was accomplished through the use of an inhumane form of slavery previously unknown to the region. Scholars generally concur that "the hunting down of men—justified in the name of economic necessity, sanctified, practiced one way or another by all the 'foreigners' and their native agents, was one factor in the destruction of the old Kongo. It perverted social relations. . . . [I]t wounded the population of the Kongo in its very substance" (Balandier 1969: 82). Afonso unsuccessfully attempted to ban the trade, which made him the victim of an assassination attempt carried out by Portuguese merchants on Easter Sunday 1540. Afonso then took his complaint directly to the king of Portugal. In a letter written in July 1526, he remonstrated against the ignoble slave trade that was ravaging his kingdom:

> We ask grace of Your Highness not to believe the evil said about us by those who have no concern but to sell what they have unjustly acquired, who, by their slave trade, are ruining our kingdom and the Christianity which has been established here for so many years and which cost your predecessors so many sacrifices. Catholic kings and princes like Your Highness are working to provide this great blessing of faith for new peoples. We are anxious to preserve it for those who have acquired it. But this is difficult to do here where European goods exert such a fascination over the simple and the ignorant that they leave God in order to obtain them. The remedy is the suppression of these goods which are a snare of the devil for sellers and buyers alike. The lure of profit and greed lead the people of the land to rob their compatriots, including members of their own families and of ours, without considering whether they are Christians or not. They capture them, sell them, barter them. This abuse is so great that we cannot correct it without striking hard and harder.[2]

The slave trade aside, Kongo's leaders found their authority undermined by Portuguese encroachments and restrictions. In a move designed to reinforce Portuguese monopoly in Kongo, the king of Portugal tried to prevent the African kingdom from establishing relations with other European nations. Christianity itself, which had been promoted to the status of a royal cult, became a powerful force of disunity as different Portuguese religious factions, Franciscans, Jesuits, Dominicans, Carmelites, Augustinians, and Capuchins, vied for influence within the court. And this competition, in turn, caused rifts within Kongo society. "Modernists" favored the new faith at the expense of local cults. They were pitted against "traditionalists," who lamented the progress of European education, modernization, and Christianization, and "syncretists," who favored blending Kongo's indigenous culture with certain elements of the new theology. Kongo's leaders unsuccessfully attempted to use Christianity as a tool of unification, only to fall victim to its divisiveness, which was compounded by external as well as internal pressures.

After the death of Afonso I in 1545, his followers were less and less able to control the affairs of the kingdom. They were beset with encroachment on their sovereignty by Portugal. The forms of encroachment included the undermining influence of Portuguese living within the kingdom, the devastating slave trade, rivalries among different religious and political factions, and poor leadership on their own part. In 1561, the succession of King Diogo I (1545–1561) set the stage for a bloody civil war that claimed the lives of several kings as the Portuguese intervened to impose their own candidate on the throne. In 1568, in the throes of chaos, Kongo was invaded by the Jaga, a group of migrant warriors who attacked the kingdom from its eastern borders. São Salvador was destroyed, and King Álvaro I (1566–1587) fled to an island in the Lower Congo River. He later appealed to the king of Portugal for military assistance to repel the Jaga. Portugal dispatched 600 men from their colony of São Tomé. This army rallied the Kongo forces, which had regrouped under the leadership of Álvaro, and drove the Jaga armies out of the kingdom.

The history of the kingdom after the restoration was marked by political improvements and some successful attempts at centralization. Kongo was now a colony loosely controlled by the Portuguese through a growing number of Portuguese merchants and their mulatto children, who by and large had the upper hand in economic activities within the kingdom. In 1606, an anonymous writer noted that Álvaro II (1587–1614) "greatly esteems the Portuguese in his city for they teach him to live civilly and aid him against his enemies. They are so important to him that it is understood that he would already have been destroyed if his enemies had not feared these Portuguese."[3] With the help of the Portuguese and the guns they provided, the *Mani Kongo* managed to keep internal disruption at bay.

This trend was undone over the course of the seventeenth century due to the rise of the Portuguese colony of Luanda, which developed new trading routes that undercut trade passing through Mbanza Kongo. The *Mani Kongo* failed to find alternative sources of revenue to make up for the losses incurred by the growth of coastal trading centers. This in turn eroded and ultimately crippled his ability to adequately respond to growing demands for autonomy by the provinces. By 1665, several provinces had seceded, and the Portuguese had seized the island of Luanda, which had provided the *Mani Kongo* with his crucial supply of *nzimbu* shells. Kongo and the weakened forces of King António I (1661–1665) were now an easy target for the Portuguese army of Luanda. The two armies met at Mbwila on October 29, 1665, in the most crucial military conflict between Portugal and Kongo. António was killed and his army disbanded. His death unleashed divisive forces. Various factions claimed the kingship and resorted to open conflict in order to impose their intended ruler on the throne. From the time of the death of António to the end of the seventeenth century, succession was chaotic and contested. Most kings did not reign for more than a couple of years before being either deposed, assassinated, or killed in battle.

In the eighteenth century, Kongo was further divided into smaller units as rival kings claimed the mantle of Afonso. In 1700, a noblewoman, Dona Beatriz Kimpa Vita (1686–1706), claimed that she was possessed by Saint Anthony. Her mission, she declared, was to find among all the rival claimants to the throne the man who would bring an end to the civil wars, restore the kingship, and repopulate the kingdom. She drew support from all sections of Kongo society because she embodied people's yearnings for peace after decades of destructive civil wars. The Antonian movement, in spite of its strong popular support, was perceived as heretical by the powerful Capuchin community, which maintained remnants of political and religious legitimacy through the *Mani Kongo*. As a result, Kimpa Vita was burned at the stake at the age of twenty. The failure of her movement precipitated the decline of Kongo. Civil wars once again broke out, ravaging all sectors of Kongo society. By the middle of the nineteenth century, the final embers of Kongo sovereignty were extinguished. São Salvador, whose population had peaked at nearly 50,000 inhabitants under the reign of Garcia II (1641–1661), was reduced to a mere village of a few hundred people. At the end of the century, the land that was once occupied by the kingdom was divided up among the French, the Belgians, and the Portuguese as Congo and the rest of Africa entered the dark age of colonialism.

Luba and Lunda

Early anthropological studies of the Lunda and the Luba tended to examine these two civilizations separately. But in recent years, scholars have demonstrated that the two should be considered jointly given that their many similarities far outweigh their differences. Kongo encompassed an area located in several modern countries. The political system developed by the Luba and the Lunda also affected cultural developments across a region that today includes parts of a number of central African nations. This kingdom spread into the southern grasslands, over a vast area stretching from the Kwango River to the Zambezi River, into parts of contemporary DRC, Angola, and Zambia. This pattern clearly demonstrates the artificial nature of colonial boundaries. In many cases, colonial authorities disregarding precolonial histories divided communities with common cultural and linguistic roots.

In the eighteenth and nineteenth centuries, the Luba and the Lunda kingdoms held sway over the entire area west of the Upper Lualaba and north of the Katanga lakes, between Lake Tanganyika and the Lomami River in the southeastern part of Congo. The two states arose initially from a single group, the Songye, that invaded the area and founded the Luba Empire during the sixteenth century. During the late sixteenth century and the beginning of the seventeenth century, they moved further west and established a second state, the Lunda Empire. Once the two empires had been established in this new environment, these migrant groups carried their political organization further east and south. By the middle of the eighteenth century, the Luba and Lunda had created a vast culture area in southeastern Congo. In doing so, the Luba-Lunda obliterated the preexisting political organization. The previous system had been based on small chiefdoms, peopled by farmers and fishermen, and interconnected through trade of various products (raffia, palm oil, fish, copper, salt, etc.), intermarriage, and exchange of gifts. By the eighteenth century, the fame and influence of the Luba Kingdom stretched across a huge area. Even populations far beyond the territories controlled by the kingdom took pride in claiming Luba ancestry.

According to Luba oral tradition, around 1500 there appeared a legendary hero, Kongolo (the Rainbow), whom many scholars believe was a Songye that migrated to the area from the northeast. Other versions collected from Luba people have Kongolo coming from elsewhere, presumably the area between the Luembe and Lubilash rivers where the small kingdom of Kalundwe had been created by a coalition of three clans. When Kongolo arrived in this foreign land, he subdued the various villages and chiefdoms he encountered there and introduced several major changes. He created the first Luba kingdom and built his capital on the plains at Mwibele, near Lake Boya, in what was to become the heartland of the Luba state. According to tradition, some time after Kongolo had established his control over the land, Ilunga Mbili (or Mbidi Kiluwe, Kiluba language for "Mbidi the Hunter") and his companions came from an area east of the Lualaba River. At first, Kongolo treated him well, even giving him in marriage two of his own half sisters, Bulanda and Mabela. Then a bitter quarrel arose between Kongolo and

Mbili. This caused the latter to depart from the land, leaving his two wives behind. After he had left, Bulanda gave birth to a son, Kalala Ilunga (the Warrior), and Mabela bore another son, Kisulu Mabele. Kalala Ilunga proved to be a gifted and fearless warrior as a young man. He gained the confidence of Kongolo and helped him to subdue the southern part of the kingdom, which had resisted incorporation until then. Suspicious of Kalala's success, Kongolo tried to kill him, but Kalala sought refuge in his fatherland. With the help of his kinsmen, he gathered a strong army and came back to wrest power from Kongolo. Kongolo was overwhelmed and outnumbered by Kalala's forces and surprised by his daring move. He fled to some caves near the Lwembe River. He was eventually captured and killed by Kalala after being betrayed by his own sisters. Soon after, Kalala took over the kingdom and relocated the capital to Munza, which was closer to a district rich in iron ore and salt mines, a few miles from Mwibele.

As is the case for many origin myths, the history of Kongolo and Kalala may not be a literal account of past events. Yet the story has found its place in Luba epic tradition and is still vividly recounted among the Luba in Congo. Many authors consider this Luba genesis story to be a political charter. It expresses an ideology that legitimized the political institutions and the sacred kingship created by Luba founding ancestors. Most Luba kings used the myth of Kongolo and Kalala to lay claim to their authority on sacred, quasi-mystical grounds. Through the story, they connected themselves to Kalala Ilunga, the embodiment of the divine king, who by might and bravery rid the land of a political order perceived as cruel and malevolent, thus inaugurating an era of prosperity. During the investiture ceremony of kings, this myth was reenacted with actors impersonating the three heroes of the Luba state. Luba kings ruled by means of a concept of sacred kingship based upon this genesis myth. The kings also controlled their territories through a political ideology of rule by proxies arranged in hierarchical order. Given the vast territories controlled by the empire, this system of loose governance, especially in remote areas, was preferred to more direct rule. In the northern and eastern parts of the kingdom, the Luba king kept in place local chiefs and kings who pledged allegiance to him.

All of Luba society was ordered hierarchically. Patrilineal relations among individuals and households dominated at the village level. Even small-scale villages were made up of several patrilineages, which included slaves and clients. The head of a village was chosen from the dominant lineage and may have been directly appointed by a territorial chief or by the king himself. Although the village head acted as a royal agent, he was assisted by a council made up of the heads of all the other lineages that existed in the village. A cluster of villages formed a chiefdom or district and was headed by a titled chief known as *kilolo*. Vested with supreme authority, the king stood at the apex of the pyramid. His authority was legally based upon the concept of *bulopwe* (royal office). The Luba king was considered a *mulopwe*, a possessor of sacred, indivisible authority to rule reminiscent of the "mandate of heaven" of Chinese emperors. *Bulopwe* conferred on the Luba king the right to rule, connected him directly to the supernatural realm, and endowed his authority with a mystical aura. From his capital he ruled his vast kingdom as a divine monarch. He appointed chiefs and village heads, sometimes for life, more often for a period of several years. A number of chiefdoms, which existed prior to the Luba Empire, were ruled by hereditary chiefs, but the king could depose any chief at his discretion. Although an absolute monarch, the *mulopwe* could not rule as a tyrant. Institutional checks guaranteed that he exercised his power for the well-being of the community. If he did not, his half brothers could always rise against him with the backing of their patrilineages and with the support of the court.

The central government consisted of titleholders, ranked according to their functions, who advised the king in all public affairs. The most prestigious title a government official could hope to gain was the *twite*. He acted as the head of an office corps, the only standing police force in the kingdom. Next to him was the *inabanza*, whose duty was to keep the sacred emblems and supervise the official rituals. The *mwana mwilamba* was the head of the army. He was expected to lead the troops in combat and received his orders directly from the king. Other titleholders included *lukanga* (senior judge), *mwine lundu* (keeper of the unwritten constitution of the kingdom), *fumwa pamba diyumbi* (keeper and maker of charms and royal diviner), *ndalamba* (queen mother), and *nsikala* (ruler during an interregnum).

The Lunda Empire was in many ways similar to the Luba state. It was created in the eighteenth century in the upper Mbuji-Mayi river valley, replacing an existing polity known as the Ruund. At the height of its power, it extended from the Kwango River to beyond the Luapula River. Kingship provided the political stability necessary for the kingdom to expand its territory, and the principle of positional succession defined the fixed relationships within the society. A successor inherited not only the political office but the personal status of the deceased, including his name, his wives, and his children and other dependents. This mechanism is the reason the Lunda Kingdom was more successful at expanding beyond its homeland than its Luba counterpart. It allowed the Lunda rulers to assimilate foreign chiefs into their own political system. The remarkable vitality of the Lunda Kingdom also stemmed from its military character and warrior tradition. The capital of the kingdom (*musumba*) was not only a center of government but also a military hub, ready to move soldiers swiftly and in an orderly way against an enemy. Given the militaristic nature of the Lunda state, it is not surprising that the Lunda leadership was more despotic and much less ritualized than the Luba kingship. Lunda's active involvement in slave-trading activities in several of its eastern territories appears to have been a by-product of this militaristic style of government.

By the 1850s, both empires had been adversely affected by international trade and could no longer control their political structures. First "Arab" ivory and slave merchants from the East African coast intruded into the hearts of the empires. Later Ovimbundu traders came from Angola. By the time the first Belgian-led expedition reached Luba land in 1891, the empire had lost most of its territories and regional clients to slave merchants.

PEOPLES AND CIVILIZATIONS OF THE FOREST

Congo's northern half, from the Kasai and Sankuru rivers in the center to the Oubangui and Uele in the north, is the site of some of the richest rainforests on Earth. The world's second largest rainforest straddles the equator here. It covers a vast expanse nearly three times the size of Texas and as large as Western Europe. It is located mainly in Congo but also in parts of Cameroon, Gabon, Equatorial Guinea, Central African Republic, and Congo-Brazzaville. Most of this area receives abundant rainfall ranging from 60 to 80 inches of rain a year. This pluvial climate is coupled with a dense hydrographic network and stable temperatures that oscillate between 23°C and 27°C throughout the year. This provides the necessary conditions for the existence of the rainforest. The climate in the rainforest, as in most of this tropical area, varies between a wet and dry season, although the dry season is relatively short, lasting an average of two months or less. Rainforest farmers who take advantage of the hydromorphic soils rely on this annual seasonal cycle to ensure successful farming.

Contrary to the common stereotype, the rainforest is not an "impenetrable jungle" but a luxuriant and varied environment. The forest does not prevent the different communities that dwell within it from communicating and sharing ideas, techniques, and cultures with one another. Indeed, as author Jan Vansina (1990: 39) points out,

> jungle is as much a myth as Tarzan is. The myth paints the rainforests as a single monotonous primeval environment, enormous in size, a 'green hell,' where wretched 'Man' unceasingly wrestles to keep the ever-encroaching foliage at bay. This glaucous universe is impenetrable, and within minutes of entering this uncharted sea of green, one is lost. Buzzing with insects, exhaling weird miasmas, the rainforest stupefies, cripples, and kills. Only pygmies ever adapted to it and their adaptation stultified them. They became living fossils: human insects caught in the amber of the green sea.

This myth has long thwarted any serious attempt to study the civilizations of the forested areas in Congo. But thanks to several researchers, based in both Congo and abroad, the dearth of historiography regarding Congo's rainforest has given way to a profusion of well-documented studies. According to Vansina (1990: xii), these studies shed light on "the workings of a powerful endogenous process, a cultural tradition that had its roots some 4,000–5,000 years ago, and that had maintained itself by perennial rejuvenation, until it withered as result of the colonial conquest." The studies also dispel the "environmental racist determinism" with its entrenched stereotype of "rainforests as a dump for the rejects of humanity," clad in the dark mantle of barbarism. This stereotype has a long history. It goes back to the nineteenth century when the first European "explorers," such as Stanley, trekked along the equator and brought back to Europe word about the so-called "dark continent" of Africa. These explorers contributed to the misrepresentations that have pervaded Western perceptions of Africa from the times of European military conquest up to the present day.

Such stereotypes are clearly untrue. Congo's rainforest has seen the unfolding over many centuries of the rich economic and cultural histories of the communities who live there. Today, some 450 ethnic groups, approximately 12 million people, live in the rainforest of equatorial Africa, interspersed throughout its various habitats. Some live in the mountainous parts of the forest; others have chosen the dry, lowland forest and have been enjoying for millennia the proximity of broad rivers, rich in countless resources; still others inhabit the patches of savanna that lay at the forest's southern fringes. Yet early anthropological accounts of these societies tended to lump them together into a single homogenous cultural unit, although the diversity of their environments alone should have compelled researchers to look for variations. Before the Bantu expansion, hunters and gatherers occupied the area, living in small nomadic communities. Although population densities remained relatively low by comparison to the grasslands at the southern fringes of the rainforest, these early communities mastered their environment without overly exploiting it. Taking full advantage of the ecosystems, they developed healing techniques based upon their extended knowledge of medicinal plants that were sophisticated by any standards. By the end of the nineteenth century, before colonial incursions, most communities of hunters and gatherers, which were later labeled "pygmies," were profoundly influenced by the new civilization introduced by the Bantu migrants. As discussed in the first section of this chapter, agriculture was one of the most important contributions of the Bantu groups to the areas they settled. Bantu migrants cleared small areas of the forest or moved into existing patches of savanna. They created compact, permanent villages and developed crafts, iron-working techniques, and farming. Soon they offered new products to the bands of hunters and gatherers, who came periodically to exchange game for iron tools, ceramics, and foodstuffs. In some areas, these villagers reduced "pygmies" to serfdom, using them mainly as a labor force in the agricultural sector. As trade relations and serfdom brought these nomadic communities in closer contact with the Bantu farmers, there was also cultural exchange and the "pygmies" adopted Bantu languages. Although the demographic expansion of the Bantu villagers was kept in check by the challenging environment, in the end they outnumbered the "pygmies" because of better nutrition and a less precarious way of life. Despite their contact, the two communities remained separate; they lived side by side, but rarely intermarried, and remain as distinct today as they were centuries ago.

Bantu farmers were not the only newcomers to the area, although they were the first group to engage in farming activities in the forest. They were followed in the seventeenth and early eighteenth centuries by Sudanic farmers who moved into the Ubangi and Uele areas from Darfur and Kordofan. These migrants rapidly took possession of the forest. They imposed their basic social organization on the Bantu villagers, and in many instances they also adopted some local cultural elements. Today, most groups living in the forest of northern Congo, including the Zande, Mangbetu, Ngbandi, and Ngbaka, have retained this triple cultural heritage in their language, economy, social organization, and political structure.

Information about the social life of these communities before the nineteenth century remains scarce. Therefore, researchers have attempted to cautiously project back to earlier centuries the wealth of information available for the nineteenth century. Most concur that the village remained the basic unit of settlement and the place where social and political institutions were implemented. Villages varied in size from 30 to 250 people. Even the smaller settlements conformed to a layout that included private rectangular dwellings built with wood and other materials collected from the forest. Adjacent to the private homes were sheds used by craftsmen. Villages were self-sufficient, although they still participated in barter, and produced most of the tools, crafts, and foodstuffs they required. In the middle of each village there was a public plaza used for ceremonies, the hearing of court cases, and the hearings that preceded all collective decisions on public matters.

In response to the challenging environment, these communities developed social institutions based upon cooperation and collective work. In the savanna, farmers, hunters, and especially fishermen could afford to live in isolated settlements and not depend too much on the community. In the forest, however, collective work was not only more rewarding and efficient but necessary. Work including trapping, fishing, and hunting was done communally. Among the Zande, for example, wealthy individuals used the collective labor of women, clients, and slaves on their plantations. In communities where iron working was highly valued, such as those of the Ngbandi, smiths were grouped into guilds and often worked together. In other villages, fishing was undertaken by small crews of highly professional fishermen. They sometimes used collective nets and also helped each other with canoe building, setting up weir systems, knotting and repairing nets, and collecting bait. They ventured along the main rivers in fishing expeditions that could last for several weeks at a time, especially when fishing was done with cone-shaped fishing traps harnessed to wooden structures built directly on the rivers. The harvesting of fish was accomplished through a gendered division of labor. Men fished and returned with their catches to the villages, where women dried or smoked the fish to preserve it.

As with the savanna dwellers, the basic social structure in each village was the extended family, or "household." It consisted of kinsmen, collateral kinsmen, wives, children (including adopted children), clients, and even slaves. A single household was big enough to make up a whole village, but in most cases there was more than one household in each village. Households were predominantly patrilineal. The leaders, or "big men," formed the ruling council in each village. The head of the council was not necessarily the eldest among the "big men" but the leader of the strongest household. He was also the headman of the village, which he represented to the outside world. But when it came to internal affairs, the head of the village was only the first among equals. Most villages were part of a larger administrative unit, which can be referred to as a "district" for lack of a better term. When a cluster of villages felt the need to defend themselves against intruders or became dependent on each other for trade or marriage, they would then create a district. The district was not dominated by a single village and did not name a chief picked from among the village heads. However, the bonds that this mode of organization created were strong enough to engender a sense of ethnicity, of "us" versus "them," among the households within the district.

The district was not the only form of political consolidation to emerge in the forest. A household would sometimes develop into a large village of several hundred kinsmen. Oftentimes, these large households would attempt to dominate the surrounding villages through a tributary system. This hegemony, however, often did not last long. Many of these strong households were ultimately weakened by crises of succession. Those groups that were successful in imposing their rule over many generations did so because they were able to keep in check the conflicts that arose after the death of a leader, that is, to create a dynastic group. Such political processes occurred, for example, in areas between the Congo and Itimbiri rivers and near the Lower Lomami. In the areas surrounding Lake Mai Mdombe, some even managed to create more centralized and less ephemeral chiefdoms based on a cult of sacred kings. The kings were vested with supernatural powers that allowed them to assert their authority over several clusters of villages, levy annual tributes, develop an administrative hierarchy based upon title holding, and implement a centralized justice system. More significantly, they were able to guarantee that heredity would be the dominant criterion for succession.

Territorial expansion sometimes meant that a ruler could no longer govern his chiefdom directly but had to appoint lesser chiefs to govern in far-flung provinces. This expansion took the process of centralization a step further. When such a development occurred it gave birth to kingdoms such as the Mangbetu Kingdom, in northeastern Congo, or the Kuba Kingdom, which emerged on the Sankuru River in the seventeenth century. These political formations were strong enough to last well into the colonial period. The Kuba Kingdom, for example, remained unchallenged until the beginning of the twentieth century, although colonial conquest was already well underway.

NOTES

1. Quoted in Balandier (1969: 181).
2. Quoted in Balandier (82).
3. Quoted in Hilton (1985: 73–74).

3

Colonial Conquest, 1885–1890

By 1800, the Congo Basin had been brought into the international trading system that was created by the Portuguese at the beginning of the sixteenth century. From the mid-1600s to late 1700s, nearly a million African captives were taken from the interior and exported from the Loango coast by Portuguese, French, British, and Dutch traders. The volume of trade expanded up until the 1830s. During this period, a large number of communities were continually challenged by foreign commercial initiatives from the Atlantic and Indian Ocean coasts. The full impact of the Atlantic slave trade on the populations of the Congo Basin is hard to document, but evidence from anthropological studies reveals that it affected various political and social institutions. In treating African captives as mere commodities, the slave trade introduced notions that were, until then, foreign to Africans. The slave trade transformed preexisting notions about humanity and disrupted social hierarchies. African states came to rely on the income generated by selling captives to European traders on the coast and not on their agriculture-based economies. Ultimately, this contributed to their own downfalls. Even the solidly built polities that had been successful in establishing dominion over large areas could not resist the new commercial patterns developed by the foreigners. Kongo, as shown in the previous chapter, virtually disintegrated as a result of intense demand for slaves on the Atlantic. As for the other major states, their ability to control vast areas was seriously undermined by foreign encroachments.

But by the turn of the eighteenth century, the Atlantic slave trade was falling out of favor with first the British and then the rest of the European nations. Instead, a new economic system was put in place that would further weaken the political and economic position of Africans in the world. The slave trade had become obsolete as a result of the overproduction of New World crops and the beginning of the industrial revolution in Europe. This prompted the British to abolish the system in 1807. They were soon followed by the Americans, the Dutch, the French, and the rest of the European slave-trading nations. After 1835 only Spanish-Cubans and Brazilians were to be found slave trading in the coastal area south of the Congo Estuary.

The main effect of the industrial revolution on the Congo region was an increase in the volume of imports from Europe. During the slave trade era, Europeans flooded the coastal areas with guns, gunpowder, and alcohol in exchange for African slaves. The presence of these goods further fueled slave traffic. With the industrial revolution in full swing in Europe, huge quantities of cheap manufactured goods produced in European factories now found their way into the remotest villages in the interior. But now it was not African captives that were in demand but Africa's raw materials. Trade in so-called legitimate products (rubber, ivory, palm oil, lumber, peanuts, etc.) replaced the old trade in captives. The new trade proved equally devastating to African economies. In many areas, slavery became the dominant mode of production as labor was needed to collect rubber and other products. The situation also caused a decline in the cultivation of subsistence crops, causing famine in some areas and great social turmoil in others. Everywhere the impact of the new economy was as devastating as the effects of the slave trade had been in the preceding centuries. In some areas, the use of European manufactured products such as industrial cotton textiles was detrimental to local textile weavers, who could no longer find a market for their products. Other areas that had prospered in spite of the effects of the slave trade were stifled by their inability to develop their economy on their own terms. In general, all of equatorial Africa was engulfed in a crisis that preceded colonialism. Decades before the actual colonial invasion, most of the groups dwelling in the Congo region were already weakened by the effects of both the slave trade and the industrial revolution. Thus, they were unable to withstand Europe's drive for overseas colonies.

The first European explorers served as a prelude to colonial conquest. In 1816, Captain James Kingston Tuckey of the British Royal Navy set off to find the source of the Congo River. After arriving at the mouth of Congo, almost three and a half centuries after the first expedition of Diogo Cão, Tuckey sailed his ships upstream. This was something that no European had done before. The first maritime expedition into the hinterland of the Congo Basin proved fateful. Tuckey and his men grew discouraged as they encountered insurmountable obstacles. First, they faced thunderous rapids rushing along the sides of the Crystal Mountains. Then yellow fever claimed the lives of twenty-one of the fifty-four men of his expedition. After traveling about 150 miles up the Congo, morale collapsed and the expedition turned around. Defeated by the powerful river, Tuckey died shortly before they reached the Atlantic. Although it did not unlock the mystery of the Congo River, Tuckey's expedition aroused great interest in Congo's other "mysteries." To some, the Congo Basin remained the land of ivory and rubber, the supplier of countless raw materials that were badly needed in European factories. To others, it came to epitomize the "dark continent." From this latter perspective, Congo was a place in need of the light of civilization, a faceless and unknown swath of land waiting to be mapped out, explored, and conquered.

STANLEY'S FIRST EXPEDITION

The man who would accomplish what Tuckey had failed to do was Welsh-born John Rowlands. Rowlands' adopted name, Henry Morton Stanley, came to be associated with Europe's ruthless subjugation of Africans. In the 1840s, one man had preceded Stanley, although with a somewhat different mission. This man was the British physician, missionary, and explorer David Livingstone. Livingstone had set off for central Africa in search of the source of the Nile, which some Europeans considered "the greatest discovery that remained to be made in the world." The Nile had long fascinated Europe. Rich and complex civilizations had developed all along its banks from the heart of Africa to the Mediterranean coast, prompting the rise of Greece, Rome, and Western civilization. Since the Greeks, Europe had sought to understand the secret of these mysterious and life-giving waters. As early as 460 B.C., Herodotus ventured to the cataracts of Assouan in search of the source of the Nile. Many other Europeans after him went even further. They pushed forward, hoping to discover what lay beyond, only to be routed by the powerful obstacles that start at the first cataracts.

Livingstone was driven by the same obsessive, insatiable curiosity to unlock the riddle of the Nile. He was also motivated by the array of impulses that fueled the "Scramble for Africa": antislavery zeal, the need for raw materials, Christian evangelism, desire for personal glory, and a craving for exoticism. Livingstone had already spent more than twenty years exploring the Zambezi region and crossing the continent from coast to coast. In 1865, at the age of fifty-two, Livingstone departed from England. He arrived at the island of Zanzibar on January 28 and set off for the interior of the continent accompanied by 130 Zanzibari porters, guides, and servants. By the beginning of 1867, his caravan was reduced to only a dozen men. They wandered aimlessly before reaching the source of the Congo River, which Livingstone immediately mistook for that of the Nile. Three years after leaving Zanzibar with his men, covering in all more than 2000 miles, he arrived at Ujiji, on the northeastern shore of Lake Tanganyika. He was seriously ill and accompanied by only nine men. During most of his wandering in East Africa, Livingstone relied on the help and hospitality of "Arab" slave-trading caravans. In addition, most of what he accomplished was only possible thanks to the staunch loyalty of his African companions, especially Chuma and Susi. After Livingstone passed away on May 1, 1873, they carried his corpse halfway across the continent to the Indian port of Bagamayo, in present-day Kenya, to hand it over to British authorities. But their courage has not elicited nearly as much admiration as Livingstone's feats. Nowhere in Livingstone's diaries do we find gratitude or even acknowledgment of their accomplishments. Had they been able to write, their narratives might have provided a different story of this early encounter between Europeans and Africans.

Meanwhile, people in Europe began to fear for Livingstone's safety, as his whereabouts were unknown. Stanley was then an ambitious young journalist who had been in Africa only once and had no experience as an explorer. He put together a rescue operation at the behest and with the unlimited financial backing of his benefactor, *New York Herald* publisher James Gordon Bennett, Jr. In 1871, the largest African mission up to that date, comprised of some 300 men in all, started out from the east coast in search of Livingstone. By then the doctor had not been seen by any European in five years. After eight months of trekking across East Africa, Stanley's expedition finally located Livingstone at Ujiji. When word of his feat reached Europe and America, it brought instant fame to the Welsh journalist.

Finding Livingstone, however, was only the first chapter of Stanley's exploits in what he would later describe as "darkest Africa." Parting with

Livingstone, Stanley returned to England in July 1872. It was not long before he organized another expedition, this time to settle once and for all disputes about Africa's hydrography. The expedition started out in Zanzibar in November 1874 and reached the seaport of Boma, on the mouth of the Congo, almost three years later. The journey included 7,000 miles of perilous walking and rowing. Stanley sometimes forced his Zanzibari porters to transport the steamboats overland. Other times he drove his men up hills and through swamps so unmercifully that some did not survive the experience. He subjected his companions to torturous treatment: "When mud and wet sapped the physical energy of the lazily-inclined," wrote Stanley, "a dog-whip became their backs, restoring them to a sound—sometimes extravagant—activity" (Hochschild 1998: 31). Flogging was inflicted upon porters for any menial offense. Some porters, after being severely flogged, were chained and left for dead while the caravan moved on. The final 220-mile stretch of the river, from Stanley Pool (later renamed Malebo Pool) to the mouth of the Congo, proved to be the most treacherous. Stanley and his men were not prepared for it in spite of their grit. This is one of the Congo River's most impressive stretches, with fast-moving, roaring waters rushing through rock gorges in a series of rapids and waterfalls. Stanley forced his Zanzibari men to carry the canoes overland (the largest of them was fifty-four feet long and weighed three tons), sometimes hauling them for miles across steep mountains. Finally, Stanley abandoned his dream of reaching the Atlantic by boat and set off for Boma by land. In August 1877, what remained of his expedition reached Boma. In all, more than half of the men lost their lives. No other white person but Stanley survived to tell the tale of the extraordinary expedition. Stanley was quick to proclaim that Europeans had finally solved the great mystery of both the Nile and the Congo rivers.

Like many of his contemporaries, Stanley was determined to translate these geographic discoveries into profitable business ensured by colonial control. Once back in England, his speeches to British manufacturers and politicians invariably included the following argument:

> There are 40,000,000 naked people beyond that gateway, and the cotton-spinners of Manchester are waiting to clothe them. . . . Birmingham's foundries are glowing with the red metal that shall presently be made into iron-work in every fashion and shape for them . . . and the ministers of Christ are zealous to bring them, the poor benighted heathen, into the Christian fold.

Most Europeans concurred with Stanley that mapping out the African interior should serve one particular purpose: to pave the way for claiming African territories.

BULA MATARI

Unlocking Congo's mysteries established Stanley's fame even more than his discovery of Livingstone. When word of his exploits reached Europe, months before he sailed back to England, Stanley was guaranteed to become not only a rich man but the most celebrated European explorer of his century. In Europe, one monarch had followed Stanley's expedition with avid interest. This monarch was eager to meet the man who many in Europe considered to have opened a new continent to commerce and Christianization. At the time when the two men met, Stanley was thirty-seven and Leopold II, king of the Belgians, was forty-two. King Leopold was a tall, imposing man with a spade-shaped beard and an enormous nose, notorious for his sexual and culinary appetites. Leopold ruled a tiny country, half the size of West Virginia, which had seceded from the Netherlands to gain its independence in 1830. It was an artificially constructed nation with no national consciousness, bitterly divided between French and Flemish[1] speakers. Leopold once referred to his adopted land as "a small country with small people" ("*petit pays, petits gens*"). It was a country with no imperial ambition, battling constantly to stay neutral so as not to incur the wrath of its much larger neighbors, France and Germany. However, against public opinion and despite Belgian politicians' apathy, Leopold was determined to find a colony for little Belgium. In his twenties, the young prince had restlessly scoured the world, from North Africa to China, in search of a colony. He stopped short of buying Fiji, considered briefly acquiring a piece of Argentina or Formosa (present-day Taiwan), and toyed with the idea of taking the Philippines from Spain. Now, thanks to Stanley's exploits, he turned his attention to "darkest Africa." If he could not buy a colony, he reckoned, he would conquer one.

The two men met in Brussels for the first time in June 1878. Stanley had long sought to influence British opinion in favor of claiming the lands he had discovered in the Congo Basin. He found in the Belgian king an attentive listener and an ambitious monarch who would spare no expense to bring the Congo Basin under his personal sovereignty. Stanley became the king's man in Africa. As the French were becoming increasingly interested in Congo, Leopold cloaked his commercial ambitions in claims of humanitarian motives. He used the cover of his Committee for Studies of the Upper Congo (Comité d'Études du Haut-Congo), which was later renamed the International Association of the Congo (L'Association Internationale du Congo). Leopold sponsored the first expedition to the Congo Basin "with an essentially philanthropic and scientific point of view and with the intention of extending civilization and finding new outlets for commerce and industry by the study and explorations of certain parts of the Congo." But the truth was obscured by this humanitarian rhetoric. In fact, Leopold so cunningly devised his scheme that the two main European contenders in Africa, France and Britain, remained unaware and did not attempt to impede his plans. In February 1879, Stanley set off for Africa, this time as Leopold's agent. His mission was to set up a station near Boma and build a road from there, around the cataracts, up to Malebo Pool. Stanley's steamer first sailed to East Africa to pick up sixty-eight Zanzibaris, three-quarters of whom had served with Stanley on his previous expeditions. So secret were Leopold's true ambitions that he only informed Stanley of his real mission when his ship drew alongside Gibraltar in passage to Congo. Stanley then received word from the monarch that part of his mission was to create a "confederation of free negro republics" in Congo. The name "Congo" now referred not only to a river but also to a huge territory that Leopold was poised to claim. Ivory and rubber were the spoils that drove Leopold's greed and his careful strategies in equatorial Africa. Since the land was home to various communities, Leopold drew on a rhetoric that by then already permeated European colonial discourse and informed Europe's relationship with Africa: Congo, as if a wasteland with no inhabitants, must be penetrated, exploited, and ruled. In Leopold's mind these so-called "free negro republics" were mere fig leaves that concealed his plan to forcefully claim Congo. In blunt terms, Stanley was told:

> It is a question of creating a new State, as big as possible, and of running it. It is clearly understood that in this project there is no question of granting the slightest political power to the negroes. That would be absurd. The white men, heads of the stations retain all power. They are the absolute commanders. . . .

Nowhere was this disregard for African culture and sovereignty more ruthless than in the building of the trail around the cataracts. To carve the trail, Stanley and his men blasted their way through the Crystal

Mountains. Bewildered and intimidated by the spectacle of these white men turning their world upside down, the Bakongo people dubbed Stanley *Bula Matari* (Kikongo for "breaker of rocks"). Although Stanley considered the term a badge of honor, it was used by the Africans with contempt. As years passed and Leopold tightened his grip over the Congo, *Bula Matari* came to convey in the popular usage a deep sense of alienation and to encapsulate the abuses of the colonial government. In Congo as in many other parts of the continent, Africans took solace in such expressions and in popular discourse that challenged the position of their oppressors.

THIS MAGNIFICENT CAKE

Stanley, accompanied by his crew of porters and workers, some of whom were recruited locally, continued breaking rocks on his way toward Malebo Pool. He supervised the construction of a fifty-two-mile road around the first stretch of rapids and cataracts from Vivi to Isangila. Meanwhile, the French, who already maintained a presence on the coast of Gabon, began to move into the interior of the Congo Basin. Savorgnan de Brazza, an Italian-born officer with French citizenship, was dispatched by the French government to explore the areas around the Ogowe and Alima rivers. In 1880, de Brazza moved swiftly along the Ogowe River directly to the pool. In September, he reached the pool's right bank at the village of Mbe, then the political center of the Bateke Kingdom, today the site of Brazzaville, capital of the Republic of Congo. De Brazza spent a month at the court of Bateke king Makoko as a guest of honor. During this time he persuaded the king to sign a treaty placing Makoko's lands and peoples under the protection of the French flag. De Brazza's goal was to lay the foundation for French colonial presence in equatorial Africa. King Makoko relinquished his power over his people and gave away ancestral lands in exchange for next to nothing to a foreign visitor accompanied only by a small retinue of unarmed West African porters and servants. This may be explained by the fact that Makoko could not read or write. He may have understood the treaty as a friendship agreement that would allow his people to inaugurate commercial relations with the French. In many of these central African societies, it was believed that people could only use the land, while ownership remained the dead ancestors' privilege. How then could African chiefs sign away their land by marking an X on a document written in a foreign language? How could one man believe that by the stroke of a pen he could appropriate lands that had witnessed the development of such great kingdoms? "Did the chiefs of Ngombi and Mafela, for example, have any idea of what they agreed to on April 1, 1884?" asks author Adam Hochschild. According to the treaty, these chiefs, in return for one piece of cloth per month for each of them and a present of cloth at the time of the signing, promised

> freely of their own accord, for themselves and their heirs and successors for ever to give up to the said Association the sovereignty and all sovereignty and governing rights to all their territories . . . and to assist by labour or otherwise, any works, improvements or expeditions which the said Association shall cause at any time to be carried out in any part of these territories. . . . All roads and waterways running through this country, the right of collecting tolls on the same, and all game, fishing, mining, and forest rights, are to be the absolute property of the said Association.

To Makoko and the other African rulers, the prospect of trading with the white man carried more weight than any other consideration in their attitude toward Stanley and de Brazza. Ngalyema was a powerful Bateke chief whose village, Ntamo, was later destroyed by Leopold's soldiers to make way for a European settlement on the left bank of the Stanley Pool. Ngalyema told Stanley, "We have no objections to trade with white men if they come for trade, but you do not come for trade; therefore you cannot come to Ntamo." Stanley and de Brazza, however, considered every treaty they established with African chiefs a cession of land and sovereignty. "The treaties must be as short as possible and in a couple of articles must grant us everything," Leopold wrote to Stanley as news about de Brazza's treaties spread in European colonial circles. As soon as de Brazza returned to France, he successfully lobbied the French parliament to ratify his dubious treaty with Makoko. This laid the legal foundation for what would become the largest French colony in Africa.

French encroachment in Leopold's domain in Congo intensified his colonial ambitions. He feared that he might be surpassed in the race to stake out claims in the Congo Basin. He became increasingly alarmed that although most Belgians were indifferent to the colonial project, the tide was turning in most European countries in favor of colonial takeover of Africa. De Brazza had the full support of both the French government and the French public, who were looking for some colonial success to off-set the humiliating defeat inflicted by the Germans at Sedan. Stanley, on the other hand, had only the backing of Leopold and lacked the moral support of Belgian public opinion. France did not believe Leopold's claims of an altruistic enterprise in Congo and was determined to impede his maneuvers in central Africa. A bitter rivalry ensued between the French and the Belgians over control of Stanley Pool, which de Brazza had secured on behalf of his government. During the early 1880s, Stanley worked feverishly to establish treaties with African chiefs from Boma to the Upper Congo area. By the time he left Congo for Europe in June 1884, he had under his belt a sheaf of some 400 treaties extorted from local chiefs. These treaties paved the way for military penetration of the Congo Basin and also ignited the "Scramble for Africa." Although he had failed to dislodge the French from the northern area of Stanley Pool, Stanley had laid the foundation for Leopold's private colony in Congo. He had secured the whole western part of the Congo river, from its mouth to Stanley Falls, near the present-day city of Kisangani.

Until it was recognized by the major European powers, Leopold's African domain remained a legal fiction. The Africans who lived there were unaware of the fate that was to befall their communities. Indeed, most of the inhabitants of the Congo Basin had never heard of Leopold or any other white man, let alone crossed paths with one. The African chiefs were unaware of the forces that were driving Stanley's expedition in Congo. For this reason, they tolerated him within their dominion and even went as far as to grant him parcels of land to set up stations. They hoped that in response to such concessions the presence of the white man on their land would boost trade. They could not imagine that behind the first explorers, and later missionaries, lurked powerful European states. For these European states, control of Africa had become a battle to enhance national grandeur and seize raw materials.

Other European nations' desires for colonies in the heart of Africa were intense. Leopold decided to act swiftly while European control in Congo was still incipient. His greatest challenge came from Portugal, which had established a colony south of the Congo Estuary in what is now Angola and had long claimed both sides of the river's estuary. By the time Stanley's expedition reached the mouth of the river, Portugal was too busy in Angola to take on Leopold. But it was nonetheless determined to see some of its interests prevail. Britain had no particular interest in Congo other than securing freedom of navigation and trade and did not take heed when Stanley urged Britain to claim the territories that he had "discovered." After de Brazza's bold moves in the Congo area, however, Britain supported Portugal's claims at the expense of its archrival France. In exchange for British recognition of Portuguese sovereignty on either side of the Congo River, between latitudes 5° 12′ south and 8° south, Portugal guaranteed Britain free navigation on the Congo. It also guaranteed the introduction of a liberal tariff in all the Portuguese African colonies and granted Britain most-favored-nation trading rights. While negotiations dragged on, Leopold used various schemes to solidify his hold over Congo and wreck the Anglo-Portuguese treaty that was established in February 1884. First, he used his European networks to rally friends in favor of his colonial designs. Second, he instructed his aides to orchestrate a press campaign against Portuguese claims on the Congolese coast. In addition, Leopold hired Henry Stanford, a former American ambassador to Brussels, to lobby the American Congress on behalf of his bogus Association of the Congo. The stated goal of the Association, according to the letter Stanford carried to the U.S. president, was to introduce civilization to Congo and suppress the slave trade. After several months of intense lobbying, Stanford's efforts finally paid off. On April 22, 1884, the United States was the first country to formally recognize King Leopold II's claim to Congo. In his message of recognition, the U.S. secretary of state stressed the "humane and benevolent purposes of the International Association of the Congo" and ordered "the officers of the United States, both on land and sea, to recognize the flag of the International African Association as the flag of a friendly government." On December 4, during his annual address to the U.S. Congress, President Grover Cleveland reiterated the United States' support of Leopold's philanthropic venture. He vowed to cooperate with other governments "to promote commercial rights and residence in the valley of the Congo, free of intervention and political control by any of the nations."

Leopold's sovereignty over Congo was secured with recognition by the United States. Leopold now turned his attention to convincing European governments that even little Belgium had the right to grab a piece of the "magnificent African cake," an expression he once used to refer to the colonial onslaught and its object. After much quibbling over Leopold's real motives in claiming Congo for his Association, Chancellor Bismarck of Germany eventually added legitimacy to Leopold's claims to Congo. Germany preferred Belgian control of Congo, with the right for German nationals to trade freely in the Congo Basin without the imposition of taxes, to French or British monopoly. On November 8, 1884, a few days before the opening of the Berlin Conference, Germany recognized the Association of the Congo. This gave Leopold the upper hand at the negotiation table to which Bismarck had invited European leaders to settle colonial disputes. By the time these European leaders convened at Berlin, Leopold had emerged as the sole and legal proprietor of his colony-in-the-making. He was soon to become its sovereign as well.

THE BERLIN CONFERENCE

The fate of Africa was decided at Berlin, among fourteen European representatives who had never set foot on African soil, without a single African present at the negotiation table. This state of affairs speaks not only to the arbitrariness of Europe's dealings with Africa but also to the rise of Bismarck's Germany. After Germany's triumph in the Franco-Prussian War, Chancellor Bismarck vowed to steer his country on an imperial course. Between 1883 and 1885, Germany set up missions and trading posts in the Tanganyika region of East Africa, in Southwest Africa, and in Togo and Cameroon on the West African coast. Bismarck claimed these territories as protectorates. Germany was the first European country to have recognized Leopold's Association, mainly because of fears that Congo might fall under the control of either France or Britain. Germany was also the means by which Leopold could realize his claims. Germany's rejection of the Anglo-Portuguese treaty put Leopold in a strong position to circumvent French and British resistance to the idea of Belgium carving out such an enormous territory in central Africa.

Against this backdrop of diplomatic activity and political rivalries, the conference opened on November 15, 1884 at Bismarck's official residence in Berlin. Although Leopold did not attend, his claims could not be brushed aside by the representatives of the other nations involved in Congo. His own representatives, Baron Lambermont, secretary general of the Belgian Foreign Ministry, and Emile Banning, a journalist turned archivist in the Foreign Ministry, worked tirelessly behind the scenes to further the Association's cause.

The agenda that all participants had agreed upon before coming to Berlin was restricted to three main issues: 1) freedom of trade in the basin and estuary of the Congo, 2) freedom of navigation on the Congo and Niger, and 3) formalities to be observed in relation to occupation of new territories on the African coast. What was at stake was 1) an enormous territory that Europeans were convinced would yield vast amounts of resources and 2) the most important commercial route between the interior of central Africa and the Atlantic coast. Europe was eager to exploit Africa's resources without the hindrance of constructing railways. Navigable rivers presented obvious advantages toward this end. These were Africa's commercial highways. Control of a major river was an asset that no European power could be persuaded to relinquish, even in exchange for larger tracts of land. In West Africa, for example, the British had tenaciously held onto the little area around the Gambia River despite France's offer to trade the much larger and richer colony of Ivory Coast.

The conference dragged on for several months and when it was finally over, the one man who did not attend, King Leopold II, had accomplished most of what he wanted. Under the "Berlin Act on the Congo," signed on February 26, 1885, Leopold's International Association of the Congo was granted sovereignty over a stretch of land of nearly 1 million square miles. It ran from the Congo Estuary to the Lualaba and encompassed more than 15 million people. Even the caveats imposed by the contending powers seemed minor when compared to the big prize that Leopold had secured. According to the treaty, Leopold had to open this vast territory to trade from all nations, to accommodate missionaries of all churches regardless of their European or American nationalities, and to administer a new independent black state. But Leopold, and not Belgium, was the sole proprietor of the territory. And the fact that he could blur the line between administration and personal sovereignty far outweighed any inconveniences. Even more important to Leopold was the fact that the legal status provided by the Berlin Act rendered the philanthropic guise of his Association unnecessary. No longer needed, the misleading humanitarian façade of the Association evaporated. In its place, Leopold established his personal sovereignty. On May 29, 1885, by royal decree, Leopold named his personal property Congo Free State (État Indépendant du Congo—EIC), discarding the already defunct International Association of the Congo. In addition to its blue flag with the gold star, the new state had its own national anthem, "Towards the Future." Leopold was now at the command of the colony he had long dreamed of, a territory bigger than all of Western Europe, nearly eighty times the size of Belgium itself. It was a land that the king of the Belgians was determined to make use of down to its last bit of wealth. How Leopold's sovereignty was to affect people in Congo was a matter of little concern in European colonial circles. So effective had Leopold's ploy been that most people in Europe still believed that Congo, under the auspices of a benevolent European monarch, was bound to become a site of international free trade and zealous Christian missionizing, a colony open to all. As Sir Harry Johnston suggested, "If ever there was a portion of Africa in which a ruler's private profits from State monopolies were precluded by an honorable adhesion to first principles, it was the Congo Free State."[2] These pretenses were unknown to the people of Congo. Further, once the diplomatic smoke cleared, a very different reality set in.

NOTES

1. Dutch language spoken in the northern half of Belgium.
2. Quote from his introduction to Morel (1906: xiv).

4

Leopoldian Congo, 1885–1908

For a long time, Leopold's one-man rule over Congo conjured up lofty images of the white man's burden. Colonial propaganda spread images of a few white men toiling together in the heart of the "dark continent" to build roads, hospitals, schools, and missions and bestow the blessings of the gospel on millions of uncivilized Africans. Above all was the dominant image of a visionary European king, who against considerable odds and by mere fiat, had created an "international state" in equatorial Africa. In his own words, "The Congo has been, and could have been, nothing but a personal undertaking. There is no more legitimate or respectable right than that of an author over his own work, the fruit of his labour. . . . My rights over the Congo are to be shared with none; they are the fruit of my own struggles and expenditure." Ironically, these noble images gained currency not during Leopold's actual rule but after Belgium took over. Belgians wanted to foster the myth of a beneficent colonial state and justify the paternalistic colonial system they created in Congo. To do so, they lionized Leopold's image. Leopold cloaked his enterprise in the Congo in the guise of philanthropy. In a similar way, Belgian rule in Congo operated behind a paternalistic façade, which guaranteed political continuity between Congo Free State and Belgian Congo.

In Belgian colonial literature, Leopold's *œuvre coloniale* (colonial work) in Congo was eulogized with unwavering conviction. The myth came to permeate Belgian policies and relations between Europeans and Africans through independence and thereafter. As recently as a decade ago, a great deal of the literature authored by contemporary Belgian historians continued to extol the virtues of the visionary king while ignoring his role in the terrible tragedy that claimed the lives of millions of Congolese. More recently, however, a burst of scholarly research is recasting Belgian colonial rule in Congo, starting with the Leopoldian era, in a less than flattering light. The myth of the "happy colony" is being gradually replaced with a less benign characterization. Looking back at this colonial myth, one wonders at its potency despite well-established evidence of atrocious mass killings. The contradiction begs reflection on the nature of Leopold's regime in Congo.

In his own country, the constitution had dwarfed Leopold's power, leaving him the constitutional monarch of a small European state with little scope for personal ambitions. In the much larger Congo, however, he was able to pursue an unwavering authoritarian path. His approach to some extent prefigured not only the colonial state but also the postcolonial dictatorship. A monarch claiming for his personal benefit nearly a million square miles of territory could scarcely qualify him as a philanthropist. Nor could the killing of millions be justified as a lofty and disinterested humanitarian enterprise. But the myth of Leopold suppressed for a time popular recognition of the atrocious events of that era. In the introduction to his poignant account of Congo's forgotten genocide, author Adam Hochschild (1998: 3) reminisces about his first encounter with Congo's genocide:

> I knew almost nothing about the history of the Congo until a few years ago, when I noticed a footnote in a book I happened to be reading. Often, when you come across something particularly striking, you remember just where you were when you read it. On this occasion I was sitting, stiff and tired, late at night, in one of the far rear seats of an airliner crossing the United States from east to west. The footnote was to a quotation by Mark Twain, written, the note said, when he was part of the worldwide movement against slave labor in the Congo, a practice that had taken five to eight million lives. Worldwide movement? Five to eight million lives? I was startled.

That Congo's genocide had been reduced to a mere footnote of history should not come as a surprise. To Leopold and other Europeans of his age, explorers, journalists, politicians, and missionaries alike, Africa was usually referred to as if it were devoid of human societies. It was considered a vast, forlorn, and empty land that begged for European civilization. To envision Africa otherwise, as a land of cohesive societies and thriving cultures, would have exposed the insidious nature of colonization itself. Twenty-four years passed from the time the first stations were erected to the time Leopold relinquished his personal sovereignty over the Congo to Belgium. During this time, rule over the newly created country was based on the violent imposition of a colonial order and the voracious pursuit of the country's valuable resources.

THE BIRTH OF A COLONIAL ORDER

Once Leopold had assumed personal power in Congo, his first and most pressing task was to map out his vast newborn state. This was a necessary step toward effective occupation and exploitation. At the time that Stanley's expedition left Congo, most of the navigable waters of the interior of the basin remained a mystery to Europeans. Several European explorers picked up where Stanley had left off. Between October 1884 and March 1885, English Baptist missionary George Greenfell traveled up the Itimbiri, the Aruwimi, and the Lomami, three major tributaries of the Congo. He gathered valuable hydrographic data that were later published by the Royal Geographical Society. In 1885, German explorer H. W. Von Wissman provided crucial information after descending the Lulua and the Kasai up to Stanley Pool. More exploratory missions followed during the years 1885–1889, each adding to the already substantial geographic literature regarding Congo. In all, Europeans mapped out more than 10,000 miles of navigable waterways in Congo. No other part of Africa was so well endowed in terms of river transport. These explorations allowed the Europeans a clearer picture of the immense hydrographic network that linked almost all parts of Congo Basin. The information from these explorations showed that with their steamboats, Europeans could penetrate virtually anywhere within the basin. Wherever they arrived, the flag of the new state was planted, native lands were seized, and administrative posts established.

One of the last regions to be explored was Katanga, in southeastern Congo. This region had remained inaccessible to Europeans because it was not served by the waterways that covered the rest of the Congo Basin. Through hearsay and the reports of early Portuguese and British expeditions, however, Europeans gathered that Katanga possessed abundant copper and gold mines. While in the neighborhood of Lake Nyasa, Livingstone witnessed the flow of caravans arriving from Katanga with their loads of ivory, malachite, and especially copper. He later wrote:

> About a month's march from here, towards the west, the natives of Katanga melting down malachite obtain large ingots which have the form of a capital I. Throughout the region these can be seen varying in weight from 50 to 100 lbs. and the natives draw them to make bracelets which they wear on their arms and ankles. Gold is also found in Katanga and samples have been offered to the Sultan of Zanzibar.

A first exploratory mission, financed by Leopold's Association of the Congo and led by German scientist Paul Reichard, reached Bunkeya on January 20, 1884. This town, located on a vast plain near the Lufira, was then the flourishing capital of a newly created state. It was ruled by a foreigner, Msiri, whose father, Kalasa, was an East African trader who often traveled from the coast to the Katanga area to purchase copper ore. Msiri, then a young man, remained in the area to act as his father's agent. With the help of a group of Bayeke people, he emerged around 1870 as the ruler of this large state, which stretched from the Lualaba in the east to Lake Mweru in the west and from the Luapula to the Congo-Zambezi watershed in the south. Msiri's state was a modern version of the state formations that had existed in the area since at least the sixteenth century. The difference was that its economy was heavily dependent upon trading activities, especially slave trading. From his base in Bunkeya, Msiri controlled a vast, intricate trading network that promoted his capital into one of the most prosperous trading centers in central Africa. Traders came from as far as Angola, Uganda, Zanzibar, the Zambezi area, and the Congo Basin to trade their products for ivory, salt, slaves, copper, and iron ore. Firearms and ammunition obtained from the "Arab" traders of the Indian Ocean coast were exchanged for copper, ivory, and slaves and sustained Msiri's position at the apex of this network.

Msiri's fame and wealth sparked the interest of many European explorers. After Reichard's unsuccessful expedition, other Europeans visited Bunkeya. First, two Portuguese explorers, Capello and Ivens, passed through Msiri's territory on their way from Angola to Mozambique. They were sent by the Portuguese government and hoped to discover a trade route that might link the two Portuguese colonies. This would provide

Portugal with a corridor across the continent between the Indian Ocean and the Atlantic coast. A little more than a year passed before another European arrived at Bunkeya. This solitary white man was the Scottish missionary Frederick Stanley Arnot. Following in the steps of Livingstone, he had decided to engage in missionary work and emulate his illustrious predecessor. He arrived at Bunkeya in February 1886 without food, or goods, or even the traveling party that most European explorers favored. Msiri welcomed him warmly and granted him authorization to settle in his domain. Arnot remained in Bunkeya for the next two years under the protection of Msiri himself, and he was well treated by the Bayeke people. However, fearing that the new religion might compromise the loyalty of his subjects, Msiri curtailed Arnot's missionary work. But Arnot remained in Bunkeya anyhow and was later joined by several other British missionaries. The continual presence of white missionaries in Bunkeya shows how powerful Msiri's state had become. It also reveals a debilitating pattern that would plague Congo far into the future. Because of its mineral wealth, Katanga was singled out by Europeans from the beginning of colonization. This profoundly affected the course of Congo's political development up through the present.

British missionaries were not the only Englishmen lured by the promise of wealth in Katanga. Leopold could not afford to effectively occupy the area in accordance with the Berlin Act. Thus, some in British colonial circles argued that unoccupied parts of Congo state could be, in the "spirit of Berlin," claimed by any other European power that had a vested interest there. Cecil Rhodes, who had already carved out a huge territory in southern Africa, decided to act on these possibilities through his powerful British South Africa Company. After an unsuccessful attempt to persuade Msiri to cede his sovereignty, he sent several of his agents to increase British presence in Katanga. It was only once the British government was poised to back up Rhodes' maneuvers in Katanga that Leopold turned his attention there. He expressed his determination to keep Katanga within the borders of Congo Free State. A military expedition of 180 African soldiers and 150 porters, under the command of Captain Le Marinel, received orders to proceed to Bunkeya. There they were to hoist Congo Free State's flag and force Msiri to recognize Leopold's sovereignty over the whole of Katanga. Le Marinel left with his column in December 1891 and reached Bunkeya on April 18. Another expedition set out from Belgium under the aegis of the Compagnie du Congo pour le Commerce et l'Industrie, owned by Belgian magnate Albert Thys. Because its objective was political as well as commercial, its command fell to Alexandre Delcommune, who had worked for several years at Boma in various colonial factories. The expedition reached Bunkeya on October 6, 1891. Delcommune failed to convince Msiri to relinquish his sovereignty to the Free State. Msiri was willing to accommodate Europeans who ventured into his country for the purpose of spreading the gospel, but was quite unbending toward those who came with demands.

European expeditions continued to mark their presence in the region. Another expedition, this time coming from East Africa, arrived in Bunkeya at the end of 1891. The English commander, Captain Stairs, was accompanied by a number of Europeans. They were ruthless adventurers who worked for a newly founded colonial venture, the Compagnie du Katanga. When they reached Bunkeya, they did not waste time attempting to strike a deal with Msiri. Instead, Stairs ordered his men to hoist the Free State flag on a little hill that dominated the capital. Alarmed at such a belligerent act, Msiri retreated to the village of his first wife. Stairs' men pursued him and murdered him.

Msiri's death ultimately brought the whole area under European domination and put an end to an authoritarian regime that had grown tyrannical. It also disrupted economic stability and weakened the political unity that Msiri's rule had maintained. At Bunkeya, famine and disease took their toll on the local population. Trading caravans no longer converged there and the people scattered, abandoning the once wealthy capital. Small African chiefs took advantage of the political vacuum to assert their independence as the authority of Congo Free State was not yet established.

In August 1892, a year after the demise of Msiri's empire, Leopold discovered that the land he had been struggling to snatch away from the Africans contained some of the richest mineral deposits in the world. This discovery bolstered his claims. On May 12, 1894, he signed a treaty in which the British government agreed to recognize the frontier between Katanga and Rhodesia.

RED RUBBER

In the following years, exploratory missions gave way to commercial exploitation. First, in 1891, the king instituted the "vacant lands" policy. Under this policy, all lands that were supposedly not occupied by native people were the state's property. In a secret decree issued in September, Leopold ordered his agents to secure on his behalf all the ivory and rubber they could find. This effectively created a monopoly that prevented

Africans from selling ivory or rubber to private traders.[1] Before roads and railways were constructed, the burden of transporting these goods to the river stations where steamers waited to load them fell on Africans. During this time, the colonial economy depended heavily on porterage. In the Lower Congo especially, local people's reluctance to assist the Europeans in hauling their spoils away to Europe proved so unyielding that they brought Zanzibaris and Kru men from Liberia to do the work. But increasing demand for carriers soon outstripped this supply, making the mobilization of local labor a necessity. Under this new system, Africans were offered no incentives and in most areas compulsory labor was the rule. Those groups who bore the full brunt of this system found themselves increasingly dependent upon an economic system that yielded no benefit to them. In the words of a Belgian observer, this system "laid so many burdens over the years on their heads and shoulders that it finished by crushing them, so that their bones mingled with the dust of the path and the whole region was depopulated." From the colonial point of view, porterage, like slavery a few decades before, was a necessary evil. Writing in the early years of the Free State as a staunch advocate of porterage, Charles Liebrechts linked this indefensible system to the well-being of the Africans:

> Some people say those who employ this system are barbarous, and load them with anathemas. But alas, in the greater part of Central Africa, this is the only means of transport, and to give it up would mean renouncing the development of civilization. Such a renunciation would engender evils as great as those of the porterage system. There could be nothing worse for Africans at present than to lose European influence, for they would only fall into a state of anarchy which would lead to the extermination of the race (quoted in Slade 1962: 72).

Even with his agents stationed in the remotest areas of his new private domain, Leopold could not effectively control such a large area unless he abided by the Berlin Act. This called for unrestricted access to the Congo Basin. Accordingly, Leopold created a free trade zone open to exploitation by any and all European private entrepreneurs. As a result, white missionaries, army officers, independent traders, and adventurers alike flocked to Congo in droves. Some of the largest trading companies included the Anglo-Belgian India Rubber and Exploration Company

(ABIR), the Société Anversoise du Commerce au Congo (Anversoise), the Compagnie du Congo pour le Commerce et l'Industrie (CCCI), and the Société Anonyme Belge pour le Commerce du Haut Congo (SAB), created in 1888 when CCCI merged with Sanford Exploring Expedition (SEE). All of these companies were registered in Belgium but maintained a motley array of trading stations all over Congo, especially along major waterways.

Table 4.1: Congo Free State Ivory Exports, 1888–1892

Year	Value (1000 Belgian francs)	% exports	Weight (kilos)
1888	1,096	42	5,824
1889	2,270	52	45,252
1890	4,669	56	76,448
1891	2,835	53	59,686
1892	3,730	67	118,739

SOURCE: Gann and Duignan (1979: 118).

The history of the transformation of Congo Free State from a liability to a highly profitable enterprise can be summed up in two words: red rubber. And these two words still strike fear into the hearts of those who heard the grisly stories of maimed hands, child labor, and mass killings that were the hallmarks of the Leopoldian regime in Congo. Fueled by rising demands for bicycle and then automobile tires in Europe and America, rubber was a valuable commodity. And it was the single most valuable commodity of Congo before Europeans could mobilize enough capital and set up the heavy infrastructure necessary to tap into the mineral wealth of Kasai and Katanga. Rubber, unlike minerals, required no capital investment, no fertilizer, no heavy machinery—just a few steamers to transport the wild rubber and, most importantly, labor. Rubber prices in the world market had more than quadrupled between the late 1880s and the early 1910s, making rubber a very hot commodity. During this period, Africa's supply of rubber went from 5 percent to nearly half the world's total production, with Congo leading the way. Rubber had gradually displaced ivory for a variety of reasons. One reason was low prices in the European ivory market as compared to the raised prices demanded by African ivory suppliers. During the last decade of the nineteenth century, colonial companies that had relied heavily on ivory saw their profits fall and shifted to the trade in rubber (see Table 4.2). One such company, SAB, created a string of rubber plantations at Busira in 1893, in emulation of the profitable rubber plantation system that had been set up in the Brazilian rainforests. However, most rubber collected in Congo came from vines that grew in the wild, snaking high into trees, throughout nearly two-thirds of the rainforests. The collection of the coagulated sap did not require any particular skill nor equipment, just a knife and a bucket. But it demanded that men, women, and sometimes children venture deep into the forest, as most vines near villages had been depleted of their sap. During the rainy season, when forests turned into huge swamplands, villagers had to spend days at a time painstakingly gathering the required quantity of rubber in an environment that harbored many dangers. Not only did rubber collection provide no profit, but it also caused a crisis of subsistence because villagers could not tend to their plots when they were most needed.

Table 4.2: Congo Free State Rubber Exports, 1888–1905

Year	Value (1000 Belgian francs)	% exports	Weight (1000 kilos)
1888	260	10	74
1890	556	6	123
1895	2,882	26	576
1900	39,874	84	5,316
1905	43,755	86	4,861

SOURCE: Gann and Duignan (1979: 219).

In order to enforce this system, a large body of troops known as the Force Publique was established, first in Vivi, the state capital, and then in the rest of the colony. Until 1894, recruits came mostly from outside the colony. These included Zanzibaris from East Africa and Kru men, Hausas, and other West African "volunteers" from Sierra Leone, Accra, Monrovia, and Lagos. In 1901, out of 12,786 soldiers of the Force Publique, who were commanded by some 350 European officers, nearly 12,500 were foreigners. After this date most recruits were drawn from the Upper Congo districts and equipped with modern weaponry. Recruiting agents obtained their recruits through armed raids upon villages and often preyed upon children (not unlike late president Laurent-Désiré Kabila, who was notorious for enrolling children in his rebel forces). These children were then sent to special "camps of military instruction," where they were trained in the most gruesome practices before being dispatched to their turfs.

Hostage taking was the preferred method for compelling villagers to collect rubber. In 1899, the British vice consul reported such a case involving a column of soldiers under the command of a Belgian officer. The soldiers arrived in a village and began looting it in retaliation for the villagers' refusal to carry out orders. The soldiers then attacked the villagers and seized their women, whom they declared as hostages until the chief could bring in the required quotas of rubber. Most of these women were repeatedly raped while their men went to collect rubber. To add insult to injury, after loading the buckets of rubber into their canoes, the soldiers sold the women back to their families for the price of a couple of goats apiece. Sometimes hostages, including women, children, and elders, were kept inside wooden enclosures in horrid conditions, without enough food or water; many died. At some villages, rubber squads forced men at gunpoint to rape their own mothers and sisters because they had refused to provide rubber.

If villagers failed to collect required quotas or, in some cases, if the quality of rubber collected was poor, soldiers customarily wiped out whole villages and brought the right hands of their victims to the white commissioner. "That was about the time I saw the natives killed before my own eyes," wrote a Danish missionary. Hands were cut off and often smoked to preserve them until they could be shown to the European officer. Force Publique soldiers acquired the habit of going on killing sprees to harvest hands in place of rubber. This happened so much that human hands took on a value of their own, becoming a sort of currency. The details of this reign of terror are too voluminous to be exhaustively reviewed here. Suffice it to say that as the red rubber system grew in scope, so did the accounts of African and European eyewitnesses who sought to expose the genocide. Writing in 1897, a Swedish missionary of the American Baptist Missionary Union, E.V. Sjöblom, recorded the following testimony:

> The natives in inland towns are, as a matter of custom,
> asked whether they are willing to gather india-rubber. . . .
> The people had never seen a white man and had
> returned from their hunt for rubber. . . . a soldier rushed
> in among the crowd, and seized an old man guilty of
> having been fishing in the river instead of gathering rub-
> ber; shoots him. . . . Right hand cut off. People flee out of
> the town. All except the old chiefs are forced to go away
> and work rubber. The sentries are from the wildest

tribes. When they get to this work they are many times worse. They are really small kings in the towns and often kill the people for the sake of the rubber. If the rubber does not reach the full amount required the sentries attack the natives. They kill some and bring the hands to the Commissioner. . . . From this village I went on another where I met a soldier who pointed to a basket, and said to me, 'look, I have only two hands.' He meant there were not enough to make up for the rubber he had not brought. He had several prisoners tied to trees. . . . Several of the natives were killed. I saw the dead bodies floating on the lake with the right hand cut off, and the officer told me when I came back why they had been killed. It was for the rubber.[2]

Another missionary, reporting from the village of Bolengi in 1896, recounted in detail the destruction of a whole village:

Describes raid of State troops upon the villages of Bandaka and Wajiko. Cause, poor quality of rubber. Questions soldiers, and is told fifty people have been killed and twenty-eight taken prisoners. Sees the prisoners taken through the mission station. Counts "sixteen women tied neck to neck." Some of these women carrying their tiny children. Several "young children were walking on before who were also prisoners." Visits the raided village. "In a little shed lay one of my late school children, a promising young lad. I lifted the leaves by which he was covered, and saw his right hand cut off. I then went through the village and saw the people burying their dead. I counted over twenty bodies and newly filled-up graves. All the bodies had the right hand cut off.[3]

Many of the accounts from Congolese eyewitnesses leave no doubt about the sadistic intents of the rubber trade enforcers. After slipping out of the hands of a rubber squad, one survivor wrote:

I myself saw a man at Likange who had had both his hands cut off. Sometimes they cut them at the wrist,

sometimes farther up . . . with a machete. Also there is a
Muboma . . . who has a long scar across the back of his
neck. There is another man called Botei at Inanga with the
same sort of scar, where they wounded him maliciously,
expecting him to die. They didn't cut his head off, they
didn't get to the bone, but expected him to bleed to death.
It was sheer cruelty; the State treated us abominably.[4]

By the early 1900s, an international campaign of protest against
Congo's red rubber economy was in full swing. In 1905, the American
Missionary Societies sent a strongly worded memorandum to the U.S.
Congress accusing Leopold of having instituted a legal form of slavery in
Congo:

The dreadful form of rubber collecting has, among other
evils, introduced a form of slavery of the worst possible
kind. No man's time, liberty, property, person, wife, or
child is his own. His position is worse than that of the
sheep or goats of the white man. . . . Even the dreadful
horrors of the 'middle passage' are completely put in the
shade by deliberate, demon-like acts of atrocity.

The demographic impact of the red rubber trade in Congo proved devastating. The trade created considerable wealth for the European companies that assisted Leopold in his gruesome scheme and replenished the
coffers of the Belgian monarch. But it wreaked havoc across the entire
colony, devastating the populations of large areas. Sifting through the
erratic demographic data of this period, suggests Hochschild (1998: 232),
"is like sifting the ruins of an Auschwitz crematorium. They do not tell
you precise death tolls, but they reek of mass murder." Venturing a personal estimate based "on innumerable local sources from different areas:
priests noticing their flocks were shrinking, oral traditions, genealogies,
and much more," anthropologist Jan Vansina has persuasively suggested
that between 1880 and 1920, Congo's population was cut at least in half.
This opinion is corroborated by the first-hand accounts of a number of
witnesses. One of these was a Belgian trader who, traveling up the Congo
River in February 1891, could only lament the ongoing tragedy:

The country is ruined. Passengers in the steamer Roi des
Belges have been able to see for themselves that from

> Bontya, half a day's journey below our factory at Upoto,
> to Boumba inclusive, there is not an inhabited village
> left—that is to say four days' steaming through a coun-
> try formerly so rich; today entirely ruined.[5]

There are no accurate figures that reflect the total revenues generated by Congo's rubber economy. This is because, as Edmund D. Morel suggests, "sown in blood, they [were] harvested in secret." Nonetheless, public records suggest that between 1890 and 1904, total Congo rubber earnings increased nearly a hundredfold, placing Congo at the top of the world's rubber-producing countries. The first beneficiary was none but Leopold himself. A conservative estimate places his revenues from Congo at no less than $1 billion in today's terms. Leopold used this fortune first of all to meet the demands of a growing administrative apparatus in Congo. Large sums were spent in rewarding his agents in Congo, in the construction of buildings and railways (which occasioned even more suffering for the African laborers), and in the maintenance of the Force Publique. But most of his fortune was lavishly spent in Europe. He showered with extravagant gifts the mistresses that he had in every major city of Europe. In December 1909, the seventy-four-year-old king secretly married his longtime mistress Carolina, a former prostitute whom he had first encountered in Paris when she was only sixteen. Having already bought her a château in France, a few days after their marriage he bequeathed a considerable portion of his fortune to her. Rubber revenues also financed the king's self-aggrandizing projects. This included the construction of monuments, promenades, gardens, parks, and the endless renovations of his many properties. The château at Laeken alone, which Leopold spent his life renovating and enlarging, siphoned off a huge chunk of his colonial earnings. Other projects included the construction of the colonial museum at Tervueren, in a suburb of Brussels, which showcased mainly Congo's fauna. Another part of Leopold's earnings was invested in real estate on the Mediterranean, especially a sumptuous property at Cape Ferrat on the French Riviera. The king also invested considerable sums in Chinese railways, in Suez Canal stock, and in other companies throughout the world from Persia to Bolivia.

At least eight main concessionary companies profited from the rubber terror. The largest of these accumulated colossal revenues through its involvement. In 1897, ABIR spent Fr 1.35 per kilo to harvest rubber in Congo. It made a profit of more than 700 percent by shipping and selling a kilo of rubber in Europe for as much as Fr 10. The net profit from red rubber between 1898 and 1903 amounted to nearly $100 million. This caused ABIR's stock to rise sharply on the Antwerp stock exchange.

BELGIUM TAKES OVER

Among the first witnesses to alert the international community to rubber terror in Congo were two African-American missionaries. They visited Congo independently in the early 1890s, unbeknownst to one another. George Washington Williams was a Civil War veteran turned missionary. He was, according to his biographer, a self-made intellectual whose extraordinary albeit short life placed him in the pantheon of black heroes. Williams was also a remarkable historian, a lawyer (although he never practiced), and an adept politician. After witnessing the abuses perpetrated by Leopold's agents, he wrote an "Open Letter" to the king based on "a list of veracious witnesses, documents, letters, official records and data." He called for the creation of an international commission "with power to send for persons and papers, to administer oaths, and attest the truth or falsity of these charges." His claims amounted to an accusation of "crimes against humanity," an expression that appeared in a letter Williams wrote to the U.S. secretary of state. In this letter he attempted to persuade the American government to spearhead an international campaign against Congo's genocide. Williams even promoted the idea of self-government in Congo, under the guidance of the international community, as a necessary step toward total independence from Leopold's authoritarian grip.

Unlike Williams, William Sheppard had genuine evangelical ambitions. He arrived in Congo in May 1890 on behalf of the Southern Presbyterian Church, and he established its first mission on the Kasai River. His interest in the "country of my forefathers," as he put it, was also a means to escape the prejudiced climate of the postbellum South. He acquainted himself well with the customs of the Kuba people and mastered their language. He became the first foreigner to reach the capital of the Kuba Kingdom, the town of Ifuca. Kuba kings had prevented Europeans from intruding on this capital, which Leopold's forces would loot and destroy a few years after Sheppard's visit. He later consigned his anthropological observations to a book entitled *Presbyterian Pioneers in the Congo* in which his admiration for the Kuba culture is clear. "They were the finest looking race I had seen in Africa," he wrote of the Kuba, "dignified, graceful, courageous, honest, with an open smiling countenance and really hospitable. Their knowledge of weaving, embroidery, wood carving and smelting was the highest in equatorial Africa."[6] Yet, a few years after Sheppard's visit, the kingdom was destroyed. The people had to abandon their crafts in order to fulfill the demands of the rubber squads. On a subsequent visit in 1899, Sheppard uncovered some of the most macabre deeds of Leopold's rubber terror, including the smoking of the hands of those killed by the state's agents. This discovery turned him into one of the most outspoken critics of Congo's red rubber trade. His outspokenness even attracted the ire of the Belgian monarch, who took him to court for an article he had written denouncing the Compagnie du Kasai's destruction of Kuba society.

Sheppard's and Williams' protests on behalf of the millions of Congolese victims of colonial abuses set the stage for what was called the Congo Reform Association. This was an international campaign led by two Europeans. The first was Edmund D. Morel, an English journalist whose humanitarian ideas were inspired by early-nineteenth-century British abolitionists. The second was Roger Casement, a protestant Irishman from Ulster who first journeyed to Congo at age nineteen. He was later commissioned by the Foreign Office to set up the first British consulate in Congo. These two men deserve full credit for their international effort to expose the near extermination of Congolese and awaken European public opinion from its ignorance and apathy. However, they remained strongly attached to the colonial ideas of their time. They neither opposed the ideological basis of the European imperial project nor championed the cause of the Congolese. Their criticisms did not suggest that Africans should be allowed to control their land and live there in peace. In fact, they were staunch supporters of a kind of "benevolent colonialism" that they felt Leopold had betrayed. Just as Leopold had, they also claimed that it was Europeans' duty to bring the "gospel of progress" to millions of heathen Africans. Where their opinions diverged from those of the Belgian monarch was in their notion that Europeans should do so in a disinterested way and not hold up the gospel as a screen to hide economic interest. In their eyes, Europe's exploitation of Africa's resources could only be justified if accompanied by a corresponding effort to civilize Africans. They were, in essence, partisans of a style of colonialism that men like Livingstone and de Brazza had promoted before them.

In 1903, their international crusade produced the Casement Report. This was a meticulous indictment of Leopold's Free State based not on hearsay but on firsthand testimonies collected by someone who was familiar enough with Congo to perform a thorough investigation. Besides

the gruesome accounts of sliced-off hands and penises, the report documented the depopulation of some of the areas Casement visited. Thriving
communities of several thousand people, which he had known in the
early 1880s, were now reduced to a few inhabitants if not completely
wiped out. The Belgian king attempted to delay the report's publication
and discredit both the author and his careful investigation. But the
Casement Report still proved damaging to the Free State. Most people in
Europe understood that the report referred not to "a few individuals and
isolated cases," as Leopold would have liked them to believe, but to a
large-scale, deliberate system of forced labor compelled by a ruthless,
coercive political machine.

   Both the Casement Report and Morel's indefatigable campaign by
means of the Congo Reform Association finally exerted enough pressure
on the American, Belgian, and other European governments for them to
scrutinize Leopold's reign in Congo. During the years that followed the
publication of the report, Congo was the subject of intense debate in
Belgium. Leopold's critics used the Casement Report to bolster their
claims that Belgium should annex Congo. They were pitted against those
who continued to believe the king's enterprise in Congo justifiable. In
1906, while the debate was raging in Belgium, evidence of Leopold's rape
of Congo continued to rise. The king spent most of the year at his estate
at Cape Ferrat in the company of his mistress, who by then no longer
went by the name Caroline but Baroness de Vaughan. He braced for the
face-off with the Belgian chamber. He worked long hours on his luxurious yacht, the *Alberta*, on a scheme that would allow him not only to
retain sovereignty over Congo but to further increase his profits. The
scheme included the creation of three large colonial companies, the
Union Minière du Haut-Katanga (UMHK), the Société Forestière et
Minière du Congo (Forminière), and the Compagnie du Chemin de Fer
du Bas-Congo (BCK). By means of these companies, Leopold hoped to
tap into Congo's mineral wealth now that red rubber had become so
unpopular.

   However, Leopold's days as Congo's absolute ruler were numbered
and resentment of his enterprise was growing among Belgian politicians.
The beleaguered king boldly announced that he would sell Congo to the
highest bidder instead of handing it over to Belgium as he had always
hinted he would. The announcement triggered negotiations as the
Belgian government strove to prevent any other European government
from acquiring Leopold's colony. Negotiations dragged on for two years
until the king finally outmaneuvered the Belgian government and

achieved most of the financial advantages he had demanded. In March 1908, the deal was officially settled. The Belgian government received full sovereignty over Congo in return for assuming Fr 110 million worth of debts that Leopold had incurred. Under the terms of the deal, the Belgian government also agreed to pay more than Fr 45 million toward completing some of the king's wayward, self-aggrandizing projects in Belgium. They were to pay Leopold another Fr 50 million, to be extracted from Congo, as a "mark of gratitude for his sacrifices made for Congo." On November 15, 1908, a solemn ceremony held in Boma, which since April 1886 had replaced Vivi as the capital of Congo Free State, marked the formal change of ownership. Congo Free State was to become Belgian Congo. This was a cosmetic change that in no way implied the amelioration of the situation of the Congolese. This series of events had provided Belgium with one of the richest colonies in the world and made Leopold the richest monarch in Europe. But despite the exchange, "Leopold's ghost would not vanish so easily," to borrow Hochschild's fitting phrase. Leopold had steered Congo onto a course that subsequent governments up to the present have firmly maintained. His enterprise was solely motivated by profit. Since the land he had cunningly expropriated yielded profitable resources in abundance, he held steadfastly onto it. He utilized all necessary means to ensure high productivity, including a political and economic system that virtually enslaved the entire population. With Belgium now at the command of this vast colony, Congo was set to experience one of the most draconian colonial regimes in Africa.

NOTES

1. Due to the brutal tactics of these agents, Congo became one of the world's leading exporters of ivory by the early 1890s (see Table 4.1).
2. Quoted in Morel (1906: 47–48).
3. Quoted in Morel (1906: 51).
4. Quoted in Anstey (1971: 72).
5. Quoted in Morel (45).
6. Quoted in Hochschild (157).

5

The Colonial State, 1908–1945

Had it not been for the wealth of Congo, Belgium would not have felt compelled to annex Leopold's imperial domain. To begin with, public opinion in Belgium opposed annexation. Belgian authorities demurred at first, citing concerns that succeeding Leopold as the supreme legislative and executive authority in Congo might be unlikely to yield profits. Finally, they decided to acquire the territory Leopold had bequeathed. The decision to take over was not motivated by what the British and American governments called "the Belgian solution," that is, the moral and political obligation of Belgium to end the cruel treatment meted out to the Congolese by Leopold's agents. Instead, the succession was motivated by the hope that Congo might provide a lucrative economic opportunity. Belgium was a poor European country. As such, it was reluctant to embark upon a costly colonial adventure when its own national institutions were still fragile and recently created. Belgium could not assume the responsibility that a colonial venture entailed in terms of the expenditures of monetary and human resources necessary for the creation of an effective colonial administration. Even the suggestion that annexation might soften the criticisms of other European nations and pave the road for reforms in Congo persuaded few in Belgium. The sheer size of Congo, with a territory eighty times that of the mother country, raised doubts among even the most zealous advocates of "the Belgian solution."

Why, then, did Belgium decide in the end to acquire Congo? Ultimately, the decisions of most Belgian politicians were informed by the economic benefit their country could derive from dominion over Congo. Congo held particular promise as a colony. Immense mineral deposits had been confirmed in Katanga and Kasai, and Leopold had entrusted their exploitation to three powerful concessionary companies, UMHK, BCK, and Forminière. Thus it was assured that Belgium would be financially compensated for its effort in succeeding Leopold in Congo. Congo's enormous reserve of both natural and human resources would boost the Belgian industrial sector, which was in dire need of a reservoir of raw materials and an outlet for its finished products. All the institutions created during Belgian colonial rule in Congo, from the tightly controlled administration to the social policies that aimed to create a loyal Congolese elite, were informed by these economic imperatives. Belgian colonial policy was designed to make Congo an asset and not a liability to Belgium.

ADMINISTRATION AND SOCIETY

The administration of Congo changed little after it was handed over by Leopold II to Belgium. Belgium's approach to Congo did not differ much from that of Leopold, and reflected more generally the manner of European countries with respect to their African domains. A Belgian version of Lord Lugard's *Dual Mandate* was implemented. The overriding concern of this policy was that the colony generate profit for the metropolis. The riches of Congo had been, after all, one of the major factors that encouraged the Belgians to go along with the annexation. Another defining principle of the takeover was that Europeans had a *mission civilisatrice* (civilizing mission) based on Christianization and education to perform in Africa. The colony was governed according to a colonial charter drafted in 1908. This charter allowed Leopold's successor, King Albert I, to exert a great deal of influence over affairs in Congo by appointing high-ranking officials and signing laws.

On the local level, most rural Congolese were ruled indirectly by native chiefs who were put in place by the local colonial administrator. Administrative policy with respect to the rural areas was formulated based on the assumption that Congolese were divided into numerous independent tribes that engaged in endless clashes with one another. As shown in Chapter 2, precolonial Congo was dominated by major polities that extended across vast territories. Each polity was organized around a solidly built administration generally headed by a king and his council at the capital. New Belgian administrative policy did not take account of these characteristics of precolonial polities. Obliterating centuries of political organization, Belgian colonial policy created small, local political units known as *chefferies* (chiefdoms). The colonial government operated under the false pretense that it would rule indirectly through supposedly preexisting traditional political structures.

Traditional chiefs who did not comply with colonial dicta were replaced. Whenever this occurred, colonial authorities dispatched territorial agents to collect local genealogies and identify potential chiefs. Appointees were usually given a medal of office symbolizing their official recognition by the colonial administration. The political implication of the administrative structure that emerged was the breakup of the larger traditional groupings found in place by the Belgians in favor of the *chefferie*, which was based on clans or families. In 1917, there were 6,095 *chefferies*, each with an average population of less than 1,000 people. They were headed by indigenous chiefs with no effective authority over their constituencies. These chiefs frequently used their position to pursue personal interests, which put them at odds with the local population and further eroded their authority.

By 1920, it was clear that something had to be done, especially as some chiefs were levying their own private taxes and abusing people who failed to comply with their wishes. Intended as a means to indirectly control the rural population through appointed chiefs, *chefferies* became a hindrance to the colonial state by interfering with its exploitation of the natural and human resources of the colony. In 1920, Colonial Minister Louis Franck acknowledged the failure of this administrative system:

> The great number of chiefs and sub-chiefs amongst whom authority is divided in many regions of the Colony is an evil and a danger. The chefferies are too small, many chiefs lack all authority. The means of obtaining obedience formerly possessed by the chief have disappeared. The time is not far distant when, if we are not careful, in many regions, the collapse of indigenous authority will be complete. Judicial anarchy will be the counterpart of administrative crumbling. . . . The chief who is no longer judge, and a respected judge, will lose what remains of his authority.[1]

Franck decided that the *chefferies* must be superseded by larger administrative units endowed with modern government institutions. This called for reducing the number of *chefferies* through amalgamation to 2,496 in 1935, 1,070 in 1940, 594 in 1945, 476 in 1950, and 432 in 1955. As the number of *chefferies* decreased, so the population of each increased. In 1922, several *chefferies* in the eastern part of the colony were grouped together to form a new, larger unit known as a *secteur* (sector). Each *secteur* was administered by a traditional chief (*chef du secteur*), who was assisted by a council of indigenous dignitaries (*conseil du secteur*). Besides routine administrative tasks of collecting taxes, administering justice and policing, and maintaining the roads, these chiefs were vested with powers far greater than those of their counterparts in the *chefferies*. The colonial state equipped these chiefs with their own budget, which was replenished regularly by the proceeds of court fines, tax revenues, and government subsidies. A complete administrative infrastructure was put at their disposal, including secretary, court, treasury, police force, agricultural staff, several schools, one or more dispensaries, and sometimes even a maternity ward and a social center.

Despite the autonomy this administrative system seemed to afford local communities, it actually brought these communities firmly under colonial control. Most chiefs were chosen by the administration not for their leadership abilities but because they were willing to collaborate with the colonial administration, acting as a link between their local villages and the central government. Indeed, one objective of this system was the demise of uncooperative traditional leaders and their replacement with amenable chiefs who would aid in labor recruitment, supervise compulsory work, and generally enforce the dictum of the Belgian colonizers in their villages. In return for their willingness to carry out the will of the colonial administration, these chiefs received a salary. Chiefs who attempted to dodge or resist these duties could not expect to hold their positions for long. Those who fully collaborated were rewarded in various ways by the colonial authority, although they found themselves at odds with the residents of their villages.

In 1933, the system of *secteurs* was generalized to the rest of the colony. The number of *secteurs* increased from 57 in 1935 to 383 in 1940, 498 in 1945, and 517 in 1950. By then, most rural Congolese lived within administrative units shaped by colonial imperatives that did not cater to the needs of their local communities. Colonial Minister Louis Franck had two aims in constructing this kind of colonial administration, which mirrored what British administrator Lord Lugard had implemented with some success in Nigeria. It ensured, in Franck's own words, "the extension of civilization and the development of outlets for Belgium and of Belgium's economic activity."[2]

Belgian administration in Congo might be described as a "colonial trinity." Three forces, namely the state, the missions, and the big companies, collaborated in the administration of the colony. Concessionary companies, such as Huileries du Congo Belge (palm oil; a subsidiary of Unilever created by the Lever brothers), Forminière (diamonds), Kilo-Moto (gold), and UMHK (copper), were not only capitalistic ventures. They also had a mandate from the colonial state to erect schools and hospitals, to build roads and railways, and to police the local people. These companies received full support from the colonial administration in recruiting labor and gaining control of the most valuable lands, even if this meant displacing local people from their villages. The colonial government's assistance to companies attracted a great deal of foreign investment to the colony, but it came at a price to investors, who performed a great amount of work in return.

The expansion of Huileries du Congo Belge (HCB) serves as an example of this. In 1911, HCB had been granted a large area to create five concessions of wild palm trees, each with a radius of 37 miles. In the operation, HCB displaced thousands of peasants and stripped them of their plantations of cultivated palm trees. According to their deal with the colonial government, HCB set up at its own expense a network of paved roads and railroads and a postal and telegraph service, which might be used or expropriated by the colonial state. There were additional sources of profit built into the deal: At least one-third of the machinery and plant as well as at least half of all other imported goods had to come directly from Belgium. HCB was also mandated to build health and education facilities for its workers and families. By 1926, these facilities included fifteen hospitals and five schools catering to the needs of 23,000 African workers and families as well as 335 Europeans. In terms of transportation, HCB created 650 miles of paved roads and 50 miles of railroad. What these figures do not reflect is that in order to create these infrastructures and still be able to pay the colonial government its annual dividend, HCB impoverished thousands of Congolese living and working within the concessions by utilizing a system of tight social control that deprived people of their freedom. It is notable that after some thirty years of activity, HCB, like most capitalistic ventures in Congo, had failed to create any substantial economic development.

The missionary presence in Congo also played an important role in creating an administrative network that facilitated political control and repression. During the latter years of Congo Free State, Catholic and Protestant missions had extended their activities to cover much of the territory. By 1935, the Catholic and Protestant denominations held, respectively, 261 and 168 posts, and there were 2,326 and 718 white clergymen dedicated to respective populations of 1,048,511 and 233,673 African parishioners.

Of all the denominations granted privileges in Congo, the Catholic Church espoused the colonial civilizing ideology with such conviction that it played a primary role as an agent of pacification and "civilization" for the colonial state. Belgian functionaries who set out for the colony were given a handbook that instructed them to work closely with the church to "civilize" the local population: "Government servants are not working alone in the task of civilization. The religious orders are participating in at least equal measure. . . . Civil servants, whatever their own religious views, are under a strict obligation to aid Christian missionaries."[3]

As Belgium was a predominantly Catholic country, the Catholic Church was given a privileged status in the colony. While the international community lambasted Leopold for his deeds in Congo, the Vatican had offered its support. In exchange for this loyalty, Leopold negotiated a concordat with the Vatican that promoted two principles. The first principle was that missionary effort in Congo was to remain not only essentially Belgian but also Catholic. The second principle called for the creation of a system of cooperation between the Catholic missions and the colonial administration. Under the agreement, Catholic missionaries working in Congo assumed a civil status and were, consequently, paid salaries by the colony. In addition, the state granted each mission station established in the colony 200 hectares to be used not only for religious purposes but also for commercial exploitation. This endowed the Catholic Church in Congo with substantial resources to carry out its activities. Since many Catholic missionaries belonged to religious orders such as the Franciscans or Capuchins, which demanded vows of poverty, their accumulated salaries went into institutional funds operated by the church. This further strengthened the financial position of the Catholic Church, which had at its disposal relatively large financial assets that greatly forwarded its colonial ambitions.

One of the church's main activities was education. Within Belgium's mission of evangelizing and civilizing Congo, education and Christianization came to be viewed as one and the same. The objective of colonial education in Congo was to create a lower middle class with limited political awareness that would staunchly support the colonial state. Toward this end, primary education coupled with professional training was standard for the majority of the population during most of the colonial period. In lieu of secondary education, the Belgian colonialists devoted particular attention to popular culture, including cinema, theater, and sports, which catered primarily to youth in the towns. In this domain, Catholic missionaries were again given a head start and the material and moral support of the administration.

Most other denominations, especially Protestant non-Belgian, were held in suspicion and regarded as agents of the European country from which they originated. As noted in the previous chapter, several American and Scandinavian missionaries spoke out about what they witnessed of the effects of the rubber trade on the Congolese. In retaliation, the Belgian administration made it a policy not to encourage or assist foreign missionary activities in Congo. Non-Belgian missionaries were difficult to control, and the Belgian colonialists suspected them of holding nationalistic views that might undermine Belgian policy toward the population. As a result, most government subsidies and assistance went to the Belgian Catholic Church, which enabled it to create a network of nearly 600 parishes serving more than 24,400 villages and small towns. By 1946, the Catholic Church could boast of 18,000 schools serving the needs of 800,000 pupils, 561 hospitals and medical centers, 19 printing houses, 24 newspapers, and a cohort of 1,432 European priests.

Concessionary companies and religious missions were instrumental in asserting the authority of Europeans in Congo. But their role in the domination was superseded by that of agents of the colonial state. Public indifference to colonial affairs facilitated a colonial policy governed by bureaucratic conservatism, blatant paternalism toward the indigenous population, and the precedence of the interests of a minority. The vast majority of the population, whether Europeans or Africans, was not permitted a place in the political organization or representation in the colony until after World War II, when reforms to integrate Africans into the affairs of the colony were gradually put into place.

ECONOMIC CHANGES

The colonial economy in Congo, as in the rest of Africa, was based on a European economic model dating to the sixteenth century. In this model, chartered and other trading companies were used by European states to enter and colonize overseas territories. The model followed a simple principle that D. K. Fieldhouse describes in the following terms:

> where an overseas territory was, from a European point
> of view, 'undeveloped' that its indigenous inhabitants
> occupied very little of the land, exploited almost none of
> its assets and did not generate sufficient products to
> form the basis of an import/export trade or a tax system,
> economic activity had to be started by Europeans. If,
> moreover, the imperial state lacked the means or will to
> restructure the indigenous economy by public action, it
> was necessary to invite private capital and enterprise to
> do so by giving large concessions with or without
> administrative authority (1978: 497).

From the time of the heyday of Congo Free State, the colonial economy in Congo did not depart from this principle. When in 1908 King
Leopold II relinquished his private domain to the Belgian government,
the colonial economy was already a brutal system of exploitation, one of
the distinctive features of Belgian colonization. This system of economic
exploitation was based on compulsory labor. The Belgian colonial administration that took over from Leopold II instituted a few changes. The
new government continued the exploitation of the Congolese population
but by means of a new method for forcing people to work: taxes.

The imposition of a heavy head tax forced able-bodied men to migrate
to work areas: plantations, mines, railway roads, ports, and white resi-
dential areas. In order to mobilize the African labor force wherever it was
needed, African able-bodied men were required by law to remain in their
chefferie of residence. Individuals who wanted to leave for another *chefferie* or move to a nearby town had to apply for a passbook (*passeport de
mutation*) issued by the territorial administration and an authorization to
migrate.

Until the 1920s, the main products generated by this coercive colonial
economy were ivory, wild rubber (and later cultivated rubber), cotton,
and palm oil. Although this economic activity triggered substantial
development and modernization in major cities, it brought little direct
benefit to the Congolese people. It benefited mostly foreign companies
and shareholders and the Belgian state itself, which had holdings in
many of the companies. The Belgian government benefited as well from
Congo's mineral industry, which became, starting in the late 1920s, the
backbone of the colonial economy. Most economic development in Congo
after the Leopoldian era took place in the Katanga region, the last area to
be conquered by the Belgians but the richest in natural resources. Its mild

climate played a significant role in attracting white settlers from Belgium, England, Portugal, Italy, South Africa, and Australia, so much so that by the late 1950s at least one-third of the 100,000 whites living in the colony resided in Katanga. For all of these reasons, Katanga held a special position in the colony. In 1910, its administration was placed by royal ordinance under a governor directly responsible to Brussels and not to Boma, the capital of the colony. This decision would have dramatic consequences in the political evolution of Congo.

The development of the mining industry in Katanga would only be possible through the construction of railroads by which Europeans might haul the mineral wealth to ports for transportation to Europe. By the 1920s, a new railway system linked Katanga with Port-Franqui, on the Kasai River. From Port-Franqui, the Kasai River was used. This route was called the *voie nationale* ("national way"), which connected Katanga to the sea. In 1931, the Belgians opened a new railway line that was more cost-effective as well as quicker. From the most important mining towns in Katanga, such as Kolwezi and Elisabethville, products were transported directly to the Angolan port of Lobito Bay via the border town of Dilolo, which connected with the Benguela railway. Economic development in Katanga was such a priority that of the 1,580 miles of new railways built between 1920 and 1932, at least 80 percent were constructed for the evacuation of mineral products from the Katanga region.

The development of the railway system during the interwar period speaks to the extroversion of the colonial economy of Belgian Congo. As described above, it was designed for the sole purpose of extracting resources from the colony. Katanga was linked to Rhodesia by a railway from Sakania to Elisabethville, to Matadi via Port-Franqui, and to Lobito Bay via one of the longest railways in the colony. By the 1930s, over 2,500 miles of rivers and an equal number of miles of railways and paved roads were being utilized to evacuate Congo's goods to Europe. As a result of this progress in the transportation system and thanks to a growing demand for raw materials in Europe and the U.S., mineral production increased markedly in the 1920s and 1930s. Between 1923 and 1930, the production of copper more than doubled, jumping from 56,221 to 138,949 metric tons. This made Congo the world's third largest producer of copper. Even more substantial was the increase in diamond production, which skyrocketed to 2,518,258 carats in 1930 from 318,979 ten years earlier. Increased mineral production was paralleled by a sizable growth in the agricultural sector, especially in the production of cotton, palm oil, palm kernels, and coffee.

This economic growth, which seemed to indicate the Belgian government's resolve to make the most out of its only colonial possession, would not have been so rapid without private investments. During the period between the two wars, the colonial government's major economic policy was to encourage private foreign investment in order to develop agricultural commodities for export. As the French did in neighboring French Congo, the Belgian government also implemented an open concessionary system, allowing large companies to exploit portions of the colony in return for their promises to create infrastructure. The Belgian colonial government concerned itself very little with social infrastructure or the welfare of the Congolese population. Instead it granted the religious missions and the large concessionary companies permission to provide health and educational services to the population.

In order to ensure adequate supplies of low-wage labor to private and state-owned companies, the colonial administration enacted compulsory recruitment, which was reminiscent of the brutal forced labor of Leopoldian Congo. Restrictions were also placed on foreign commercial activities, which might have stimulated the farmers to produce surpluses that could be sold for cash instead of taking low-paying jobs on plantations and mines.

Congo's increasingly dependent economy suffered greatly during the turmoil caused by the Great Depression of the 1930s. The copper industry, which acted as the backbone of colonial economy, especially suffered the effects. Production fell drastically due to the drop in the price of copper from an average of one hundred British pounds before the Depression to only thirty pounds. The collapse of the copper industry weakened Congo franc to the point that devaluation was warranted. Imports dropped almost 70 percent between 1929 and 1933. In some places economic activity came to a standstill, which resulted in huge layoffs of skilled and semi-skilled workers. Between 1931 and 1934, an annual average of 6,000 workers who had lost their livelihoods were repatriated by force from Leopoldville, a major economic center before the Depression, to their respective villages. The city's population dropped from 37,054 in 1929 to 22,184 in 1933. In Katanga, the Depression reduced the African workforce by 70 percent from its level in 1929. In the year 1932 alone more than 72,000 African wage earners employed in industrial centers and commercial towns throughout the colony were dismissed without severance pay.

The years after World War II witnessed the growth of the copper, gold, and tin industries, whose output had picked up during the war as part of

Belgian Congo's efforts in favor of the Allied forces. American and British armies demanded more rubber for the manufacture of tires for military trucks, uranium for bomb making (American atomic bombs dropped in Hiroshima and Nagasaki were built with Congolese uranium from Shinkolobwe mines), and cotton to clothe the armies. Profits flowed out of the colony and coercive measures, such as *chicotte*, or flogging, were used to force workers to mine. Working conditions in the mines were abysmal. Scores of workers died each year from brutality, disease, and despair, and methods of recruitment differed little from those employed in Leopold's time. These conditions attracted few migrants even though male heads of households were hard-pressed to raise cash to pay taxes. Recruiters from the mines ventured to remote villages accompanied by soldiers and used bribery of village chiefs as well as force to coerce people into migrating to the mines. Oftentimes, local government administrators assisted company agents in recruiting and holding villagers through the imposition of penalties. Those who resisted were rounded up, chained, and taken by force to the mines. When a recruit fled, a member of his family was imprisoned until he turned himself in to the recruiting agents. Fines and imprisonment were imposed upon workers for breach of contract.

World War II stimulated Belgian Congo's economy and led to a shift in foreign trade. As ties with Belgium were severed by German occupation, new markets were found abroad, and new industries were established to supply the colony with consumer goods previously imported from Belgium (clothing, tobacco, beer, furniture, radio sets, bicycles, sewing machines, etc.). These new industries catered to the rising African middle class, which consisted of servants, teachers, qualified artisans, and foremen who had acquired their skills in the big mining and industrial companies. Also included were the Africans who had set up businesses of their own, operating bars or selling goods and crafts in small shops. The colonial government recognized this growing group of relatively prosperous Africans and supported wage increases and steps toward the development of an African middle class.

At independence, many observers considered Congo one of the most thriving colonial domains, where, according to a European visitor, "lived the most *embourgeoisé* negro of all Africa." But behind this façade of a "*colonie modèle*" (model colony), the real picture looked entirely different. The actual situation was that Africans were confined to the most menial and unskilled tasks while more than 90 percent of the high-skilled positions, managerial posts, and economic wealth were monopolized by foreigners and expatriates. The roots of Congo's economic dependency and weakness are to be found in the colonial period. In a matter of seventy years, a territory of more than 10 million inhabitants was transformed into a class-divided society with a fragile economy.

URBANIZATION AND SOCIAL CHANGES

European colonization in Congo, as elsewhere in the continent, brought about an unprecedented urban revolution. Most historians and archaeologists agree that before the arrival of Europeans, the majority of the sub-Saharan African population lived in agrarian, noncapitalistic societies organized in small villages of no more than a few hundred inhabitants. Although some urban centers existed in some precolonial areas, such as along the Nile River, in the Sahelian area of West Africa, in Hausaland in northern Nigeria, in Zimbabwe, Uganda, and Angola, less than 5 percent of the African population lived in towns and cities before the nineteenth century. By 1960, the year that witnessed the independence of a large number of African countries, one in three Africans resided in cities, most of which had been built by Europeans. Historically, African colonial cities acted not only as industrial nexuses and trading centers, which attracted the capital and labor needed to boost colonial economies, but also as tools of colonization and loci of social change. Most of what the West deemed indispensable to its civilizing mission (schools, churches, hospitals, administrative buildings, sports facilities, etc.) was concentrated in the colonial cities. These cities were intended to showcase European civilization and its technological superiority. Thus, Congolese cities shared similar features with most newly created colonial cities. Here as in the rest of the continent, urban growth picked up immediately following the end of the Great Depression. The total population living in the cities increased to 971,907 in 1939, to 1,569,195 in 1947, and to 3,240,000 by the end of 1958 (see Table 5.1).

At the beginning of the nineteenth century, urban growth depended mostly on compulsory migration. The early colonial economy relied heavily on African forced labor for the completion of public works projects such as the construction of railways, paved roads, and administrative buildings. Labor shortage was at that time the common lot of state companies and private employers alike. In the early 1920s, renovation of the railway from Matadi to Leopoldville suffered direly from lack of available labor, which prompted the government to enact compulsory recruitments. In 1926, for example, 13,000 additional workers were needed to build the new docks in Leopoldville, but only 6,000 could be found. Even recruitment patrols sent to the rural areas to force reluctant villagers to the city did not yield enough recruits. As a last resort, the Belgian colonial authorities unsuccessfully attempted to hire foreign workers from French West Africa. Except for a brief resurgence during World War II, forced labor no longer played any significant role in the migration of young villagers to the cities after the late 1920s. Young male migrants now flocked to the city voluntarily for a variety of reasons, among which the desire to find an urban professional occupation dominated.

Table 5.1: Urban Population, 1940–1970

City	1940	1950	1958	1970
Kinshasa	100	406	827	2,814
Lubumbashi	100	366	677	1,177
Mbandaka	100	170	580	1,080
Kisangani	100	446	686	1,513
Bukavu	100	947	2,736	7,105
Kananga	100	306	2,224	8,755
Matadi	100	200	700	1,222

Source: Ndaywel è Nziem, histoire générale du Congo (1998: 373).

In the early years, few towns had the amenities characteristic of urban centers. They consisted simply of a number of lots of land granted by the municipality to newcomers to build their houses. Migrants often used traditional modes of construction. Mud-walled and thatched-roofed houses were a common sight in most colonial cities before the 1940s. These structures sometimes housed as many as six or seven workers in a single room without running water or sanitation. In some cities, where large companies such as UMHK (Elisabethville) or OTRACO (Office des Transports Coloniaux, Leopoldville) concentrated a sizeable workforce, it was customary for the colonial administration to direct these companies to provide durable housing for their workers.

Until the late 1930s, native townships looked more like worker camps than full-fledged urban centers. What promoted them to towns and cities was a radical change in the demographic pattern of rural-urban migrations. Until then, the typical migrant was young, male, single, lacking the skills that could fetch him a relatively decent wage in the city, and with little or no formal education. He remained fundamentally attached to his rural mode of life and his migration to the city was generally temporary. After a few months of accumulating meager earnings, the young migrant would pack up and go back to his village to resume agricultural activities. Migration to the city was part of a strategy to acquire the bridewealth necessary for marriage and did not reflect a desire to settle there permanently and adopt an urban way of life. Geographical and professional mobility were two of the most striking characteristics of the early Congolese urban population. Also notable was the unbalanced sex ratio, with men outnumbering women four to one in the largest cities until the 1930s.

The transformation of African townships owes much to the female migrants who came to the cities in droves after the war. Single women who had been dissuaded from migrating earlier were now permitted to move to the city. The colonial authorities had tried to keep women in the villages for fear that once in the city they would take advantage of the overwhelming presence of single male wage earners by engaging in prostitution. Therefore, before the war, only married women were allowed to reside in the city. Single women, legally attributed the awkward label *femmes indigènes adultes et valides vivant théoriquement seules* (indigenous able-bodied adult women officially living alone), were burdened with heavy taxes. In Leopoldville, a municipal decree required that they pay fifty francs annually (roughly the wages a domestic servant earned for ten days' work). In Stanleyville, from 1939 to 1943, this tax was the second highest source of revenue for the city. Consequently, the number of women in the urban centers remained particularly low. In 1928, one of the biggest townships in Leopoldville was home to 21,500 men but fewer than 5,000 women. Among these only 358 were legally married while the majority had illegally slipped into the city. This demographic situation was part of the precarious urban life depicted by a Belgian priest: "I walked around the immense black city, where live, only God knows in which moral indiscipline, 20,000 negroes . . . it's a camp, it's not a village. There is little greenery, even fewer children . . . not many mothers, little joy. Of all the places that I went, I have only seen two children."

During World War II and thereafter, women were at last allowed to reside in the towns. At first this was done to meet the needs of white male urban dwellers. In the early twentieth century, the distribution of the European urban population was strikingly unbalanced. In Leopoldville in the late 1920s, for example, there were only 600 white women (mostly associated with the religious missions and therefore unmarriageable) compared to 2,500 white men. Until the 1930s, contact between European men and African women was heavily stigmatized. But as industrial activity picked up after the Depression, the number of white male settlers and interracial couples increased.

The colonial authorities also encouraged the arrival of women at the workers' camps in order to promote family life there and to stabilize the male working population. Colonial officials feared that the growing presence of tens of thousands of young male workers in townships designed to shelter only a few thousand individuals would breed unrest and epidemics. The authorities worried that enforced celibacy and high labor turnover were a detriment to health and morality and would thwart social advancement. More than any other, this was the reason the colonial administration decided to remove all legal obstacles to women moving into the cities.

There is evidence to suggest that the improvements made to the African townships after World War II owe much to the increasing female presence in towns. Efforts by both employers and workers to give a human face to the townships stemmed from the necessity of accommodating the growing population of women and, shortly thereafter, the first generation of children born in the cities. Old townships were redesigned to create new ones that were more Western in character and provided public amenities and community buildings. Buildings and amenities that had not existed in these cities before the 1930s were erected, including maternity wards, social centers, dispensaries, hospitals, churches, schools, markets, and other public facilities. The colonial government spearheaded these urban developments by creating the Office of African Townships (Office des Cités Africaines—OCA) in 1952. By April 1957, OCA had completed a little more than 25,000 dwellings in the five most important cities, including almost 14,000 in Leopoldville alone. Had the Belgian father mentioned above seen Leopoldville twenty years after his first visit, he would have witnessed a very different scene, that of a bustling city of almost half a million people, populated by numerous families and scores of children, who drew on the schools, markets, and businesses the city offered.

African urban dwellers had to adapt quickly to this new way of life marked by the presence of Western cultural symbols and institutions. These migrants also had to get used to one another and find ways to coexist as they came from different ethnic backgrounds. The cities were not ethnically homogenous but were instead a mixture of various peoples and cultures. Urban life differed greatly from community life in the villages. It involved a whole new series of relationships based on new criteria. Marriage in the city, for example, was interethnic and not based on common cultural mores. It no longer symbolized an alliance between two lineages or a political relationship between two communities but became the union of two independent individuals. Marriage underwent these profound transformations as Christian ideals gained currency in the cities. One of the most fundamental features introduced by these so-called Christian marriages, as opposed to customary marriages, was the stress on the ideal of monogamy.

The colonial city precipitated the social transformations brought about by colonization. These transformations were not just imposed upon passive African city dwellers. On the contrary, they were the product of the Europeans' imposition of a new urban order and Africans' efforts to take hold of the city, to interpret and appropriate urban life, symbols, and spaces. The urban revolution set in motion by Belgian colonization was pushed forward by Africans themselves, who positioned themselves on the frontlines of change, in the streets, markets, beer halls, schools, social centers, and soccer fields, and through their initiative produced a totally new, yet typically African urban milieu.

RESISTANCE TO THE COLONIAL SYSTEM

African resistance to the Belgian colonial system took many forms and shapes. Africans responded to the imposition of European administration, economy, and religion on their lives and customs according to their own priorities. Some were compliant, others defiant, and still others avoided the confrontation altogether. Responses ranged from collaboration to open resistance, and the most radical responses were found in areas where heavy taxation, compulsory recruitment, and low wages had driven the population into poverty. Instances of armed resistance occurred among the Azande in northeastern Congo, the Yaka and Pende in the southwest, the Luba in the southeast, and the Lele between the Lulua and the Loango rivers. In several cases religious movements took on overtones of political protest.

One of the first uprisings pitted new African recruits against their European officers at Luluabourg in 1895. The newly created post of Luluabourg had a mission outpost, local government buildings, and a military garrison housing mostly war veterans who had fought on behalf of Congo Free State under the leadership of their chief, Ngongo Luteta. On September 15, 1893, this African chief had been executed after being found guilty of treason and rebellion by a martial court set up by the colonial government. After his death, most of his soldiers were transferred into the regular colonial army and stationed in Luluabourg. There, they found themselves victimized and confined to the most menial tasks by their white officers. Flogging was common as a way of disciplining those who refused to go along with army regulations and colonial discipline. The grievances of these African soldiers included their unfair treatment as well as the fact that their wages were sometimes withheld for months. Discontent mounted, and in early July some of the soldiers deserted their garrison after a clash that resulted in the death of one European officer and left another severely wounded. These soldiers had originally intended to return to their respective villages. But when the government gathered a force of more than a thousand African soldiers led by fifteen white officers to track down the mutineers, the rebellion gave way to a full-fledged guerrilla war that lasted until 1908.

The revolt of Luluabourg stands out in the history of colonial Congo as the first violent response to colonization. It set the pattern for subsequent revolts that challenged the colonial system. A common feature shared by these revolts was the absence of a clear nationalistic project. Like the Luluabourg rebellion, later uprisings staged by soldiers of the Force Publique or members of the rural population lacked a visionary leader or a clear political objective. Their demands, as in the case of the Shinkakasa revolt of April 1900, had more to do with a desire to improve their social conditions than with a desire to end the colonial system. Most wanted to escape the exploitation of the colonial system, not end it. This fact alone is testimony to the dominance of the colonial state. Within a couple of decades of the first contact between Europeans and Africans in this region, the colonial state had succeeded in dominating the lives of millions of Africans and imposing itself as the only viable political institution.

However, the domination of the colonial state did not go unchallenged. The unsuccessful violent resistance of the early colonial period, examples of what historian T. O. Ranger has termed "primary movements of resistance," later gave way to more subtle forms of everyday resistance. Historians of colonial Congo have yet to investigate the use of popular culture by Africans in the urban centers of Belgian Congo to circumvent colonial subjugation and voice their frustrations with the colonial system. Such domains include sports, popular music, dancing, religion, fashion, the use and abuse of alcohol, and illegal migrations, which until the 1950s were perhaps the only avenues open to Africans as both recreational outlets and political sounding boards.

One example is the revivalist movement launched by Simon Kimbangu in Lower Congo region in the early 1920s. Kimbangu's movement played an important role in the history of modern Congo and illustrates the nature of African resistance, which in many cases took the form of ethnic allegiances. The example also shows the historical continuity between pre-colonial and colonial cultural developments. Kimbangu was transformed into a charismatic leader by the colonial repression that threatened to destroy his movement. Because Christianity was such a critical element of the colonial civilizing mission, Kimbangu's attempt to create an indigenous Christian church met with unprecedented colonial oppression.

Kongolese Christianity goes back to 1491, when the king and queen of the Kongo Kingdom were baptized by Portuguese missionaries. Later, in the early eighteenth century, a Christian revivalist movement led by a Kongolese noblewoman, Kimpa Vita (also known by her Christian name Dona Beatriz), attempted to reconfigure Christianity within a Kongolese ethos. She was burned at the stake, in 1706, at the age of twenty.

Continuing with this Christian influence of Lower Congo, colonial missions, including the British Missionary Society (BMS), established their first centers there. Simon Kimbangu was born on September 24, 1889 at Nkamba, near Thysville (now Mbanza-Ngungu), in Lower Congo. Kimbangu, whose name in the Kikongo language literally means "the one who reveals what is hidden," belonged to the Bakongo people, who had long experienced Christianity and Christian revivalist movements. Kimbangu was brought up within the religious realm of the BMS and became a Christian as a young man. In July 1915, after thorough instruction by the missionaries, he was baptized along with his wife, Marie Mwilu. For a short period he was a teacher at the mission school in Ngombe Lutete, where he gained a strong command of the Bible. He also acted as an evangelist at Nkamba. Kimbangu enjoyed a particularly favorable reputation among the white missionaries, who described him as a good and thoughtful man who read his Bible and performed his tasks conscientiously. Kimbangu received his first call to "tend Christ's flock" one night in 1918. He declined the call and sought refuge in Kinshasa, where he worked at various menial jobs. But he did not find peace of mind, for even in Kinshasa the voice called him to minister the gospel. He returned to Nkamba and, on the morning of April 6, 1921, performed his first healing by laying his hands on a critically ill woman in the name of Jesus Christ. A second miracle took the form of healing a child. Many more healings of the sick and prophecies followed. At first, people thought Kimbangu was using charms. Eventually he convinced people by insisting, "It is Christ who has performed these miracles through me. I have no power to do these myself." From then on, pilgrims flocked to Nkamba in search of healing and instruction.

Kimbangu commanded people to renounce their non-Christian ways. His movement combatted polygamy, "profane" dances, and "fetishes." Kimbangu and the movement he initiated represented a Christian African reaction against colonization and colonial evangelization. However, Kimbangu never opposed the colonial authorities but championed obedience to the powers that be, which in the case of Lower Congo included yielding to forced labor and burdensome poll taxes.

Faced with the staggering desertion of workers and servants who flocked to Nkamba, the colonial administration branded Kimbangu an *illuminé* (visionary) who sought popularity and might later organize a rebellion in a region particularly prone to such outbursts. A state of emergency was declared in the districts of Mbanza Ngungu and Luozi. After hiding for a few months, Kimbangu gave himself up and was arrested in September of 1921, less than six months after opening his ministry. A military court charged him with sedition and civil disobedience, and he was sentenced to death in what appears a legal travesty. Later, however, the sentence was commuted by King Albert to life in prison. Kimbangu was transferred to Elisabethville (Lubumbashi), where he spent thirty years in solitary confinement.

Lacking a leader and faced with relentless colonial repression, including the destruction of places of worship (Nkamba was totally destroyed by government forces) and massive deportations, the movement went underground. It later sprung up in the form of various splinter groups (Nguzism, Mpadism, Kakism, etc.) and spread to French Congo and Gabon.

Kimbangu's movement found itself at the forefront of African resistance to the colonial regime. The movement, which was even labeled a "communist-led anticolonial movement," triggered a swift and repressive response from the colonial government. The powerful response that the movement elicited, both from the colonial authorities and from African participants, speaks to the role that popular culture played in undermining the foundations of the colonial system. It also shows the extent to which *Bula Matari* (the colonial state) strove to quell any African-led initiative, whether religious, political, or in the realm of popular culture, that might challenge the colonial order.

The 1950s constituted a major turning point in the way colonial authorities dealt with their colonized subjects. For many years the social policy toward the local population could be described as purely paternalistic. Congolese were considered children, and white administrators, employers, and missionaries their fathers. The Belgians successfully promoted the idea of a "happy colony" where there were no upheavals or discontent, only peace and progress under the humane and benevolent care of the colonial government. But education brought about the political awakening of the Congolese, and both this policy and the propaganda that sustained it were brought into question. Under the pressure of the *évolués*, the Congolese social and intellectual elite, native councils were set up in which Africans acquainted themselves, albeit remotely, with colonial affairs. Some *évolués* were also invited to sit on various advisory boards such as the Fonds du Bien-Être Indigène, a social welfare organization, and the OCA, which was concerned with native housing. But these cosmetic changes did not satisfy the *évolués*, especially since in many other African colonies, including neighboring French Congo, Africans were more intimately involved in the administration of their countries and the political process of emancipation that was underway.

NOTES

1. Quoted in Anstey (1966: 62).
2. Quoted in Anstey (1966: 102).
3. Quoted in Young (1965: 14).

6

The Crisis of Decolonization, 1945–1960

On June 30, 1960, the largest crowds ever seen in any urban center in Congo poured into the streets of the capital city of Leopoldville to celebrate emancipation from the former Belgian colonizers. For Congolese, independence meant not simply regaining control of their country. It heralded the new era of prosperity and freedom promised by the elite and aspired to by the Congolese masses. Belgian colonization of Congo had brought about tremendous economic change, unequaled in any other African colony, owing largely to the huge mineral resources and vast expanses of land the country possessed. The standard of living of Africans in Congo compared favorably with that in other colonies, and the average African income surpassed that of Nigeria, Kenya, Senegal, and the rest of the French and British African territories. This lent credibility to the myth that Belgian Congo was a "happy colony." Economic prosperity had given rise to an African middle class consisting of artisans and skilled workers. After World War II, the new economic environment produced an even more prosperous class of Africans, who had created businesses of their own as owners of shops and bars, building contractors, transport operators, craftsmen, and dealers. The state provided comfortable, modern housing for this emerging elite in the native townships.

Belgian Congo seemed ahead of other colonies in terms of medical and educational services as well. Improved health services had dramatically increased the birth rate and decreased the mortality rate. In terms of education, the colony boasted the highest primary school attendance levels in Africa.

Behind this façade of progress and peace lay a different picture, which prompted some members of the African elite to push for independence. They realized that economic development had benefited mostly the European colonists and their home countries. Under colonization, Africans were viewed as second-class citizens who could only rise to subaltern positions within the colonial society. There were no African mayors, deputies, doctors, lawyers, or judges as there were in many other African colonies, and any sort of independence for Africans was out of the question. In 1956, when most African colonies were following a fast track toward emancipation and political autonomy, the Belgian colonialists maintained their paternalistic role in Congo. Even as other colonies moved toward granting Africans the right to govern themselves, colonialists in Belgian Congo still thought of themselves as bearing the "the white man's burden." The story of the path to independence provides insights into the contradictions of colonial society in Belgian Congo.

POLITICAL CHANGES AFTER WORLD WAR II

Most African historians agree that without the upheavals brought about by World War II, decolonization in Africa would have been delayed for at least another decade. The war encouraged European colonizers to grant rights of political participation to their African subjects, whose war efforts on behalf of the Allied forces had proved so crucial. On May 27, 1940, the Belgian army was forced to surrender as the German Wehrmacht marched through Belgium. This military occupation put the economy in the hands of the Germans and sent the Belgian government into exile. As with France, which also fell to the German army, the Belgian government-in-exile carried on the fight for the Allied side by relying on the colonial domain.

On the military front, Congo made a significant contribution in comparison with other colonial territories. The Force Publique called up reserves and recruited new forces in order to have battalions ready to assist the Allies. At its peak in 1943, Congo's colonial army included more than 40,000 soldiers. In 1941, Italy entered the war on the side of Germany and annexed Ethiopia. This prompted the Allied forces to incorporate three battalions from Belgian Congo into a military operation led by the British and intended to prevent the Axis powers from reinforcing their presence on African soil. In March 1941, the Congolese colonial army won two critical battles in Abyssinia, Ethiopia (at Assosa and Gambela), which greatly contributed to the victory of the British-led forces. In July 1942, another military expedition of nearly 13,000 Congolese soldiers of the Force Publique went to Nigeria to protect French interests in West Africa. They participated in exercises with troops from Nigeria, Ghana, and Sierra Leone. A third expedition of 8,000 men was sent to North Africa (Egypt and Libya), the Middle East (Lebanon, Syria, Iraq, and Palestine), and the Far East (Burma and India), where they were deployed in garrisons and support duties.

In Congo, the war effort relied on production by Congolese peasants, who were compelled, sometimes through forced labor, to work harder to support the war economy. Africa's importance as a source of raw materials for the Allied armies was the result of the fall of Southeast Asia to the Japanese and the ensuing shortage of important raw materials. The Allied armies needed tin, cotton, palm oil, rubber, sisal, coffee, tea, cocoa, and other goods, whose prices had skyrocketed in Europe. African peasants bore the full brunt of this economic war effort. The colonial government kept prices low so that raw materials were readily available and affordable to the Allied forces. In many cases this meant that Congolese peasants were not compensated for producing more. Forced labor, which had been abolished in the early 1930s, was restored. By 1944, the maximum amount of compulsory labor had been increased to 120 days for all rural workers. It is important to remember how critical Congo's economic activity was for the world during the war. It provided large quantities of strategic materials for the Allies, which played a decisive role in the war's outcome. Most significant was the production of mineral resources, which more than doubled between 1939 and 1945 (see Table 6.1). The mines of Shinkolobwe, in Katanga, which contained the world's largest deposits of uranium, provided the essential component of the first atomic bomb, which sealed the fate of the war.

The war had psychological and intellectual effects on the African soldiers who participated. African soldiers returned from the war fronts knowing that they had fought a battle to liberate Europe from the evils of racism. Hitler's rhetoric about racial "purity" awakened Africans to issues of racial politics. The war also showed Africans that Europeans did not possess divine attributes that made them different from Africans. In the war, Africans saw Europeans without their imperial and colonial masks, in moments of hunger and thirst, courage and cowardice, and they found them all too human. Through these contacts, Africans took white people down from the pedestal of racial superiority.

Table 6.1: Production of Raw Materials in Congo, 1939–1944

	1939*	1940	1941	1942	1943	1944
Copper	100	122	132	136	128	135
Tin	100	128	146	135	174	176
Gold	100	107	107	98	83	77
Zinc	100	107	148	84	208	158
Diamond	100	115	70	72	58	90
Lumber	100	141	157	213	226	233
Coffee	100	107	107	109	101	136
Rubber	100	70	131	157	788	1050
Cotton	100	104	112	95	104	74
Gum copal	100	98	129	138	156	148
Fibers	100	147	112	228	267	167
Mean	*100*	*113*	*129*	*133*	*208*	*222*

*1939 = 100

Source: André Lederer, "Les transports au Congo pendant la seconde guerre mondiale."

Congolese soldiers also made contact with fellow Africans, some of whom came from countries where African political participation had been initiated. These encounters afforded Congolese the opportunity to exchange ideas and experiences with other Africans, which had profound political implications. This was noted by an American observer who served with lese army during that period:

> Flogging was permissible in the Congo Army and was, in fact, administered at a daily parade. Offending soldiers were treated exactly like children and had to take their punishment in the presence of their colleagues. . . . Amongst the British and French forces at this time, the striking of an African soldier, for any reason, meant court martial. The Belgian troops became aware of this and made an unfavourable comparison with their own conditions,

which later fermented great hatred of Belgian colonialism (Hennessy 1961: 53–54).

Once they came back to Congo, these war veterans of the Force
Publique became the driving force for colonial emancipation. The colonial government could no longer afford to ignore their demands for
reforms that would promote some Africans to better jobs. These veterans
did not limit themselves to peaceful protest. On February 20, 1944, one of
the most serious postwar rebellions occurred when Force Publique soldiers stationed at Luluabourg brought the economy of the area to a standstill. Their grievances reflected the poor treatment they had received
since their return home: Some did not receive their pay and others had to
surrender to their white officers the shoes and clothes they had pur-
chased with their own money while on duty in North Africa and the
Middle East. More generally, they complained of the lack of African participation in the administration of the colony, the absence of an independent African press, and the lack of consideration they received from
whites. In short, they demanded that participation replace paternalism.
There were other similar upheavals, some of which took on religious
overtones. One example occurred in Kivu, where in February 1944 a spiritual leader named Bushiri proclaimed himself "Yesu Mukombozi wa
Dunia" (Jesus, savior of the world) and incited the population against the
economic war effort. In other areas, such as along the Leopoldville-
Matadi railroad, African workers staged strikes and paralyzed one of the
main arteries of the colonial economy.

In most French and British territories, colonial authorities reacted to
growing African nationalist demands by formulating a broad range of
policies. In Belgian Congo, however, the administration was determined
to resume old patterns of colonial government and blocked African aspirations for political reforms. Yet even from the perspective of their short-
sighted colonial doctrine, some colonialists realized that politics as usual
ran counter to the new political mood set by the war. The war period also
saw the emergence of an intellectual elite in Belgian Congo. This was due
partly to a shortage of Europeans in Congo. With Belgium falling into the
hands of the Germans, recruitment of civil servants and skilled workers
for Congo did not take place. In addition, a certain number of Europeans
established in Congo went to combat in Europe, leaving behind skilled
jobs that could only be filled by Congolese from low-level positions. With
this new social status, these so-called Congolese *évolués* took their places
as the vanguard of the new civil society.

It would be misleading to equate this new elite with a political force in the years immediately following the war. During the war, the Belgians had created a special Bureau of Information and Propaganda to counter external influences. After the war, this bureau worked single-handedly to foster public expressions of African opinions. These government-controlled initiatives included clubs, newspapers, radio, and film programs, all dedicated to the new African urban elite. Chief among these initiatives was the first African newspaper, *La Voix du Congolais* (*The Congolese Voice*), with articles and editorials exclusively written by Africans.

But this reformist path of more freedom and participation had its limits. This is exemplified by the fate of Lomami Tchibamba, a journalist at *La Voix du Congolais*. In one of the very first issues of the newspaper, he wrote a critical article asking rhetorically what would be the place of the Congolese in a new Congo. ("Quelle sera notre place dans le monde de demain?"). The article was a cautious but categorical indictment of the slow pace of Belgian reforms. The author argued that whereas in neighboring French Congo and many other territories Africans were moving steadily toward emancipation, Belgian Congo appeared stuck in a colonial status quo. For his comments, Tchibamba suffered the ire of the government. He was censored and flogged and had to seek refuge in neighboring French Congo in order to avoid prosecution. This and many other examples indicate Belgium's reluctance to deal with the timely issue of emancipation of the colonies. Nationalism, reforms, and emancipation of colonized peoples were some of the harvests of World War II and signaled the end of the old-fashioned colonial mindset. In Belgian Congo, however, this mindset remained in place for another decade following the war.

THE RISE OF ETHNIC NATIONALISMS

The period from 1945 to 1956 witnessed the rise of ethnic nationalisms in Belgian Congo. The way this phenomenon played out during the first years of independence reflects the cultural diversity of Belgian Congo and the nature of the Belgian administration itself. Political parties as such did not exist in Congo before 1956. Belgian response to the international pressure of the postwar period was articulated mostly in terms of social, not political, reforms. However, in the words of Maurice Hennessy, "Welfare was a poor substitute for the intellectual craving which was lying dormant in the African."

Thus, when Congolese *évolués* started to formulate nationalistic demands, the channels of expression open to them were not political but cultural, social, and ethnic. The greater freedom of speech and of the press after the war did not immediately translate into the creation of political parties. On the contrary, it gave way to a proliferation of nonpolitical associations whose goals, structure, and leadership were unlike those of typical political parties.

Until the 1940s, nativistic and messianic movements, such as Kimbanguism, were virtually the only independent African movements. These movements loosely qualify as political because they depended to some extent on the social and political structures of the societies from which they originated and because, as René Lemarchand points out, "[they] provided alternative outlets for the discharge of grievances and tensions." But relentless repression by the colonial state pushed these movements further into the realm of mysticism and, in most cases, confined them to one ethnic group. Nevertheless, these movements affected subsequent political developments by sustaining a climate of social and political unrest that fueled nationalistic feelings among the local population. When political parties were at last permitted, political leaders capitalized on these feelings to mobilize their own constituencies.

For example, after the death of Simon Kimbangu in 1951, his movement went underground and took on messianic overtones. Kimbangu was believed to be a messiah. By this time most Kimbanguists belonged to the Kongo ethnic group. Kimbanguism served as a catalyst for the growth of ethnic sentiments and allegiances among the Bakongo people and political consciousness among the Bakongo urban elite.

Ethnic associations that grouped Congolese along ethnic, regional, and professional lines were another type of nonpolitical organization that developed before political parties. These associations tended to enlist individuals from one or more ethnically related groups who found themselves together in the growing urban centers of the country. Ethnic groups that had not lived together before colonization sought to conform to the new urban values without losing sight of their ethnic backgrounds. Ethnic organizations provided just such a possibility, as membership was determined through ethnic and linguistic ties. Leadership of these organizations often fell into the hands of Westernized individuals who understood the necessity of preserving or strengthening ties between the members and the traditional milieu. They used both their personal clout and urban resources to increase the social, economic, and cultural status of their ethnic communities.

Most of these associations appeared in the late 1940s and early 1950s as a result of the postwar mass migration from the countryside to the urban centers. Leopoldville, which received more migrants belonging to a greater variety of ethnic groups than any other Congolese city, had as many as eighty-five officially registered ethnic associations by 1956. Chief among these associations was the ABAKO, founded in 1950 by Edmond Nzeza-Nlandu, a former student in theology and accountant at HCB, and officially recognized by the colonial authorities three years later. As its original name indicates—Association des Bakongo pour l'Unification, la Conservation, le Perfectionnement et l'Expansion de la Langue Kikongo— the main objectives of the ABAKO were the unification, preservation, and spread of the Kikongo language. Some Bakongo contended that Kikongo was threatened by Lingala, a language spoken mostly by people from the Upper Congo area. ABAKO leaders established various programs dedicated to the cultural advancement of the Bakongo people through the preservation of their language. One program dealt with the cultural history of the Bakongo people, starting with the legendary Kongo Kingdom. Another program produced a newspaper, *Kongo dia Ngunga*, which acted as the mouthpiece of the organization. Members of the ABAKO were drawn exclusively from the Kongo and Kongo-related ethnic groups (Bantandu, Bandibu, Bambata, Bazombo, Besi-Ngombe, Balari, Manianga, etc.), including Bakongo from Angola and French Congo.

A host of other associations similar to ABAKO, in which ethnic affiliation was the only criterion, sprang up in Leopoldville during these years. The Fédération des Bangala, better known by its Lingala name, Liboke lya Bangala, appeared in 1954 under the leadership of Jean Bolikango and other Bangala *évolués*. This association never displayed the unity and strength that had made the ABAKO so powerful in Leopoldville, because it was intended for a group, the Bangala, which had been more or less created by colonial ethnologists. However, by 1958, due to its increased popularity among ethnic groups such as the Lokele, Basoko, Bapoto, Ngombe, Bangbandi, Ngbaka, and others, the association had at least thirty-five branches throughout the country. As with the ABAKO, the Liboke lya Bangala strove to foster among its members a sense of identification with their traditional culture.

The Fédération Kasaïenne, or Fédékaléo, originated as early as 1915. In 1949, Eugène Kabamba and Joseph Ngalula, both members of the Luba ethnic group, revived the old Luba organization. But in the end the enterprise went dormant again for a variety of reasons, including lack of resources and failure to build a strong constituency. In 1954, the Fédékaléo resurfaced in a more conducive environment. Between 1954 and 1957, through the effective leadership of Joseph Ngalula and Paul

Kabayidi, the association increased its branches from twelve to forty-three. In addition to Luba people, the Fédékaléo included people from three other ethnic groups, the Lulua, Tetela, and Songye. Unlike the Liboke lya Bangala, which managed to accommodate a multitude of ethnic groups and early on agreed on Lingala as its lingua franca, the members of the Fédékaléo could not resist the divisive forces of the various ethnic components. In 1957, after an unsuccessful attempt to impose Tshiluba as the main language of the association, Lulua, Tetela, and Songye members broke off and founded their own ethnic associations, the Lulua Frères, the Fédération des Batetela, and the Assobaléo. Just as the Fédékaléo originally drew its members from the main ethnic groups located in the Kasai area, the Fédération Kwango-Kwiloise, founded by Gaston Midu in 1953, included members from groups found in the Kwango-Kwilu area, such as the Bambala, Bapende, Batshokwe, Bayaka, Bayanzi, and others.

It might be argued that these organizations facilitated their members' transition from the traditional milieu to the urban centers. There is evidence that they also heightened the migrants' political expectations as the struggle for emancipation approached. As the associations included both elites and commoners, they provided the model and the constituencies for broad-based political parties. Thus, they can be regarded as the immediate precursors of the organized political parties that came into being after 1956.

Another type of nonpolitical organization that allowed Congolese, especially the *évolués*, to acquaint themselves with the political issues of their time, was the alumni associations (*associations d'anciens élèves*). These associations provided the connections that allowed some members, who later created political parties, to gather a critical mass of advisers and collaborators. By 1956, Leopoldville had eighteen such associations, including the two oldest and most influential, the Adapès (Association des Anciens Élèves des Pères de Scheut) and the Assanef (Association des Anciens Élèves des Frères des Écoles Chrétiennes), founded in 1925 and 1929. Most major Congolese politicians who emerged in the late 1950s were members of one of these associations, including Joseph Kasavubu, Congo's first president, Patrice Lumumba, the first prime minister, and other political figures such as Cyrille Adoula, André Delvaux, Jean Bolikango, Antoine Ngwenza, and Paul Bolya, all of whom held governmental positions after 1960. The membership of these two organizations reached nearly 30,000 individuals by 1946, which reflects the esprit de corps fostered in Christian religious congregations and passed on to Congolese *évolués* who attended Christian schools.

The *cercles d'études et d'agrément pour évolués* that burgeoned in most cities after the war represented yet another type of organization that prepared the Congolese elite for the political confrontation to come. Their purpose, as described in the statutes of the Cercle d'Évolués de Stanleyville, which was headed by Patrice Lumumba until his official entry into politics, was to "group all the évolués of Stanleyville, to create an atmosphere of understanding and solidarity among its members, to organize their leisure according to their level of education, and to improve their intellectual, social, moral and physical formation." By 1956, when most *évolués* left these *cercles* in order to direct their energy to the newly created political parties, the number and membership of the *cercles* had reached 317 and 15,245 respectively, up from 113 and 5,609 in 1947.

Nationalist ideas were not a part of Congolese political life until relatively late, and when they did appear they were immediately elided with ethnic sentiments and interests. One reason for the delay in nationalist consciousness in Congo was the Belgian policy of sheltering the Congolese elite from any external influence. For example, before 1958, the year when more than 700 Congolese attended the Brussels Colonial Exposition, only a handful of educated Congolese had been abroad. However, the main factor was Belgium's resolve to maintain control of Congo for economic reasons or at least to postpone for as long as possible the inevitable independence.

VAN BILSEN'S THIRTY-YEAR PLAN

In early December 1955, Belgian professor A. J. Van Bilsen published a treatise under the ominous title "Thirty Year Plan for the Political Emancipation of Belgian Africa." Van Bilsen was a professor of colonial legislation at the University Institute for Overseas Territories at Antwerp. He had visited Africa on a few occasions and was critical of Belgian resistance to political reforms in Congo. This may have qualified him in the eyes of Congolese *évolués* as a champion of African emancipation. But Van Bilsen was not pro-African nor a firebrand liberal, and some came to resent him while others lauded him. Van Bilsen was responding to United Nations disapproval of Belgian colonial policy by urging a move away from the old colonial mindset and toward more reforms and eventually self-government in Congo. In Article 73 of its charter, which the Belgian parliament had unanimously ratified, the United Nations advocated the right to self-determination for non-self-governing territories. Belgium found itself at odds with this policy, which was backed by the two superpowers, the United States and the Soviet Union. For this Belgium came under intense criticism from the United Nations. In 1953, after the United Nations had called for more reforms, especially in the field of education, Governor General Léon Pétillon dismissed these demands as illegitimate and ill advised. He declared:

> We know these tendencies. They are inspired by ideologies that, at first glance, seem generous, but are utopian. They are built on impatience, they are calculated to incite us to do things, no matter how, in impatient haste. They are calculated to lead us to ignore the lessons of long experience, dearly acquired, for reasons of political opportunism.

Van Bilsen's plan called for a progressive political, social, and economic emancipation. It provided a timetable that would have ended colonization in 1985, a hundred years after the creation of Leopold's Congo Free State. Why thirty years? According to Van Bilsen, this was the time needed to create an educated elite capable of replacing the Belgians at the reigns of power. The new African state—a nonracial Congolese nation composed of Africans and Europeans—would then have become an independent country though still strongly attached to Belgium through a *confédération belgo-congolaise*. But it was soon clear to most Congolese *évolués* that accepting the thirty-year timetable would have allowed Belgium to remain in a position of control.

Van Bilsen's project, couched in paternalistic language and centered on Belgium's interests, surprised everyone involved, including the colonial administration, which reacted with disbelief and suspicion. In retrospect, it is surprising that this proposal elicited such a negative response from the colonial government. Although it had no plan of its own, the colonial government dismissed Van Bilsen's plan as nonsense. As Belgian historian Georges Brausch has pointed out, by refusing to consider the plan, "the Belgian colonial administration, which until then had always kept ahead of social and political claims, was passed by them and it would never catch up with them again."

Without waiting for the government to formulate its official response, a group of Catholic *évolués* published their own reaction in an occasional journal, *Conscience Africaine*, known for its moderate views with regard to such issues as the Belgian-Congolese community. This African response would go down in history as the *Manifeste de Conscience Africaine*. It was the first published document in the history of colonial Congo in which Congolese intellectuals openly voiced their criticisms and demanded to be included in the process of decolonization. However daring this manifesto, its tone remained moderate, even timid, and its spirit did not depart much from Van Bilsen's appeal for Belgian-African cooperation. As such, it was a clear endorsement of the Van Bilsen Plan. It called for social, economic, and political emancipation to be pursued according to Van Bilsen's twofold program: (1) a timetable of thirty years and (2) the cooperation of Belgium, which should not only be willing to go along with the emancipation project but also to facilitate it.

In comparison with later manifestos, the *Conscience Africaine* manifesto was a moderate document. As many have noted, it had been drafted in part by some Belgian liberal intellectuals who mentored those at *Conscience Africaine*. Although its authors clearly indicated emancipation as their main goal, they were willing to abide by the timetable devised by Van Bilsen: "We demand in the most explicit terms to be directly involved in the elaboration of the Thirty-Year Plan now under discussion. Without this participation, such a plan could not have our consent."

Only a few weeks later there came the ABAKO manifesto, which did not merely distance itself from its predecessor but set a rather vehement and unyielding tone for future African responses to Belgian colonial reforms. The authors declared: "We do not aspire to collaborate in any way with the conception of this [Van Bilsen] plan. We demand nothing less than its withdrawal, for its implementation could only further impede Congo's progress." Although the word independence was never mentioned, the counter-manifesto brushed aside all solutions short of immediate self-government and urged the formation of several political parties in Congo. This last demand ran counter to the unified position favored by most Congolese intellectuals, who believed that only one strong national party could overcome ethnic sentiments and allegiances. But ABAKO had to fight on several fronts, and its radical position can also be construed as a distrust of any colonial attempt at solving the decolonization conundrum. Because all the African members that sponsored the *Conscience Africaine* manifesto were either Baluba or Bangala, the ABAKO also felt it necessary to stake a more radical claim and retake the initiative.

A conciliatory plan devised by a Belgian professor and intended for the Belgian public captured the attention of educated Congolese and triggered their public opposition to the Belgian colonial system. This series of events speaks volumes to the inhibitive and coercive nature of colonial rule in Congo. However, once unleashed, African drive for independence could not be impeded.

THE ROAD TO INDEPENDENCE

Until 1959, the Belgians officially ignored the political developments unraveling in Congo. The policy of inertia that persisted despite the Van Bilsen Plan was unlike what was going on in other colonial territories except perhaps for apartheid South Africa, which still clung to a colonial past. While the Congolese elite was considering the Van Bilsen Plan, some Asian countries, including India, had recovered their independence, and others were in the process of winning theirs. In British West Africa, significant reforms helped countries such as Ghana to gain their independence as early as 1957. France, which had accorded representation in the National Assembly to the African populations under French rule, was drafting a program, the *loi cadre*, intended to confer a great deal of autonomy on these populations. In 1956, just across the river from Leopoldville, Brazzaville, the capital of French Equatorial Africa (FEA), had a new mayor, elected in a landslide victory by the African population. Fulbert Youlou, a young African Catholic priest turned politician, won the vote of the majority of Brazzaville's Bakongo population to become the first black elected mayor in FEA. This was at a time when residents of Belgian Congo did not even have the right to vote. This important development made Congolese feel even more frustrated with the state of affairs in Belgian Congo.

In 1958, however, Belgian colonial attitude shifted from immobilism to controlled gradualism. This change was the result of general elections in Belgium, which brought to power a Social Christian government with liberal support. One of the first symbolic gestures of the new government was to rename the position of minister of colonies. The new "Minister of Belgian Congo and Ruanda-Urundi," as he came to be known, was Belgian Congo's governor general. Instead of a more vigorous, far-reaching program, he set up, in August 1958, an all-European commission (Groupe de Travail). The commission was to undertake a fact-finding inquiry whose results would serve as a blueprint for new governmental policy in Congo.

Meanwhile, African protest had coalesced into full-fledged political parties. Starting with the ABAKO, Congolese ethnic organizations moved in a matter of a few months from advocating the social promotion of an ethnic group to demanding the abolition of the colonial regime. Rather than creating new structures for these new demands, Congolese used the same structures that had served so well in promoting ethnic sentiments. Thus, ethnic associations were transformed into political organizations, retaining their constituencies and allegiances.

There is one exception to this general evolution, which put Congo in a position to undergo the transition to African self-government without the divisive effects of ethnic politics. In October 1958, the group that had authored the *Conscience Africaine* manifesto decided to "give a more precise form to the advancement of the ideas they wished to promote." The Congolese National Movement (Mouvement National Congolais—MNC), as the new party was called, demanded the rapid democratization of institutions, the granting of fundamental liberties as called for by the charter of the United Nations, and independence within a reasonable period. It advocated national unity as a means to achieving emancipation and vigorously opposed the division of Congo into separate political entities. The party included members from different ethnic groups. Some Bakongo *évolués*, namely Gaston Diomi and Alphonse Nguvulu, who had come to oppose the exclusiveness of the ABAKO, joined the MNC committee. By providing an alternative to the separatist discourse of the ABAKO, the MNC thought it might win if not the support at least the tolerance of the colonial government. Until February 1959, it was the ABAKO and its leader Joseph Kasavubu that were lambasted as extremists, and the MNC was considered by all to be a moderate party. This changed with the arrival of Patrice Lumumba as the head of the MNC. In the words of René Lemarchand, "Thanks to his own charisma, Lumumba rejuvenated the MNC and gave a fresh élan to its cause." From then on, ABAKO had a formidable political rival to contend with. Other minor parties appeared on the political scene at the end of 1958, and by mid-1959, when it became evident that colonization was coming to a close, new parties proliferated in Leopoldville and other major cities. Many of these groups proved ephemeral, without any sizeable constituency or real organization in the countryside. Besides the MNC and the ABAKO, other political parties included the PNP (Parti National du Progrès), PSA (Parti Solidaire Africain), CEREA (Centre de Regroupement Africain), CONAKAT (Confédération des Associations Tribales du Katanga), and PUNA (Parti de l'Unité Nationale).

On August 24, 1958, General de Gaulle's famous speech in Brazzaville —indicating his intention to give French overseas territories the choice between "immediate independence" and participation in the French community—was not lost on the Congolese elite. Two days later, some of them presented Minister Pétillon with a petition deploring "the anachronistic political regime" and demanding that a date be set for complete independence. But the Belgian government, still convinced that gradualism should prevail, kept on dodging Congolese demands. In November 1958, it promised a declaration of government policy to be made public on January 13. This brought rumors in Leopoldville's African quarters that independence was to be granted on January 13 and that the Belgian authorities had already picked some Congolese personalities for key cabinet positions.

At the end of 1958, African protest in Congo, besides responding to the "paternal gradualism" of the government, was also responding to external developments such as the All-Africa People's Conference, held in Accra in December 1958. This first pan-African conference convened on African soil brought together, in Africa's first independent nation, political leaders from several African colonies. Among the delegates to the conference was Patrice Lumumba, then the leader of the MNC. Upon his return to Leopoldville, Lumumba enflamed a crowd of more than 7,000 people with a speech that presented the major themes discussed at Accra. Delivered in French and translated into Lingala and Kikongo by Gaston Diomi, this speech struck a deep chord with the populace. "Independence was not a gift," Lumumba stated, "but a fundamental right of the Congolese."

Leopoldville remained in this condition of agitation into January 1959. Aside from political agitation, the causes of tension in Leopoldville included the overpopulation and unemployment that had driven a large section of the local population into poverty.

Unimpressed by the pace of reforms and frustrated with their social conditions, Leopoldville's mass of unemployed and working poor decided to take matters into their own hands. On January 4, 1959, riots broke out in the streets of the capital after the police disbanded a meeting of the ABAKO. Armed with clubs and rocks, rioters wreaked havoc on the city for two consecutive days. They attacked European motorists and passersby and destroyed churches, hospitals, schools, and social centers. According to the official Belgian report, 47 Congolese were killed and about 330 Africans and 49 Europeans were injured.[1] Casualties among the Europeans—no dead and only fifteen seriously injured—might have been much heavier had some of them not been sheltered from the rioters by individual Africans, including ABAKO members. The government, however, decided to arrest the leaders of the ABAKO and dissolve the party.

There is no way of knowing the impact the Leopoldville riots may have had on the government's decisions, but it must have bolstered the cause of pro-independence advocates in Brussels. The much-awaited governmental proclamation finally dispelled any uncertainties regarding Belgium's decision and Congo's political future. A declaration announced the holding of elections by universal suffrage at the end of 1959 to endow Congo with provincial councils, a House of Representatives, and a Senate. More important was the unequivocal message from King Baudoin that preceded the declaration. "It is our intention," he announced, "without undesirable procrastination but also without undue haste, to lead the Congolese populations forward towards independence in prosperity and peace."

While the majority of Europeans in Congo clearly opposed the declaration as an act of capitulation, among Africans the use of the word "independence" for the first time in a government document was enough to arouse much hope. But the ambiguity of the declaration in terms of the nature of this independence and its timetable also aroused suspicion. Belgium hoped to buy more time—a five-year grace period in order to devise a constitutional structure that would guarantee a peaceful transfer of power without depriving Belgium of most of its economic interests in Congo.

As a result of Belgium's resolve to pursue gradualism, during much of 1959 nationalist parties hardened their positions, reiterating their demand for immediate independence, and federalist parties became even more forceful in their demands for a federal state. The two largest parties, the MNC and the recently reinstated ABAKO, threatened civil disobedience and elections boycott. Meanwhile, ethnic tensions flared up between the Lulua and the Baluba in the Kasai province. Exacerbated by Europeans who resented the influence of militant nationalism, this ethnic conflict claimed the lives of thirty Baluba people and spurred the migration of tens of thousands of Baluba refugees toward the southern part of the province.

These events forced the government to commit to an Independence Roundtable held in Brussels in January 1960. At this conference, forty-four Congolese political leaders met Belgian members of Parliament to discuss the transfer of power in Congo. Within the first week after the talks began, the Congolese delegates outmaneuvered their Belgian counterparts and obtained a guarantee that the Belgian Parliament endorse the decisions of the conference. They then demanded that Lumumba, who had been imprisoned for his role in riots in Stanleyville, be released and flown to Brussels to attend the roundtable. As soon as he arrived,

Lumumba used his influence to steer the discussion toward setting a date for independence and ensuring that the new government would retain power in all matters, including defense, security, and foreign affairs. After tedious negotiations, Auguste de Schrijver, then minister of Belgian Congo and Ruanda-Urundi, announced that independence would be granted on June 30, 1960, a month after the general elections.

When the roundtable disbanded on February 21, 1960, independence was no longer a fantasy. To ease the transition and with only a few months remaining before the established date, Belgium sent a resident minister, Walter Ganshof van der Meersch, to Congo to uphold authority during the transition period and supervise the legislative elections. As predicted by many observers, Lumumba's party came out ahead but without winning the majority of seats in national and provincial assemblies. As the winner of the elections, Lumumba was guaranteed to become prime minister and had to form a coalition government. A compromise was worked out with Ganshof van der Meersch to appoint Kasavubu as the head of state.

Congo's political compromise was tested and found lacking in strength. Beset by tensions and antagonisms, it was bound to unravel. Both the prime minister and the president enjoyed the support of the Parliament. Kasavubu was voted head of state by the Parliament, and Lumumba's government received a vote of confidence from the same institution. But the two men remained at odds with one another regarding the future of the new country. While Lumumba favored an undivided Congo with a strong central government, Kasavubu aspired to exhume the old Kongo Kingdom. Under his term as president, "the embers of Bakongo nationalism continued to smolder," according to political scientist Stephen Weissman. To make matters worse, Belgium had its own plans for independent Congo. At the closing of the roundtable, King Baudoin had declared:

> More than ever our thoughts turn to Leopold II, who founded the Congo State some eighty years ago. From a completely unexplored wilderness, unknown to most of the world, from a variety of races and tribes mainly hostile to each other and victims of the slave trade and disease, a mighty empire has grown.

How could Belgium let go of a land that most Belgians believed had been rescued from savagery and transformed into one of the richest colonies in the world? How could they let independence undo what had been created? For Belgium and the rest of the Western world, Congo's attainment of unity and democracy could not take precedence over their economic interests. With the Soviet Union looking to Africa for new adherents to communist ideas, the stage was set for Congo to become a battleground in the Cold War between the two superpowers, the Soviet Union and the United States.

NOTE

1. This official report was disputed by the MNC, which, in a document published on January 9, established the casualties at 530 dead.

7

The First Republic, 1960–1965

The five years that followed Congo's independence proved, in the words of John Clark, "disproportionately influential" in Congo's political development.[1] This period provides eloquent testimony both about the responsibility of Western powers for Africa's turmoil and about the troubled nature of African governance. Many have argued that Congo's leaders were unprepared to take over, and that this should be regarded as the most significant factor in the civil war that ensued. In early April 1960, Professor Van Bilsen, who had become one of Kasavubu's advisers, cited three serious impediments to the success of the new state: a lack of elites, a lack of political experience by the population, and adverse economic conditions. These were not the only factors working to turn Congo from a prosperous colony into a chaotic state. The situation was aggravated by the growing fear among Western countries that Congo's woes might compel its government to look for help to the Soviet Union, and that in order to prevent this situation from occurring it was necessary to intervene in Congolese politics. The "Congo Disaster" of these years—to borrow Colin Legum's expression—was spurred not only by a crisis of leadership but also by an array of outside economic and political forces, which ultimately contributed to the demise of the First Republic.

THE LACK OF UNIVERSITY-TRAINED ELITE

The question most commonly asked about events that have transpired in Congo since independence is, Why did the transition from European to African rule fail considering the wealth of the country and the relative peace it enjoyed during Belgian colonial rule? One answer is the lack of reforms, as was stressed in the previous chapter. However, another key factor in Congo's shaky beginnings was the absence of an elite that might run the administrative system and business sector inherited from the Belgians. The data in Table 7.1 speaks for itself. At the time of independence there was not a single Congolese administrator capable of overseeing the complex administrative system left in place by the Belgians.

Table 7.1: African and European Civil Servants in June 1960

Ranks	Europeans	Africans
High-ranking functionaries	5,900	0
Mid-level functionaries		
Office managers	1,690	9
Assistant managers	1,976	24
Clerks	774	726
Low-level functionaries	0	10,791
Total	10,340	11,550

In addition, not a single Congolese lawyer, doctor, or judge was trained according to European standards before independence. It was only in 1952 that the first Congolese student to register in a university left Leopoldville to attend the University of Louvain in Belgium. In 1954, after much deliberation as to whether higher education was suitable for Congolese, Belgians opened the University of Lovanium[2] under the auspices of the Catholic University of Louvain. Belgian Colonial Minister André Dequa and Governor General Léon Pétillon finally agreed to the demands of both Congolese évolués and Belgian Catholic officials on the condition that law, philosophy, and letters be excluded from the curriculum. They assumed that these subjects would lead the Congolese astray. Thus, initially, the curriculum included only agriculture, medical sciences, and pedagogy. It was not until the fall of 1958 that the first contingent of Congolese students enrolled in the newly organized law program.

In 1956, a second university was established in Elisabethville, at the behest of some members of the Université Libre de Bruxelles, as an alternative to the dominance of the Catholic Lovanium. As Table 7.2 indicates, the great majority of students enrolled were the sons of European colonists.

Table 7.2: Number of Students Enrolled in Congolese Universities, 1954–1959

Year	University of Lovanium		University of Elisabethville	
	Africans	Europeans	Africans	Europeans
1954	30	3	—	—
1955	77	10	—	—
1956	122	47	8	86
1957	177	72	17	107
1958	248	117	44	155
1959	344	136	77	199

SOURCE: Lemarchand (1964: 136).

As a result of the slow progress in introducing higher education in the Congo, in June 1960 only thirty Congolese held university degrees, earned at home and abroad. Only 466 African students attended the universities of Lovanium and Elisabethville and 76 were enrolled in Belgian universities. The dearth of university-trained individuals explains the difficulties experienced by the new government in filling key positions in the administration. For many years, the government had to rely on Belgian personnel for high-level positions in the civil service, universities, hospitals, and army.

Of all the institutions at the new government's disposal, the Force Publique remained the most rooted in its colonial ways. Until 1960, it had served as a well-disciplined native army that carried out military operations as well as a police force that crushed nationalist movements such as in the Leopoldville and Stanleyville riots in 1959. The Force Publique remained impervious to the social and political changes that affected the country in the 1950s, mostly due to the way it continued to be staffed. By 1960, the Force was comprised of nearly 24,000 African recruits, the bulk of whom were illiterate, often drawn directly from the remotest areas of the colony. They were ruthlessly commanded by 1,000 European officers. Until independence, Belgians refused to promote to the rank of officer the few educated African soldiers despite their long experience in the army. After independence, although in some areas progress was made to incorporate Congolese, the army and the civil service remained the two most segregated and least "Africanized" institutions in the country.

CIVIL STRIFE

From the beginning, the new country faced a situation which would have tried even the most stable democracy. Congo had won its independence, but its new leaders lacked the human capital and the political clout to put this into action. The morning following the festivities of independence, the Belgian commander in chief of the Congolese Force Publique, General Émile Janssens, reminded his African troops of this painful truth. He summoned his troops and wrote on a blackboard "before Independence = after Independence." Janssens was not a man to hide his bitter feelings about Belgium's loss of Congo. Staunchly loyal to his country and a notorious white supremacist, he bemoaned the end of colonial rule and vowed to continue to treat his African troops as if independence had not occurred. Independence, he contended, may have removed the Belgians from power and replaced them with Congolese politicians, but business would continue as usual in the army.

In response to Janssens' attitude, Congolese troops mutinied. This can be considered the prelude to a protracted political and military crisis that engulfed the whole country. Starting on July 5 at Camp Hardy (near Thysville), Congolese troops threatened their European officers and sent a wave of fright through the European civil population. The mutiny spread to Leopoldville the next day and then to the rest of the country despite Janssens' dismissal and the nomination of Victor Lundula, who had been hastily promoted from sergeant major to general, as commander in chief of the new Armée Nationale Congolaise (ANC).

The incidents reported usually involved the looting of European properties, the beating of European officers and civilians who refused to yield to the demands of the mutineers, and the rape of European women. Aware of the dissatisfaction in the army, Lumumba had announced publicly before the mutiny that the newfound political liberty of the Congolese did not imply total license. Lumumba had also reassured the European population that the new authorities intended to safeguard the personal security and property of everyone—black and white—and that law and order would be maintained at all costs. But his words went unheeded, and he had to assert his authority more vigorously. It was not until both the prime minister and the president personally intervened that the mutineers surrendered their arms and released their officers in Leopoldville and Thysville. But in the rest of the country the mutiny went on unabated. The rebellion took its first European victims in Katanga on July 10, when mutinous Congolese soldiers allegedly ambushed and killed six Europeans, including the Italian vice consul. The government disapproved of the atrocities perpetrated against Europeans and tried to quell the mutiny. Still, Belgium grew alarmed at the situation in Congo, especially when European civilians began seeking refuge in northern Rhodesia, Uganda, Portuguese Angola, and the neighboring Republic of Congo.

Instead of seeking a diplomatic solution to the crisis, Belgium decided to airlift in thousands of troops, who came to join the 2,500 Belgian troops already in Congo as part of a military agreement signed between the two countries. Belgian intervention contributed to the escalating violence and also fueled latent tensions between Lumumba and Kasavubu. While President Kasavubu welcomed the intervention, Lumumba denounced the Belgian decision as a reckless move that would only fan the flames of violence. But, on July 11, while visiting Luluabourg to appeal to the mutineers, Lumumba agreed to the presence of Belgian troops as long as they restricted themselves to their initial mission of protecting the lives and properties of Europeans.

For the first few days, Belgian troops seemed to be doing just that. Then on July 11, after completely evacuating the European population of Matadi, Belgian naval forces bombarded sections of the city, killing at least nineteen Congolese civilians. News of the Matadi massacre sparked renewed attacks throughout the country, targeting the Europeans who had chosen to remain in spite of the violence. After the events in Matadi, Belgian troops moved swiftly to occupy other cities, including the capital, where they clashed with Congolese soldiers.

KATANGA SECEDES

The most contentious event leading to the rupture between Belgium and Congo was the secession of Katanga. This series of events provided proof of Belgium's insincerity in granting independence to Congo and its determination to dominate Congo in a neocolonial way after independence. From the early days of Belgian rule, Katanga had enjoyed special treatment because of its economic status and large European settler community (31 percent of the total European population of Congo). During the colonial period, Katanga had cultivated affinities with southern Africa more than with the rest of Congo. The proximity of southern Rhodesia (present-day Zimbabwe) and South Africa, with its apartheid system, had encouraged separatist ideas on the part of Katanga's white community.

The sheer wealth of the province was unmatched. During the 1950s, mineral production soared by nearly 60 percent, allowing UMHK,

Congo's largest operating company, to gross enormous profits. UMHK—which held an absolute monopoly of Katanga's mining industry—was controlled by the Société Générale de Belgique, a powerful Belgian financial company that controlled at least 70 percent of the Congolese economy. This meant that economic interests in Belgium would be jeopardized by adverse political developments in Katanga. According to unofficial figures provided by Catherine Hoskyns, a break with Congo, and especially Katanga, would have cost the Société Générale about "30 percent of the overseas operations of transport and insurance firms, and the loss of about 77 million dollars in revenue from investments." For Belgium, the loss of Congo would have amounted to a drastic reduction of annual budget plus the huge expense of reintegrating approximately 10,000 administrative officers and former colonial servants who remained on the payroll of the Congolese government. Other Western countries also had a large stake in Katanga's economy and remained attentive to the political events there. Heavily dependent on Katanga as a source of raw materials such as copper, France, Italy, and West Germany worried that political chaos in Congo might put at risk their access to Katanga's vital mineral reservoir. American involvement in Congo, according to Stephen Weissman, was also motivated by an "access interest rather than an investment one." American officials considered Katanga to be part of a larger geographical area known as the Copperbelt, an area including the Rhodesias that was responsible for a quarter of the world's copper output. Like other Western countries, the United States had a vested interest in the mineral activities of the Katanga-Rhodesia Copperbelt. In 1960, the U.S. imported from Katanga alone three-quarters of its cobalt and one-half of its tantalum—two minerals used in the aerospace industry. Using declassified documents, David N. Gibbs takes Weissman's analysis a step further by arguing that during the late 1940s and 1950s, the U.S. pursued procolonial policies and even opposed Congo's independence on the grounds that an independent Congo would not guarantee access to Congo's minerals as Belgian rule did. Private economic interests, contends Gibbs, was the impetus that dictated American policy toward Congo.

Besides these economic uncertainties, Western powers were fearful of the political implications of Belgium's haphazard retreat from Congo, a land highly coveted by European colonialists because of its size, location, and mineral wealth. With its descent into anarchy, American policymakers feared that it would be coveted by the Soviet Union, which began working through the Belgian communist party to influence Congolese leaders. Concerned about the possibility of a communist takeover in Congo, Western countries had first assumed that the best answer was a strong central government headed by Patrice Lumumba, whom they believed to be the only Congolese politician with enough clout to keep separatist propensities in check, guarantee political stability, and safeguard Western economic interests in Congo. But Lumumba proved to be a fierce and uncompromising nationalist leader who considered his main task to be restoring the dignity of the Congolese people. During the independence celebration, Lumumba had made a fiery speech responding to Belgian king Baudoin's characterization of Congo's independence as the "culmination of the work conceived by the genius of Leopold II." He started his impromptu speech by saluting the "fighters for independence, today victorious." He went on to indict Belgian colonial rule and excoriate Belgian paternalism:

> We have known mockery, insults, blows which we had to endure from morning to night because we were 'Negroes' . . . . We have known that the law was never the same for whites and blacks. . . . We have known the atrocious sufferings of those banished because of their political opinions or religious beliefs. . . . Who will forget the firing squads, the brutal arrests of those who refused to bow to the regime of injustice, oppression and exploitation?

From the moment these words were uttered Lumumba fell out of favor in Western financial and political circles. In the words of one observer, a "consensus quickly crystallized that Lumumba was unreliable, anti-Belgian, antiwhite, perhaps a Communist, and probably crazy."[3] U.S. officials, including President Eisenhower, vilified him as a "very difficult if not impossible person to deal with . . . dangerous to the peace and safety of the world." Lumumba was viewed as dangerous, as an irrational and erratic politician who might recklessly foil Western neocolonial projects in Congo. This explains why Lumumba's opposition to Belgian intervention and his intransigence about the secession of Katanga were met with such strong reactions by Western nations.

Lumumba reacted swiftly to the Katanga affair. He denounced Belgium for carrying its initial mission of protecting Europeans too far. It became clear after the first clashes between Congolese and Belgian troops that Katanga's decision to break away from Congo could not have succeeded without the political and military support offered by Belgium.

During the first two months of the secession, Belgium flew more than one hundred tons of arms and ammunition from Brussels to Katanga and gave twenty-five of its own military planes to build up Katanga's air force. Belgian troops helped Moïse Tshombe, the leader of the CONAKAT and self-declared prime minister of the new independent Republic of Katanga, to neutralize the ANC and assert his authority. On July 12, the day following Katanga's declaration of independence, Belgian troops moved to put down the few pockets of rebellion in Katanga. In Jadotville, what was supposed to be an operation of disarmament turned into a bloodbath when Belgian soldiers attacked Congolese mutineers and killed fifty of them.

At first, Katanga's secession helped Kasavubu and Lumumba mend their differences. The two men flew to Katanga to persuade Tshombe to rescind the secession. But after consulting with his Belgian advisers, Tshombe refused to allow their plane to land safely in Elisabethville, which remained under Belgian military control. In retaliation, Kasavubu and Lumumba issued a joint appeal to the United Nations soliciting technical assistance and military aid to put an end to Belgian aggression. On July 15, the Congolese Senate passed a resolution calling for immediate withdrawal of Belgian troops. A few days later Kasavubu and Lumumba gave the United Nations an ultimatum, which convinced the West of the imminence of a Soviet takeover: Belgian troops must withdraw from Congo within seventy-two hours or else the government would appeal to Soviet forces. Evidence suggests that every step made by the government to bring the secession to an end was the product of collective decision making. But in the end, Lumumba bore the brunt of Western criticisms alone. State Department officials in Washington described Congo's actions as a result of Lumumba's "desperate, self-contradictory, unpredictable, irrational mood."[4]

Belgian troops officially withdrew from Katanga on August 14, a few days after a contingent of Swedish UN forces led by UN Secretary General Dag Hammarskjöld had entered the province. But Katanga still enjoyed military protection from Belgium, which ordered hundreds of Belgian officers to remain in Katanga to instruct the gendarmerie. Belgium also continued to provide Katanga with all the financial, technical, and diplomatic assistance it needed. Other Western powers also bolstered Tshombe's position. France, for example, helped Katanga recruit white mercenaries and buy military aircraft. France also bolstered Katanga's international legitimacy by convincing President Fulbert Youlou of Congo-Brazzaville to recognize Katanga's sovereignty. Angola and southern Africa eased the export of Katanga's mineral commodities by providing access to their roads and coastal facilities.

Katanga's secession devastated the ability of the central government in Leopoldville to assert its authority and deter further secessionist movements in other provinces. On August 9, after secession attempts in Equateur and Kivu provinces failed, the same process that had taken place in Katanga occurred in the rich mining province of Kasai under the leadership of Albert Kalonji. Although backed by the Belgians and financed by the Forminière diamond company (another subsidiary of the Société Générale), Kalonji's "mining state" was short-lived. Before Kalonji could recruit enough mercenaries to build up his army, Lumumba ordered Congolese troops to occupy Luluabourg and Bakwanga. On August 28, overwhelmed by the Congolese army, Kasai's soldiers retreated without ever regaining control of the major cities.

These secessionist movements took their toll on the unity of the central government. Berating Lumumba's inability to restore order in Congo, Kasavubu declared in early August that only a confederation could provide a peaceful resolution to the conflicts that ravaged the country. This announcement broke the tenuous alliance between the two Congolese leaders and tilted the political balance toward the federalist cause. Lumumba's days in office were numbered. As long as he had the backing of President Kasavubu, his vision of a strong and united Congo maintained the political legitimacy that Katanga's secession lacked. But now that Kasavubu had joined forces with other opponents of Lumumba's regime, Lumumba became the last obstacle preventing Western governments and companies from making Congo their own neocolonial state.

LUMUMBA'S ASSASSINATION

By the end of August 1960, it was clear that Lumumba had fallen out of Western favor as a result of his disagreement with UN handling of Congo's crisis. He had repeatedly remonstrated to UN Secretary General Hammarskjöld that sending white troops to Congo amounted to substituting "UN colonialism for Belgian colonialism." The main bone of contention was the UN's reluctance to get involved in what it regarded as Congolese internal problems. Lumumba had unsuccessfully tried to compel the UN to help his government solve the Katanga imbroglio even if this meant a long-range, UN-led military operation. Only by resolving the secession, he argued, could his government restore the integrity of the national territory and regain authority over it. His persistent demands that UN troops intervene in Katanga failed to distract the UN from its objectives: to prevent the country from being a site of military confrontation between foreign powers and to avoid the internationalization of the Congolese conflict.

In July, Lumumba made his first trip to the United States. He hoped to dispel American fears that he was under strong leftist influence and to convince the Eisenhower administration to support peacekeeping efforts in Congo. However, this trip convinced Lumumba that the United States had no intention of frustrating Belgian neocolonial objectives in Congo. As a last resort, he turned to the Communist bloc for military equipment and diplomatic support, further distancing himself from the United States and its Western allies.

Lumumba had even lost the support of his own cabinet, which started to show signs of division. The reconquering of southern Kasai by the ANC, led by Mobutu, started as a military operation. By August 29, it had turned into the massacre of thousands of Baluba civilians. This failed military operation alienated Lumumba from a large portion of the population, not only in Kasai but also in other provinces with strong federalist sympathies. Lumumba was unbending toward the secessionist movements of Kasai and Katanga and uncompromising in his commitment to the nationalist cause. This stance cost him the support of some moderate politicians who would have liked to see the crisis dealt with around a negotiating table rather than by force. This opposition was compounded by Lumumba's lack of a strong constituency in Leopoldville. His earlier popularity, based on his abilities as a political leader who could unite Congolese regardless of their ethnic background, had disappeared. Once this dream of a unified nation was shattered by rising ethnic sentiments, people in Leopoldville and the rest of the country rallied behind their ethnic leaders. With its population of primarily Bakongo and Bangala, Leopoldville was hardly a place where Lumumba could draw the support he needed.

Furthermore, Lumumba's convictions that the church should not have a major role in public life and his flirtation with the Communist bloc had set the powerful Catholic Church against him. Two of the most widely read newspapers in Leopoldville, *Courrier d'Afrique* and *Présence Africaine*, were controlled by the Catholic Church. They did not fail to lambast Lumumba's government for its inability to solve the crisis.

It was against this background that the CIA and the Belgian secret service concluded that only the physical elimination of Lumumba could prevent Congo from ending up in the hands of the Soviets. The new leader chosen to replace Lumumba was Joseph-Désiré Mobutu, one of Lumumba's lieutenants, a young, ambitious army officer with no political talent or ideas but a reputation for ruthlessness. He could be persuaded to espouse virtually any political agenda if bribed with money. From the beginning of the Congolese crisis he had been used by the CIA to create, in the words of David Gibbs, a devoted "freelance strike force" in the army. According to Madeleine Kalb's account of Mobutu's connections with the West, "money supplied by the CIA and by the Western embassies in Leopoldville kept him in business." Mobutu had been a favorite of Western secret services since his beginnings as an obscure journalist. While representing Lumumba's party in Brussels in 1959, he was enticed to work for the CIA by Lawrence Devlin, the head of the CIA bureau in Leopoldville. When the time came to dispose of Lumumba, Mobutu played into the hands of Western powers. But as long as Kasavubu was leading Lumumba's opponents, Mobutu remained a behind-the-scenes player.

In a preemptive move prompted by Lumumba's break with the UN, President Kasavubu made a national radio address on September 5 revoking the prime minister from his functions and replacing his government with a cabinet headed by Senate leader Joseph Ileo, a conservative known for his federalist views. Kasavubu acted under a constitutional provision that granted the president the legal power to name and revoke the prime minister. Lumumba immediately reacted with a radio address denouncing his dismissal as an illegal action, accusing the president of betraying the interest of the country, and declaring his decision to remove Kasavubu as head of state. Kasavubu's decision encountered strong opposition in the Parliament, where a large majority voted to annul Lumumba's revocation on constitutional grounds. On September 8, the Senate went even further and reinstated Lumumba's government in a landslide confidence vote of 41 to 2, with 6 abstentions.

As the political elimination of Lumumba had failed, it became clear that only physical elimination could neutralize him and clear the way for a conservative government. On September 14, Mobutu staged his first coup d'état, announcing in a press conference that the army was "neutralizing" both the president and the prime minister. Having also suspended the parliament and the constitution, he designated a *Collège des Commissaires* composed of university students, most of whom hurried back from Belgium to serve in a provisionary government that would handle affairs until the end of the year. His regime was later endorsed by Kasavubu, who lauded his efforts to save Congo from an "explosive situation."

Western influences encouraged Mobutu's subsequent decision, on September 15, to confine Lumumba to the prime minister's residence and deny him access to the main means of communication with the Congolese population, whereas his main opponents, Kasavubu and Tshombe, used respectively Radio Brazzaville and Radio Elisabethville to further their objectives. Although protected by a cordon of UN troops and closely watched by ANC troops, Lumumba remained a threat to Mobutu and his Western backers. One State Department official echoed the American opinion of Lumumba as a dangerous demagogue by noting that Lumumba "had this tremendous ability to stir up a crowd or a group. And if he could have gotten out and started to talk to a battalion of the Congolese Army, he probably would have had them in the palm of his hand in five minutes."[5] Lumumba was to be arrested, but several attempts by Mobutu's troops to apprehend him were warded off by UN troops stationed around the residence. Lumumba never trusted the protection offered by UN troops and knew himself to be at the mercy of Mobutu's dictatorial powers and determination to heed the CIA's orders to arrest him.

On November 27, Lumumba left his residence by car according to an escape plan that would have taken him to Stanleyville, where nationalist supporters had regrouped. Arrested in Mweka, near Port-Franqui, with two of his comrades, Senate Vice President Joseph Okito and Youth Minister Maurice Mpolo, he was transferred back to Leopoldville and imprisoned at the military camp in Thysville. On January 17, there were reports that Lumumba's presence at the camp had turned a large group of soldiers in favor of the nationalist cause and that soldiers had taken hostages and some officers were demanding the liberation of Lumumba. Harold d'Aspremont de Lyden, Belgian minister for African affairs, ordered that the three prisoners be flown to Elisabethville. What followed was long held in tight secrecy, but a recent study[6] based on UN and Belgian Foreign Office archives as well as information provided by key actors has shed new light on the circumstances that led to Lumumba's death. Orders to eliminate Lumumba had been issued by President Eisenhower during a National Security Council meeting in Washington in August 1960. One National Security Council staff member testified a few years after the fact that Eisenhower's words "came across to me as an order for the assassination of Lumumba. . . . There was no discussion; the meeting simply moved on." Eisenhower's order was immediately cabled to CIA station chief Devlin, who attempted, although unsuccessfully, to carry out the assassination of the Congolese premier. As Jonathan Kwitny (1984: 62) notes, the U.S. sought to "replace by force the legally constituted government of the Congo—a nation with which the United States was not at war and had no cause to be." However, according to Ludo de Witte's recent study, direct U.S. involvement in the assassination is unlikely. Although the U.S. was responsible for setting the stage and providing the impetus, the assassination itself was endorsed by the Belgian government and orchestrated by the Belgian secret service. It was during an informal meeting of Tshombe's cabinet attended by several of his Belgian advisers that Lumumba's fate was sealed. The night of their arrival in Elisabethville, Lumumba and his two companions suffered severe torture at the hands of their captors, including Tshombe himself and his interior minister Godefroid Munongo. They were then executed by Katanga soldiers under the command of two Belgian police officers, Frans Verscheure and Julien Gat. Tshombe, who kept the news from leaking to the press for three weeks, finally announced Lumumba's death on February 10, sending waves of protest across several world capitals and ushering in a period of open war between the Lumumbists and the federalists.

MOBUTU TAKES OVER

Lumumba's death cleared the way for the political rise of Mobutu and the establishment of one of the most staunchly pro-Western regimes in postcolonial Africa. But first Mobutu had to contend with a situation over which he had little control. Lacking the support of the masses and a legal mandate, he was forced to reinstate Kasavubu as president immediately following the official announcement of Lumumba's death. In theory, Congo reverted to civil rule, but in effect it remained divided into two rival governments, Leopoldville and Stanleyville, each claiming to be the country's legal capital. Meanwhile, two of its richest provinces, Kasai and Katanga, defiantly claimed to have seceded.

Holding less than half the country's territory and only a fraction of its natural resources and industry, Ileo's government in Leopoldville failed to draw enough support to bring the rival parties to the negotiating table. Similarly, the Stanleyville government led by Antoine Gizenga, who served as vice premier in Lumumba's cabinet, never attracted much international support. Despite its territorial expansion and the military threat it posed to Leopoldville, it functioned as a government in exile without any extensive administrative structure.

The stalemate finally came to an end in August 1961 when the Parliament rejected both governments and chose Cyrille Adoula to form a new government. Adoula had served as interior minister in the Ileo government and had strong connections in Leopoldville. However, he opposed the Katanga secession on the same nationalist grounds that informed Lumumba's political action. It was during his tenure as interior minister that prosecution of pro-Lumumba elements in Leopoldville came to a halt. The single achievement during Adoula's tenure was to bring the Katanga secession to an end.

On February 21, 1961, a UN Security Council resolution authorized UN forces to use arms as a last resort to prevent a full-scale civil war and to remove from Congo all foreign military personnel and political advisers not employed by the UN. Given that Tshombe's administration was filled with Belgian officers and advisers, the resolution came as a blow to the secession movement. Until January 1963, Tshombe dodged UN plans to dismantle his regime, threatening to use scorched-earth tactics in the event of a UN military operation against Katanga. Even after being offered the post of premier in a unified Congo, Tshombe unflinchingly reiterated his opposition to reunification. As pressure mounted from the United States and Belgium, which had reversed their policies and now considered secessionist Katanga a factor of instability for the entire country, Tshombe finally announced the end of the secession on January 17.

Unending civil and political strife had taken its toll on the social welfare of the population. The end of Katanga's secession brought little respite to a country in dire need of peace in order to resume economic activities. The year 1964 saw little economic improvement and the intensification of violence and rebellions throughout the country. In July, President Kasavubu asked Tshombe to form a new cabinet with a twofold agenda of national reconciliation and economic recovery. However, by this time half the country had fallen into the hands of rebellious Lumumbist factions, headed by Victor Gbenye, Pierre Mulele, and Gaston Soumialot. They had formed the National Liberation Council (Conseil National de Libération—CNL) under the protection of Congo-Brazzaville's leftist government of President Alphonse Massemba-Debat. The intensification of rebel attacks hardened Tshombe's position. After November 1961 he vowed to crush the rebels and enlisted Belgian and American assistance to supplement ANC troops commanded by General Mobutu. When Tshombe failed to make forays into the rebel territories, General Mobutu decided to act. On November 25, 1965 he deposed President Kasavubu and assumed the presidency for what he initially claimed would be a five-year tenure until new elections were held. In the end, Mobutu's dictatorship lasted for more than thirty years, during which time Congo spiraled into economic chaos.

NOTES

1. John F. Clark, "Ethno-Regionalism and Democratization in Zaire," in *Ethnic Conflict and Democratization in Africa*, Harvey Glickman, ed. (Atlanta, GA: The African Studies Association Press, 1995), p. 360.

2. When compared to other African colonies, the educational situation of natives in Belgian Congo was particularly difficult. In South Africa, the first college for blacks opened its doors as early as 1914. In the late 1940s, the British began to establish universities in their African colonies of Uganda and Nigeria. Although the French did not set up universities in their colonies, Africans from French colonies were allowed to attend French universities as early as the 1920s.

3. Quoted in Gibbs (1991: 81).

4. Quoted in Weissman (1974: 62).

5. Quoted in Gibbs (1991: 98).

6. Ludo De Witte, *De Moord op Lumumba* (Louvain: Uitgeverij van Halewyck, 1999).

8

The Second Republic, 1965–1990

Proponents of realpolitik in Washington and elsewhere supported Mobutu, justifying his protracted reign with the threat of anarchy. These supporters claimed that an absence of authoritarian rule in Congo would lead to chaos because underlying ethnic tensions could burst at any time into full-fledged civil war. The strong political and financial support that followed from these claims buoyed Mobutu's regime for more than three decades. Despite his supporters' claims, Mobutu's reign was characterized by a rapid decay of the Congolese state accompanied by unprecedented economic deterioration. He did manage to forge a national identity that helped the country avoid the kind of ethnic tensions that devastated so many African nations. But this was accomplished at the expense of freedom of expression and democracy. Ironically, Mobutu came to symbolize the chaos from which foreign powers had sought to protect the country. Some scholars have compared Mobutu's corrupt and brutal tenure to the Leopoldian era of terror in Congo, arguing that it was nothing other than the reincarnation of *Bula Matari*.

THE COLLAPSE OF THE FIRST REPUBLIC

Following his first military coup, Mobutu relinquished power to civilians. But he continued to wield substantial control within the army, and he acted as an éminence grise under Adoula and Tshombe. For four years, he waited for civilian rule to be discredited. He knew the civilian government would be unable to strike a bargain with the Lumumbist insurgent groups or to restore the integrity of the national boundaries. On August 1, 1964, President Kasavubu ratified a new constitution with some major changes. These changes strengthened presidential prerogatives and ushered in a new period of political stability, although the constitution hardly drew unanimous praises. Kasavubu changed the name of the country to the Democratic Republic of Congo, a change that was well received by authorities in Brazzaville. They had long disagreed with the claim of Leopoldville that the name "Republic of Congo" should only be used in reference to the former Belgian Congo. The new constitution also introduced a new flag. It bore the yellow star of the Leopoldian flag, symbol of the mineral wealth of the country, and a red diagonal stripe, symbolizing the blood of martyrs. The new flag mirrored the contradictions as well as the challenges the country faced. The balance of power tilted toward the president with the new constitution, although Congo remained a parliamentary regime. Another constitutional innovation granted more autonomy to the twenty-one provinces, endowing each with its own provincial government, its own budget, and the right to share the revenues from the export of raw materials with the central government. The new constitution was an attempt to reform a parliamentary system that had failed to keep in check the divisive ethnic forces that the end of Belgian rule had unleashed.

As the presidential elections drew nearer, the political climate between Kasavubu and Tshombe soured. The latter had been in exile in Madrid and came back to replace Adoula as the new head of the central government on July 6, 1964. Many perceived Tshombe's position of control in the central government as a prelude to greater decentralization and thought this might lead to some form of federalism. Tshombe intended to initiate a dialogue of national reconciliation. But many within the nationalist groups could not forget that he had orchestrated Lumumba's assassination. In late July, following a successful campaign to ingratiate himself with the population of Leopoldville, Tshombe turned his attention to the provincial capitals. He toured several Congolese cities to rally regional constituencies that remained suspicious of his apparent good will. While in Stanleyville, he visited Lumumba's monument and bowed his head in a moment of silence before it. At first, Tshombe's gesture won him the sympathy of the populace in that area, which was considered the stronghold of Congolese unified nationalism. Then, a week after his visit, Stanleyville fell to CNL rebels. The rebels captured several European hostages, including four CIA agents and the American consul, and sent Mobutu's ANC troops into hiding. Despite Tshombe's symbolic gestures and conciliatory rhetoric, the CNL was offended by some of his policies. It particularly abhorred Tshombe's decision to exclude all the prominent nationalists from his government, choosing instead to staff his cabinet with staunch federalists and to recall some of his former Belgian advisers. As a result, CNL nationalists announced that they would not recognize the Tshombe government. Their political opposition to Tshombe's regime meant that guerrilla operations would go on, and the insurgents showed renewed military vigor. However, in early 1965 foreign military intervention curtailed their momentum. A military operation spearheaded by white South African mercenaries and Belgian paracommandos captured Stanleyville in November 1964 and freed most European hostages.

With the insurgent movements receding, Congo's political scene was dominated by an intense conflict between Kasavubu and Tshombe. Both vied for power as the elections approached. To undercut Tshombe's position, Kasavubu made a bold move and dismissed him on October 13, 1965. He selected Évariste Kimba, a former ally of Tshombe, to form a new cabinet. But Prime Minister Kimba lacked both the constituency and charisma to establish his new cabinet. The Belgians found Kimba's government and its nationalistic outlook to be less amenable than that of Tshombe. Kimba also lacked the backing of other foreign governments, who could not afford to jeopardize their interests in Congo. All these factors prompted Mobutu to stage a second military coup. On November 24, he deposed president Kasavubu and assumed the title of chief of state, justifying his actions on the grounds of the administration's inability to rein in civil unrest. He placed Kasavubu immediately under house arrest at Kokolo camp before allowing him to travel to his rural home in Lower Congo. The next day, in an extraordinary session, the Parliament approved Mobutu's seizure of power with a unanimous vote of confidence. The First Republic had essentially ceased to exist. Most Congolese welcomed the new regime, hoping that it would bring a new era of political stability and economic recovery after the chaotic beginnings of the First Republic.

POLITICAL CONSOLIDATION

Mobutu took power at a time when the rebel factions had ceased to pose a real threat to the central government. He took advantage of this period of truce to transform his supposedly transitional regime, which he himself had promised would last for only five years, into a full-fledged dictatorship that would rule Congo for over three decades. Because he had no ethnic-based constituency[1], Mobutu created a broad-based, inclusive government. For the first two years, he relied on the institutions of the First Republic rather than creating new ones. For example, the premiership continued to exist though with far less authority than previously. Mobutu entrusted this position to Colonel Léonard Mulamba, whom he gave the task of forming a government of national unity consisting of twenty-two ministers, one each from Leopoldville and the twenty-one provinces. The Parliament unanimously approved this government on November 28.

Mobutu's regime was backed by the army. However, it still ran the risk of falling apart unless it continued to receive massive foreign support. The United States, which had approved and helped Mobutu carry out the coup, was among the first foreign countries to recognize the new regime. Recognition by some African countries and most Western European countries followed. A few African countries, including Zambia, vehemently disapproved of the military dictatorship. But their recriminations went unnoticed as the tide gradually turned against democratic regimes in the whole of Africa. Within a few months of Mobutu's takeover, several other African countries experienced the same brutal shift toward military dictatorship. This gave a boost to Mobutu's regime and allowed him to attend the 1966 African summit convened in Nairobi by Kenyan president Jomo Kenyatta. Promising to rid Congo of all foreign influences, Mobutu convinced Congo's neighboring countries to help him put an end to the rebellion. They agreed not to let Congolese rebel factions use their territories to establish operating bases for launching military attacks against Mobutu's regime. A second meeting held in Kinshasa in February 1967 gathered leaders of nine East and central African nations, who vowed to reinforce political and economic ties.

Mobutu was accepted as Congo's new leader. He had great confidence that his regime enjoyed the protection of Western countries and felt he could rely on the loyalty of the army. This bolstered his determination to obliterate the institutional framework established by the First Republic. Despite the Parliament's approval of his regime, Parliament itself was to be the first target of Mobutu's authoritarian rule. In March, after only four months of activity under the new regime, the Parliament was stripped of most of its legislative powers. It remained in a state of suspension until May 22, when by presidential decree Mobutu gave himself "full powers." This effectively obliterated the office of prime minister. In October, Mobutu dismissed General Mulamba and abolished the premiership altogether. As a pretext for the dismissal, Mobutu cited Mulamba's lax attitude toward rebellious military units in Stanleyville. Mobutu thus made himself head of both state and government.

Mobutu's general mode of operations across the years of his dictatorship was to either co-opt or repress his political opposition. On May 30, this repression took an ominous turn. Mobutu arrested former Prime Minister Évariste Kimba and three of his "acolytes," former ministers Alexandre Mahamba, Jérôme Anany, and Emmanuel Bamba. They were arrested on the grounds that they had conspired, in what became known as the "Pentecost Plot," to overthrow the government and assassinate Mobutu. The military court that Mobutu had appointed deliberated for only ten minutes and found the four men guilty. Three days later, on June 2, they were hanged before 50,000 spectators in one of Leopoldville's busiest squares. Appeals by several governments had failed to deter Mobutu from carrying out the public executions. These events sent a chilling message to the opposition and ushered in a long reign of terror. During this period, assassinations, tortures, and betrayals were used as political tactics to maintain power.

Abuse of political power and co-optation became the hallmarks of Mobutu's regime. Presidential nominees generally lasted for only brief periods. Political careers amounted to nothing but an opportunity for graft. The first contingent of politicians drafted by the new regime were First Republic figures such as Nendaka, Bomboko, Mungul Diaka, and Adoula. Munongo and Kamitatu were imprisoned, Kasavubu confined to his home village, and Tshombe jailed in Algiers after being kidnapped in Spain. Tshombe's nephew, Nguza Karl-I-Bond, was also co-opted, serving intermittently as Mobutu's foreign minister, ambassador to Washington, and prime minister in the 1970s and 1980s. In the words of Young and Turner (1985: 56):

> Cooptation, a device used with remarkable effect through the Mobutu era, was early developed into a fine art, as the far-flung apparatus of the state offered a large reservoir of positions for those willing to pledge faithful

service. University graduates were the object of particular solicitation; a number were absorbed into the ramify-
ing services of the presidency itself, including several
who as student leaders had been articulate spokesmen
for intransigent nationalism.

The regime ensured loyalty and submission through the threat of
political disgrace, which hung ominously over the heads of those
involved. Political positions were ephemeral. Periods of dismissal could
also be brief, as long as those who fell from presidential favor were
remorseful and ingratiating enough.

Like his predecessors, Mobutu had to face fierce opposition from
inside and outside the country. His power continued to depend on his
ability to eradicate the threats posed by rebelling groups. Although
unrest and violence persisted in several parts of the country, Mobutu
managed to reduce rebel zones to small pockets of insurgency, some of
which lasted until the late 1980s, for example in the southern part of
Kivu. But Mobutu managed to control them such that they no longer
posed a threat to the stability of his regime. In 1968, Mobutu outsmarted
one of the last insurgent leaders, Pierre Mulele, who had led the Kwilu
rebellion in southwestern Congo. Mobutu promised Mulele amnesty. In
response, Mulele came from Brazzaville aboard Mobutu's presidential
ferry. When he arrived, Mulele was greeted in Kinshasa by Foreign
Minister Justin Bomboko, who declared, "We welcome Mr. Mulele as a
brother. He will work with us toward the total liberation of our country."
Mulele was then taken to the residence of General Louis Bobozo, where
there was a reception in his honor attended by several prominent figures
of the regime. The next day, however, Mulele was arrested, tried as a war
criminal by a military tribunal, and sentenced to death, despite his plea
for clemency. On October 9, he was executed by firing squad. Mulele's
execution signaled Mobutu's resolve to deal harshly with rebels and initiated a wave of executions of rebels throughout the country. This lasted
until 1971, when some exiled opponents were finally granted amnesty
and allowed to return to Congo.

Repressive measures characterized Mobutu's policy toward Lumumba's
legacy. However, Mobutu also tried to mollify the opposition. He wanted
to draw support from politicians who adhered to Lumumba's vision of a
free, independent, and harmonious nation. In 1966, for example, Mobutu
declared Patrice Lumumba a national hero and vowed to continue his
nationalistic project. This declaration was made at a time when tensions

between Mobutu and Tshombe had escalated. In order to discredit Tshombe, Mobutu portrayed him as a neocolonial element serving the interests of the West. Mobutu was then able to position himself as a nationalist leader who had remained true to Lumumba's ideals. As part of this political maneuvering, he built an impressive monument to Lumumba's memory in one of Leopoldville's busiest districts. The monument still stands as testimony to Mobutu's recuperation of Lumumba for political reasons.

In 1969 Mobutu cleared the last hurdles that had impeded his attainment of complete personal power. In April, Kasavubu died. This removed the accusations of illegality and usurpation that had so haunted Mobutu's first years in power. On another front, Tshombe's mercenaries and Katangan soldiers were on the verge of launching a military operation against the ANC. However, in June news came from Algiers that Tshombe had succumbed to a heart attack. There is no evidence that links Mobutu to the demise of these two prominent First Republic figures. But their deaths came at a propitious time for the consolidation of his regime. Tshombe, especially, had remained a serious contender, as he had the kind of political clout and ethnic constituency Mobutu could not match. While in detention in Algiers he continued, rather successfully, to drum up financial and diplomatic support for his political comeback. Tshombe had resolved to depose Mobutu, preferably through a military operation, in sharp contrast to Kasavubu's docile and passive approach. Even after he was tried in absentia for treason and condemned to death, Tshombe continued in his determination to overthrow Mobutu's regime. Now that he no longer posed a threat, Mobutu could concentrate his attention on strengthening his authority.

GOVERNMENT AND POLITICS

Some had assumed that Mobutu would abide by his initial claims. They anticipated that after five years of Mobutu's transitional regime, elections would be held to designate a new president. These anticipations were utterly disappointed. On April 17, 1967, Mobutu announced the creation of his own political party, the Popular Movement of the Revolution (Mouvement Populaire de la Révolution—MPR). All other parties, including the MNC/L (Mouvement National Congolais, Lumumba wing), upon which Mobutu had relied during his first year in power, were banned. Article 4 of the new constitution, drafted by Interior Minister Étienne Tshisekedi, contained a provision that authorized the creation of a second political party of opposition. According to Mobutu's own interpretation of the constitution, this party should be from among "those who do not share our ideas, those who do not agree with our political and economic program." However, this proved to be a deceptive façade. Several parties vied with one another to be recognized as the legal opposition party. These included the MNC/L and the UNARCO (Union des Nationalistes de l'Afrique Révolutionnaire du Congo), a loose coalition of First Republic parties that had adopted a low profile after Mobutu's coup. However, it soon became clear that Mobutu's regime could not afford its own claims of multipartyism. Although the constitution called for a second party, Mobutu argued that this did not mean that a second party had to be established. Thus Congo became a single-party regime. All citizens were de facto members of the MPR because the party and the state formed the same entity. This situation continued until 1992, when pressure from opposition politicians and Western backers led Mobutu to announce the end of MPR's monopoly over Congo's political life.

The creation of the MPR and the ban of all other parties was part of a careful plan aimed at curbing the country's incessant ethnic conflicts. The establishment of a single party precluded the existence of ethnically based parties, the sort of party that had fueled devastating ethnic conflicts during the First Republic. Mobutu wanted to do away with regionalism, which he considered a vestige of the defunct First Republic. Toward this end, he took several significant steps. He eliminated all the provincial legislatures. He transformed the provincial governors into mere representatives of the MPR without a local army at their disposal. He also reduced the number of provinces from twenty-one to twelve and then to eight large administrative units. These administrative units ceased to enjoy their previous partial autonomy.

Internal opposition came mainly from university students, but as it did with rebels and political opponents, the new regime dealt harshly with students. A small but vocal group of Lovanium students had organized an autonomous student movement, the Union Générale des Étudiants Congolais—(UGEC) in 1966. This group alone remained unbending toward Mobutu's repressive policies and actions. During its few years of activity, the UGEC fought for its autonomy. It demanded the right for students to create a real intellectual community, one that would not be stifled by the regime. But the government curtailed the Union's activities and attempted to disband it altogether. In January 1968, students staged a demonstration around the Lumumba monument to protest U.S. Vice

President Hubert Humphrey's visit to Leopoldville. The vice president had laid flowers at the monument honoring the memory of the late Congolese prime minister, a gesture that the students considered hypocritical. As soon as students converged on the square, military units moved in to disperse the demonstrators and arrest their leaders. Mobutu decided to dissolve the UGEC and force its members to enroll in the JMPR, the youth wing of the MPR party. Despite government intimidation and attempts at co-optation, most Lovanium students did not back down nor did they join the JMPR.

During the first months of 1969, student agitation gained momentum in Leopoldville, although it remained disorganized. The grievances of the students concerned the regime's authoritarianism. These frustrations came to a head on June 4, 1969, when the students staged a demonstration. They meant to defy the government and demonstrate their dissatisfaction with its unwillingness to address their needs. Mobutu refused to listen to the students' complaints, and he decided not to take any chances with what he considered an intolerable affront to his autocratic rule. A unit of armed soldiers was dispatched to disperse the unarmed students. This military response quickly turned violent and at least one hundred students were killed.

Military repression, however, did not deter the students. They continued to manifest their opposition to the regime in the aftermath of the killings. In 1971, they organized another march to commemorate the second anniversary of the demonstration. The regime again reacted with brutality. This time it also took a further step toward eradicating the student movement altogether. All Lovanium students were conscripted into the army and sent to military camps for "training," a euphemistic term for disciplinary action. In the aftermath of the confrontation, the government decreed drastic reforms in higher education that curtailed students' abilities to organize and protest. All three independent universities (Leopoldville, Stanleyville, and Elisabethville) were consolidated into a single national university, which became known as UNAZA (Université Nationale du Zaïre). Student protest was effectively shut down by these measures. It was not until the 1980s and 1990s that students were again in the streets demonstrating against Mobutu's regime. By then the prospect of democratic reforms and the collapse of the economy had galvanized Congolese civil society.

By 1970, Mobutu's power was total. The party, the army, the administration, and state companies were under his strict control. The population had been led to believe that the new regime was responsible for ending civil unrest and was in the process of restoring the state and the economy. One of the major obstacles to Mobutu's power had been removed the year before when Belgium agreed to support Mobutu's regime in a reconciliation agreement signed by both countries. This support encouraged Mobutu to renege on his earlier promise to lead a transitional military government for five years and then cede the government to civilian rule. Instead Mobutu organized a parody of presidential elections with himself as the only candidate. He launched an intimidating campaign designed to draw a massive voter turnout. Armed soldiers were posted around each voting booth on election day to make sure that voters picked the right ballot. Thus the outcome of the elections was predetermined.

Table 8.1: Congo's Prime Ministers and First State Commissioners, 1960–1997

Patrice Lumumba	June 24, 1960 to September 5, 1960 (d. 1961)
Joseph Ileo	September 12, 1960 to July 27, 1961 (d. 1994)
Cyrille Adoula	August 2, 1961 to June 30, 1964 (d. 1978)
Moïe Tshombe	July 10, 1964 to October 13, 1965 (d. 1969)
Evariste Kimba	October 18, 1965 to November 14, 1965 (d. 1966)
Léonard Mulamba	November 25, 1965 to October 26, 1966
Mpinga Kasenda	July 6, 1977 to March 6, 1979 (d. 1994)
Bo-Boliko Lokonga Mihambo	March 6, 1979 to August 27, 1980
Jean Nguza Karl-I-Bond	August 27, 1980 to April 23, 1981
N'singa Udjuu Untubu	April 23, 1981 to November 5, 1982
Léon Kengo wa Dondo	November 5, 1982 to October 31, 1986
Mabi Mulumba	January 22, 1987 to March 7, 1988
Sambwa Pida Nbagui	March 7, 1988 to November 26, 1988 (d. 1998)
Léon Kengo wa Dondo	November 26, 1988 to May 4, 1990
Lunda Bululu	May 4, 1990 to April 1, 1991
Mulumba Lukeji	April 1, 1991 to September 29, 1991 (d. 1998)
Étienne Tshisekedi	September 29, 1991 to November 1, 1991
Bernardin Mungul Diaka	November 1, 1991 to November 25, 1991 (d. 1999)
Jean Nguza Karl-I-Bond	November 25, 1991 to August 15, 1992
Étienne Tshisekedi	August 15, 1992 to March 18, 1993
Faustin Birindwa	March 18, 1993 to January 14, 1994 (d. 1999)
Léon Kengo wa Dondo	July 6, 1994 to April 2, 1997
Étienne Tshisekedi	April 2, 1997 to April 9, 1997
Likulia Bolongo	April 9, 1997 to May 16, 1997

Critics attacked Mobutu for implementing one of the most brutal dictatorships in postcolonial Africa. But Mobutu's regime did manage to make some inroads among some of the less fortunate segments of the population. These were Congolese who did not benefit from the regime's largesse but fell prey to its propaganda. Mobutu himself promoted this by carefully nurturing his persona as "le Guide," a Zairean version of what other charismatic leaders like Stalin and Mao Zedong imposed on the people they ruled. Because of his grip on both the media and the army, many were led to regard Mobutu as the father of the Zairean nation. He was a paternal figure who retained both the attributes of the village chief and the symbols of authority that he had inherited from the colonial state. There is evidence to suggest that Mobutu's rhetoric, which presented him as an enlightened autocrat, gained credibility among a large segment of the population. This acceptance allowed him to deflect blame for Zaire's political and economic failures onto his cabinet members, whose positions, as a result, were extremely unstable.

Within the regime, there was a high turnover rate for political appointees, which was explained as both a precautionary and punitive measure against incompetent high-ranking officials. Cabinets were in charge of public affairs for an average of only six months before being dismissed. In 1988, for instance, Mobutu reshuffled his cabinet five times and put three successive ministers of finance in command of the country's economy. Mabi Mulumba held that position for less than three months before losing it as a result of a cabinet reshuffling. Ephemeral and precarious tenures were the norm in virtually all areas of government in Zaire, including the party, the army, the provincial administration, and the state companies. Still, these positions were coveted because nominations to high-level positions usually served as opportunities for graft. Political reshuffling did not seriously alter the ethnic makeup of the government, which was strongly dominated by Mobutu's Ngbandi group. But it allowed the regime to showcase ethnic balance and unity by rotating key cabinet positions among the major ethnic groups.

Only five years after taking over, Mobutu had installed a new one-party political order, which was backed by foreign countries and sustained by a personality cult. By 1970, Mobutu's artificially constructed national unity did not resemble at all the political mayhem that had characterized the First Republic. Although Mobutu had been successful in constructing this political order, he had failed to provide the country with a stable economy despite its immense resources. For all of these reasons, the history of Congo during the Mobutu era could be said to have been that of a crippled giant, of a "rich country where people starve."

"AUTHENTICITY"

In 1971 President Mobutu embarked on a series of political campaigns aimed at "decolonizing" the country. Mobutu contended that this was necessary in order for the country to modernize and become more egalitarian and democratic. It entailed a drastic, albeit cosmetic, societal transformation. On October 27, 1971, he announced that the name of the country would be changed from the Democratic Republic of Congo to Zaire.[2] This was the first step in Mobutu's endeavor to obliterate all vestiges of colonialism in Congo. Place names that had been imposed under Belgian colonial rule were replaced with African ones. Leopoldville was renamed Kinshasa after a precolonial village destroyed by the Belgians in the 1880s to make room for the European settlement. Other major cities, Elisabethville, Stanleyville, and Luluabourg, were renamed Lubumbashi, Kisangani, and Kananga, respectively.

This new ideology came to be known as "authenticity" (*authenticité*), or Mobutism. Its author defined it as Zaire's unique and distinctive brand of nationalism. Authenticity, according to its proponents, was the road to progress. They argued that the society's development could only be achieved through returning to the precolonial heritage and turning away from the alienating materialism of the Western world. In order to create this progressive, authentic society, Mobutu conjured up mythical images of the precolonial village. He presented the village in idealistic terms of communal ethos, as an idyllic community blissfully living under the benevolent authority of a patriarchal, yet strong-willed chief. Mobutu used this image to legitimize his quest for absolute rule. Precolonial Congolese polities had enjoyed a system of checks and balances that provided for the removal of an abusive chief. However, the new "authentic" Zaire allowed for no such thing. Nor did it encourage democratic decision making or allow room for disagreement. Dissent and opposition to Mobutu's authority were regarded as crimes punishable by imprisonment or even death. Speaking to delegates at a UN meeting in New York on October 4, 1974, Mobutu spelled out the fundamentals of authenticity:

> Authenticity has raised the awareness of the Zairean people and prompted them to go back to their own roots, to seek their ancestors' values in order to appreciate those values that can contribute to their natural and harmonious development. It is at the same time a

refusal by the Zairean people to follow blindly foreign ideologies.

Nothing more clearly demonstrates the radical change brought about by the new ideology than the decree Mobutu issued on January 5, 1972. This decree required all Zairians to drop their Christian first names and adopt authentic African names. Setting the example himself, he changed his name from Joseph-Désiré Mobutu to Mobutu Sese Seko Kuku Ngbendu wa za Banga. Besides demonstrating his project of "authenticity," Mobutu's new name conveyed other political messages, including nearly divine grandeur (*Sese Seko* in Lingala means "forever lasting") as well as fear (*Banga* literally means "fear" in Lingala). This decision alienated the powerful Catholic Church, which perceived the "return to authenticity" as a threat to Christianity and denounced it as an anachronistic concept. Cardinal Malula, Zaire's most prominent Catholic cleric, publicly criticized the president's actions. He wrote in the Catholic weekly *Afrique Chrétienne*, "It is not by resuscitating a discredited philosophy that we will win the battle of the modern world." However, the church's strong rhetoric abated when the regime cracked down on religious activities in the country. First, all religious broadcasts came under attack as Mobutu attempted to suppress any dissent. He needed to shore up popular support for his new revolution. Next, all church-sponsored youth movements were dissolved. This left the church without one of its most valuable constituencies. Finally, in January 1975, religious instruction in primary and secondary schools was abolished and replaced by civic education. At this time the Catholic Church controlled nearly half the nation's primary and secondary schools. Mobutu's radical decrees pushed the church further away from a regime it had initially accommodated.

This ideological campaign represented a concerted effort to purge the country of any Christian influence. It was also an attempt to remove all obstacles that might have obstructed Mobutu's hegemonic objectives. Many observers have linked Mobutu's personality cult and obsessive quest for power to the totalitarian regimes that arose in many countries after World War II. There are noticeable similarities between Mobutism and Maoism. Mobutu's three-week visit to China in December 1974, during which he met with Chairman Mao Zedong, seemed to have influenced the way he approached his political project. This influence can be seen especially in the emphasis on mass political mobilization, which in later years would acquire great prominence in the political life of the country.

ZAIREANIZATION

On the economic front, Mobutu sought to enact his nationalistic agenda in a radical way. During his first years in power, he remained at loggerheads with Belgium over who was to control the country's mining industry and how the profits were to be shared between Zaire and Belgium. During the colonial era, the Belgian colony had successfully supplied the demands of Western countries for raw materials and strategic minerals. This international interest in Congo's natural resources played a crucial role in the elimination of Patrice Lumumba. The West handpicked Mobutu because he had proven more amenable to Western demands than Lumumba. But once his power was secured, Mobutu tried to alter the balance of economic power in favor of the political needs of his regime.

In 1966, a year after the coup, Mobutu decided to bring all former colonial companies under the control of the state. In doing so, he appropriated Lumumba's nationalist economic agenda. Some companies, such as Forminière and Kilo-Moto, were no longer profitable. These companies bore the brunt of this new policy, much to the indifference of Belgium. When Mobutu moved to take over UMHK, however, Belgium entered a protracted and bitter conflict with its former colony. Mobutu had unilaterally declared that on January 1, 1967, UMHK would be incorporated into the country's public sector. Belgium seemed equally determined to retain control over the production and export of Zairean copper. Mobutu accepted a settlement, which came to be known as the *contentieux belgo-zaïrois*, in which Belgium agreed to break up its mining conglomerate into two entities. One entity would be directly under the control of the Zairean government. However, Belgium refused Zaire's demand that UMHK headquarters be transferred to Kinshasa. Mobutu responded by announcing that UMHK could no longer operate in Zaire and that management of the country's mining industry would be entrusted to a state-owned company called GECOMIN (later renamed Gécamines). These maneuvers failed to deter UMHK. In February 1967, an agreement was reached in which UMHK recognized Gécamines' monopoly in mining operations in Shaba, but retained some control over the management of the state company. Mobutu's negotiations with UMHK resulted in some gains for the Zairean economy and signaled a growing trend toward what many scholars have termed "patrimonialism." Under the patrimonialism of Mobutu's regime, appointments to high offices were used to reward individuals who provided loyal service to their ruler. Strong centralization and expansion of the bureaucratic sector in Zaire under Mobutu allowed for the patrimonialization of public offices.

The same can be said of Mobutu's Zaireanization measures of November 30, 1973. These measures expropriated most foreign-owned plantations, small and medium-sized companies, and wholesale and retail shops with little or no compensation. According to Thomas Callaghy, "roughly 1,500 to 2,000 enterprises were taken from their non-Zairean owners, and members of the political aristocracy . . . acquired them" (Callaghy 1984: 191). According to Young and Turner (1985: 328), "The president perhaps viewed the seizure of commercial establishments and plantations as a way of creating a new reserve of prebends to be used for the manipulation and control of the political bourgeoisie." Zaireanization provided needed resources, which buttressed the support of clients under patrimonialism. The politics of patrimonialism was enacted through Zaireanization, as illustrated by the way confiscated foreign companies were allocated to members of the Zairean political elite. Most beneficiaries were not people involved in the economy or entrepreneurs but were instead members of Mobutu's political clique, including MPR leaders, deputies, local notables, and their relatives and clients. These were all people who lacked the vocational and managerial skills to operate these economic ventures productively. In Lubumbashi, one-third of all confiscated businesses were given to local politicians. Mobutu himself acquired a huge agricultural conglomerate consisting of fourteen different plantations located all over the country. CELZA (Cultures et Élevages du Zaïre), as this presidential conglomerate came to be known, was the third largest employer in the country in 1977. It employed 25,000 workers, including 140 Europeans occupying managerial positions. As shown in Table 8.2, CELZA was a successful venture and provided the president with an enormous reserve of cash.

Zaireanization was politically useful to Mobutu. It won him a cohort of devotees and strong supporters among those who benefited from the measures. Economically, however, it was a disaster. Some foreign entrepreneurs, mostly Portuguese and Greek traders, were able to maintain their small businesses by ceding them to their Zairean spouses. However, many were dispossessed. These individuals had no choice but to leave the country, which deprived the economy of its most skilled operators. The economy entered a long period of decay as foreign businessmen left the country, leaving their businesses in the hands of local politicians who had little if any business or managerial experience.

Table 8.2: CELZA Share of Total Zairean Production of Agricultural Commodities
in 1976 (in metric tons)

	CELZA	Zaire	CELZA % of production
Palm oil	20,898	155,000	13
Palm kernel	4,298	59,000	7
Coffee	5,547	86,000	6
Cocoa beans	1,161	5,000	23
Rubber	7,053	27,000	26
Tea	921	6,000	15

SOURCE: Young and Turner (1985: 180).

Observers have emphasized the obvious and disastrous economic
effects of Zaireanization, effects that included "dislocation of economic
circuits, shortages, layoffs in Zaireanized enterprises, pay arrearages,
inflation, tax evasion" (Young and Turner 1985: 343). But few analysts
have paid attention to the psychological devastation that resulted and
that remains one of the scourges of Congolese society. Zaireanization
failed to harness the energy of the people or reinforce a work ethic. This
led the population to adopt several behaviors that continue to hinder economic development. Chief among them is corruption, which has encouraged unscrupulous foreign entrepreneurs to set up ventures in the country
and has warded off more serious investors. Corruption in Zaire has meant
that any sort of economic or legal service, including obtaining common-
place legal documents such as driver's licenses, birth certificates, or pass-
ports, requires paying a bribe. Rarely can anything be obtained from legal
authorities through legitimate procedures. The name given to corruption
in Zaire is *madesu ya bana* (Lingala for "beans for my children"). The
phrase demonstrates the extent to which, for many workers, daily bribes
rather than sporadic wages provide the majority of their income. Other
behaviors that are detrimental to the economy include nepotism, which
became widespread in the wake of Zaireanization. The new owners of
Zaireanized businesses laid off thousands of workers in order to replace
them with members of their own kinship and ethnic groups. Many of
these businesses fell pray to embezzlement and pilfering because workers no longer abided by the work ethic that prevailed in the traditional
setting. All these characteristics were unleashed by the economic debacle
that ensued in the wake of the Zaireanization measures. Even though, in
1974, Mobutu softened and even reversed some of these measures, the

psychological damage could not be so easily undone. Scores of businesses reverted to their original owners. The state took over a number of large-scale companies that were attributed to individuals through Zaireanization. But the country had already sunk into a moral, social, and economic crisis. Many suggested that this crisis could not be overcome without an all-out effort to strengthen civil society and introduce a new work ethic.

CIVIL SOCIETY

Mobutu's rule in Zaire spanned more than three decades. His longevity was rivaled only by that of Ivorian president Félix Houphouet-Boigny and Hassan II of Morocco, who remained in power for thirty-three and thirty-eight years respectively. Given the high political turnover during the First Republic, Mobutu's long reign at the helm of this vast, divided country might seem a feat. Mobutu maintained his position through military force and a personality cult, by stifling internal opposition while also gathering staunch allies within Zaire. One of the main obstacles to Mobutu's total power was Zairean civil society, which had gained strength in the wake of the first anticolonial manifestos and developed a vibrant independence movement in the 1950s and early 1960s. Repression during Mobutu's first decade in power cut this vibrancy short. But civil society experienced a resurgence after the collapse of the Zaireanization measures.

In general, civil society provides a site for democratic contestation and mobilization outside the realm of the state's influence. It provides the possibility for the empowerment of the population at large by creating independent organizations, such as churches and voluntary and professional associations. These are organizations that might truly represent the interests of the people, realize their aspirations, and equip them with the tools to curb the state's abuse of power. Civil society is an indispensable component in any democratic system and a driving force for democratization in many societies. The more vibrant and visible a civil society, the more democracy can truly thrive. Within the context of the Zairean state, civil society continued to be active despite the lack of democracy and the threats and repression by Mobutu.

During the first decade of the Second Republic, Mobutu was relatively popular. His regime was able to muzzle internal dissent, and he managed to discredit those exiled politicians who sought to voice their opposition from abroad. Some organizations lent their support to the regime in exchange for access to its resources. This was the case for the Kimbanguist movement. As shown in Chapter 5, this movement opposed the colonial state and was later forced to go underground. In 1959, after several decades of concealed activities, Kimbanguism was finally recognized by the Belgian colonial administration and placed on the same footing as the Catholic and Protestant churches. By then the church was led by Joseph Diangienda, Kimbangu's second son. The Kimbanguist Church adopted the name The Church of Jesus Christ on Earth through the Prophet Simon Kimbangu (Église de Jésus-Christ sur Terre par le Prophète Simon Kimbangu—EJCSK). After Mobutu's takeover, EJCSK became one of the regime's clients and its most fervent defender. The church shifted from an explicit policy of not interfering with politics to supporting Mobutu's regime and promoting *authenticité*. In return, the church received preferred treatment. In December 1971, Mobutu banned all the religious "sects" in the country. EJCSK was spared from this persecution, and even benefited from it, because dissident religious groups had to either disband or integrate into EJCSK. Mobutu's regime guaranteed the church financial prosperity and political protection. This enabled EJCSK to become the third largest organized religious denomination in Zaire. The church became a powerful financial institution with hundreds of schools and temples across the country.

The Catholic Church, on the other hand, took a less accommodating stance toward the regime. In the early 1970s, it became clear that Mobutu had failed to deliver on his promise of peace and stability. He had grown intolerant of any doctrine that might compete with the tenets of *authenticité*. In response, the Catholic Church spearheaded Zairean civil society's resistance to the regime's repression. Since the implementation of *authenticité*, the church and Mobutu had been at loggerheads over the cultural transformation of Zairean society. In March 1976, Lubumbashi's archbishop Eugène Kabanga wrote a pastoral letter indicting the regime and its use of *authenticité* to mask the failure of the economy. He observed, "In the past the colonizers crushed our dignity as human beings and as Africans. Today our situation is much worse, brought about by the behaviors of our own brothers." He went on to decry corruption as the defining characteristic of Mobutu's regime. He asked rhetorically:

> Why is it that in our courts justice can only be obtained by fat bribes to the judge? Why are prisoners forgotten in jail? They have no one to pay off the judge who sits on their dossier. Why do our government offices force people to come back day after day to obtain services to

which they are entitled? If the clerks are not paid off, they will not be served. Why, at the opening of school, must parents go into debt to bribe the school principal? Children who are unable to pay will have no school.

A year earlier, another prominent Catholic archbishop, Monsignor Bakole wa Ilunga, denounced what he called "an internal colonialism" forced upon "millions of citizens . . . rejected on the margins of society" by the greed of Mobutu's cohort.

These harsh criticisms forced the government to reconsider those of its policies that had crippled the church's ability to carry out its mission. The government met with a delegation of Catholic bishops in September 1976 to hear their grievances and later decided to reverse its policy toward mission schools and religious teaching in public schools. In February 1977, Catholic, Protestant, and Kimbanguist churches officially regained their responsibility for operating mission schools.

In 1979, Mobutu visited the Vatican and was granted an audience with the pope. The following year, Pope John Paul II visited Zaire. This contributed to mending the relationship between the president and the country's Catholic hierarchy. However, this truce proved to be short-lived. Tensions between the two mounted because the church recognized that the economic deterioration of the country was the work of Mobutu's regime. During the 1980s and early 1990s, the church did not miss an opportunity to criticize the state. And so the church remained, in the words of Michael G. Schatzberg (1988: 122), "a significant latent threat to an insecure state."

ECONOMIC DETERIORATION

By the mid-1970s, Zaire's economy had sunk into the doldrums of recession. Serious reforms were required. The state, however, seemed neither willing nor able to implement these reforms. In addition to the ill-fated Zaireanization measures of the early 1970s, other developments contributed to the economic crisis that beset the country. In late 1975, the price of copper, Zaire's main export, dropped dramatically. The price fell from $1.40 per pound in 1973 to as low as $0.53, which destroyed the state's ability to generate revenues. At the same time, there was an upsurge in world oil prices and other industrial imports, which limited Zaire's access to strategic commodities. There was a shortage of industrial spare parts, fuel, agricultural products such as pesticides and fertilizers, and other manufactured goods that had previously been affordable by means of the country's copper revenues.

The economy was also affected by Zaire's involvement in neighboring Angola's civil war. The Angola-Benguela railroad, Zaire's main copper transportation route, was closed. This adversely affected the nation's economy, especially when the Angolan faction that Mobutu had supported lost the war. In March 1977 and May 1978, Mobutu's own armed forces (Forces Armées Zaïroises—FAZ) suffered their first military defeats at the hands of the last of the Katanga soldiers of Tshombe's secession. These forces operated from bases in Angola and called themselves the National Front for the Liberation of Congo (Front National de Libération du Congo—FNLC). The Katangese rebels made a successful foray into Shaba, the province that held most of the country's mineral wealth, and cut the province off from the capital for several weeks. Although the FAZ forces were larger and much better equipped, they were rapidly overwhelmed by the assailants. In both instances, foreign troops (Moroccans in 1977, French and Belgians in 1978) and foreign logistical support (mainly from the United States) had to come to the rescue of Mobutu's regime. Shaba I and Shaba II, as these two wars were dubbed, eroded the regime's legitimacy. The wars also emboldened external and internal opposition and further increased the country's dependence on Western powers and Third World allies. In economic terms, the use of resources to drive off the rebels led the economy to the brink of bankruptcy. Moreover, after the failure of the first invasion, a wave of refugees fled Shaba by the hundreds of thousands to escape Mobutu's death squads, contributing further to the economic disruption.

By the end of the 1970s, economic indicators showed that the country's economy was in a comatose state. Congo's economy has not been able to recover since that time. Between 1974 and 1978, imports were cut in half and inflation doubled. Industrial output was reduced by 40 percent during these years and continued its steep decline in the 1980s and 1990s. As the economy shrank, the state could no longer repay debts contracted from international banking institutions. By the late 1970s, this debt totaled nearly $5 billion, at least 80 percent of which was owed to bilateral government creditors. In 1978, Mobutu gave in to the demands of international partners, and the International Monetary Fund (IMF) was allowed to overhaul the Zairean economy. A team of IMF experts, led by retired German Bundesbank officer Erwin Blumenthal, virtually took control of Zaire's financial sector. The IMF team suggested that credit and foreign exchange procedures needed the most scrutiny. They endeavored to prevent the abuses that had depleted the nation's banking and financial institutions of badly needed foreign currencies. The IMF financial reforms also aimed to increase tax revenues, curb the regime's reckless spending, limit imports, and improve the way the country had been servicing its growing external public debt. Less than two years after the first reform package had been implemented, the social effects were clear. Inflation, high prices, layoffs of thousands of civil servants, and continuing shortages of basic goods made these reforms unpopular. They even earned Blumenthal the nickname "Bula Matari." Questions still remain as to whether these measures could have benefited the nation's economy. There is general agreement that the IMF's inability to salvage the economy and prevent Zaire's economic downfall was the result of Mobutu's policies. The regime was determined to block all efforts by international financial institutions that might have challenged its control over the nation's revenues.

In the early 1980s, Mobutu was pressured into allowing another team of IMF experts to visit the country. On December 5, 1983, the government signed a formal agreement with the IMF, which paved the way for the country's debt to be rescheduled and arrears to be paid. But this economic truce lasted only a few years. Mobutu claimed that the IMF's reforms had increased Zaire's trade deficit. In 1986, he unilaterally reduced the servicing of the debt to 20 percent of the annual budget. In the following years, the economic crisis reached alarming proportions, with the rate of inflation exceeding 100 percent. This was accompanied by a disastrous budget deficit, dwindling foreign investments, and a foreign debt of more than $10 billion. Zaire had once again lapsed into the convenient, yet self-destructive habit of not meeting arrears and accumulating delinquent payments. Under these circumstances, Mobutu had no other choice but to appeal once more to the IMF for assistance. In May 1989, Zaire agreed to abide by yet another economic reform package. As before, international experts had to fight an uphill battle. It was difficult to implement these policies in a system in which political leaders used economic mismanagement as a political asset to tighten their control of the country.

Ultimately, the IMF failed to resuscitate the nation's economy, which is a testimonial to the resilience of Mobutu's patrimonial regime. The IMF's structural adjustment policies could not curb the regime's drive to monopolize the nation's revenues for its own purposes. Within Mobutu's inner circle, it was assumed that the income collected by the state belonged to a handful of individuals, including Mobutu himself, who had free reign to spend it as they saw fit. Mobutu's personal fortune was estimated at $5 billion in private bank assets, company shares, and property investments around the world. This fortune was accumulated at the expense of the nation's economic development.

The early 1990s marked Zaire's final economic downfall, at least by the standards of international monetary institutions. The IMF and the World Bank shunned Zaire as a pariah state, and the country lost all credibility in the eyes of most of its lending partners. The state, according to Clark (1998: 9), had never served "any socially meaningful purpose that could promote the interests, however defined, of the Zaïrian people. Rather, it exists, to the extent to which it exists at all, to enrich and empower the small group that controls it." Mobutu's corrupt government pilfered the nation's wealth, encouraged by the interests of Western powers. The real tragedy of Mobutu's Zaire, however, is the millions of Zaireans driven into destitution and despair. The future of whole generations was destroyed in the process. In Mobutu's Zaire, wealth was the mother of misery.

TRANSITION TO MULTIPARTY DEMOCRACY

By 1990, Mobutu's popularity had long since waned. His ability to remain in power depended solely on his external backers and internal reign of terror. Even these foreign backers now had second thoughts about continuing to lend their support to Mobutu. They could no longer ignore the martyrdom of millions of Zairean people. There had been a geopolitical shift caused by the fall of the Berlin Wall and the end of the Cold War, which meant that Mobutu's Zaire had lost its strategic position as a bulwark against the spread of communism in central Africa. At first, Mobutu failed to heed the ominous changes that were sweeping Eastern Europe, even after his long-time friend, Romanian strongman Nicolae Ceausescu, was executed in December 1989 after being deposed by a popular uprising. He took no notice of Washington's new attitudes toward Third World proxies that had been instrumental in keeping the threat of communism at bay.

But Mobutu's unrestricted exploitation of the nation's resources had unleashed forces that he could no longer ignore. On January 15, 1982, a group of thirteen parliamentarians, led by Étienne Tshisekedi—who held the post of interior minister in Mobutu's first government—responded to the regime's abuses. They wrote a manifesto indicting the regime on several counts, including corruption and human rights abuses. Their action gave birth to a clandestine opposition party, the Union for Democracy and Social Progress (Union pour la Démocratie et le Progrès Social—UDPS). This party suffered governmental repression until 1990, when Mobutu finally caved in to popular demand for a multiparty democracy in Zaire. The UDPS played a crucial role in shoring up popular support against Mobutu's regime. During the late 1980s and early 1990s, the UDPS was the major pro-democracy political force that overtly challenged Mobutu's dictatorship.

The role of the military was equally critical in bringing the regime down. In colonial times, the military (the Force Publique) served as a police force intended to keep the native population in check, and this was the role it continued to play under Mobutu's regime. During his first years in power, Mobutu relied heavily on the military to crush any form of dissent. Zaire was a military dictatorship where the president held the titles of both minister of defense and head of the armed forces. But the promotion of the MPR as the supreme organ of the regime alienated some army officers. They had been indoctrinated during the colonial period to distrust politicians, and they could not tolerate the party's monopoly of public life. Fearing that well-trained and well-equipped armed forces might become a threat to his personal power, Mobutu instituted a number of policies that proved disastrous. They included a divide-and-rule policy that exploited rivalries within the FAZ as well was occasional purges targeting officers from the Kasai and Kivu regions. High-level positions were staffed with people of Mobutu's own ethnic group. Most importantly, in 1986 Mobutu created a separate Special Presidential Division (Division Spéciale Présidentielle—DSP), an elite military unit entrusted with his personal security. The DSP included mostly Ngbandi soldiers, drawn from Mobutu's home region. They received military training from Israeli officers, the most sophisticated military equipment, and enjoyed high pay. All of this came at the expense of the FAZ and was a deliberate effort to reduce the risk of a coup by the regular army. The FAZ were unable to respond effectively when confronted with armed opposition because of outdated second-hand equipment and lack of training. They went for months without being paid wages. As a result, ragtag FAZ soldiers preyed on ordinary citizens by demanding money and foodstuffs at roadblocks. By the time Mobutu was unseated by Kabila's rebels, the FAZ had been transformed from an effective fighting force into several groups of armed ruffians totally unprepared for war but unsurpassed when it came to highjacking vehicles, stealing provisions from the markets, and gang-raping defenseless civilians. They remained a source of instability in the country throughout most of the 1990s.

On April 24, 1990, faced with mounting domestic as well as international pressure, Mobutu took an important step that paved the way for the transition to multiparty democracy in Zaire. He declared the end of single-party rule and called for the opening of a Sovereign National Conference (Conférence Nationale Souveraine—CNS), which would be responsible for creating the blueprint for a new constitution. As when independence was proclaimed in 1960, people were elated as the long reign of an oppressive regime came to a close. But just as in 1960, people's aspirations for a better life remained unanswered. Instead of democracy and economic recovery, Zaire remained mired in a situation of chaos reminiscent of the climate that bred Mobutu's dictatorship.

NOTES

1. Mobutu's Ngbandi ethnic group represented less than half a percent of Congo's total population.

2. Most authors agree that "Zaire" is a Portuguese deformation of the Kikongo term "Nzari" or "Nzadi," which means an expanse of water. When the first Portuguese reached the mouth of the River Congo in the early 1480s, they enquired about the name of the river. The Kongo people who occupied the land uttered the word "Nzari," which the Portuguese mistook for the name of the river and transformed into "Zaire."

9

Transition to Democracy, 1990–1997

Throughout the 1990s, the political and economic situation in Zaire was disastrous. The country was plagued by the same impediments that had prevented any long-range development since the country gained its independence in 1960. Many observers expressed pessimistic views regarding the future of one of Africa's largest and wealthiest nations. The end of the Cold War had eroded Zaire's pro-Western position. But it did little to diminish foreign interest in the country's mineral resources. Zaire remained a rich source of countless minerals. But nowhere in Africa has mineral wealth been so mismanaged as in Zaire. In fact, most Zairians believed that their country would have fared much better had it not been for its abundant natural resources. The management, or mismanagement, of Zaire's mineral wealth is at the root of the chaos that has prevailed in the country since Mobutu relinquished power in 1997. Today the country is a battleground for Western as well as regional powers, including Zimbabwe, Rwanda, Uganda, and Angola. These neighboring countries have involved themselves under the guise of promoting African mediation of the Zairean internal conflict. They have used this opportunity to insinuate themselves into Zaire in order to tap into the country's resources while continuing to thwart any peace effort.

THE CNS AND THE DEMOCRATIC TRANSITION

In 1990, Mobutu conceded to a transition to democracy. Zaire seemed to have awakened from a long nightmare and was poised to meet a new future. But the transition turned out to be similar to the period that followed the proclamation of the First Republic in 1960. It was fraught with confusion and deception, much to the chagrin of many Zairians who were eager to embrace the long-awaited change.

Following Mobutu's declaration, several ominous events cast a shadow over the new multiparty process. On May 11, 1990, Mobutu sent some of his DSP commandos to suppress student protests on the campus of the University of Lubumbashi. This was part of Mobutu's carefully orchestrated plan to stall the democratic process. Between 50 and 150 students paid with their lives during the nighttime rampage on the Lubumbashi campus. It was one of the most violent acts of civilian repression of the Mobutu era. More armed attacks against civilians and opposition leaders followed. The regime targeted those who demanded an official investigation of the incident. Also targeted were those who pressured Mobutu to make good on his promise to convene the Sovereign National Conference.

Mobutu finally agreed. In August, 2,850 delegates, including representatives from over 200 political parties, attended the opening of the CNS. Catholic archbishop Laurent Mosengo was chosen as its chairman. The two main political contenders at the conference represented a rift between the regime's apparatchiks and its opponents. This latter group was drawn from a variety of opposition groups. Some were longtime foes of the regime, most of whom had been in exile and returned. A number were former political cronies of Mobutu who had grown disenchanted with the regime. A third group were young reform-minded firebrands. They formed a loose umbrella organization, the Union Sacrée de l'Opposition (USO), led by Tshisekedi's UDPS. The USO had 42 percent of the delegates. The coalition found itself in a favorable position to influence the debates and the decisions at the CNS. This was despite the fact that Mobutu had packed the conference with hundreds of his staunchest supporters. Mobutu had also bribed certain opposition delegates in an attempt to sway their votes.

Not long after the debates at the CNS had started, angry FAZ soldiers went on a looting spree because they had not been paid their salaries. They complained that they had not received any salary increases in months, whereas CNS delegates received lavish per diems. They targeted stores and private homes as well as public properties in Kinshasa and a few other cities. The FAZ soldiers were joined by huge crowds. Three nights of systematic looting and rioting brought the nation's economy to its lowest point ever. Estimates suggest that from $700 million to $1 billion in damage was sustained. An estimated 1,400 businesses were seriously attacked or burned to the ground during the looting frenzy.

The government was undecided as to how to respond to public fury. It was wary that military mutiny might pave the way for a coup. The regime decided to buy peace by promptly meeting the soldiers' demands. The mutinous troops received their salary increases rather than punishment for their actions. The government also hired 50,000 more civil servants. However, the reopening of the CNS was blocked. The work of the CNS had been suspended after a controversy over the accreditation of delegates. On Sunday, February 16, 1992, several religious organizations took their protests to the streets of Kinshasa in what was dubbed the "March of Hope" (Marche de l'Espoir). Mobutu's military intervened and killed at least forty-five unarmed civilians.

Mobutu's actions were an attempt to prevent the CNS from drafting the texts that would guide the transition to democracy. Despite these efforts, in August 1992 CNS delegates established a transitional government. On August 15, they overwhelmingly elected opposition leader Étienne Tshisekedi as prime minister. The conference adjourned in December 1992 after establishing a provisional legislature, the High Council of the Republic (Haut Conseil de la République—HCR), to continue its work. During the first week following the inauguration of Tshisekedi's transitional government, Mobutu appeared willing to abide by the new democratic rule. This prompted some observers to conjecture that he would eventually accept a figurehead presidency. There were also rumors that he would choose a comfortable exile in France or Switzerland, where he owned hefty real estate properties. Few understood that he intended to maintain his grasp on power, and that this depended on maintaining anarchy.

In a preemptive move intended to undermine the transitional government, Mobutu appointed as governor of Katanga a controversial figure, Kyungu wa Kumwanza, known for his hostility against Tshisekedi. Immediately after taking office Kyungu announced that he would not recognize a government headed by Tshisekedi and that if Tshisekedi were to be elected prime minister Katanga would not recognize his authority.

Nothing served Mobutu's immediate interests better than the disarray of the transition period. In a preemptive move that baffled most Zairians, Mobutu put an end to the transition process initiated by the CNS. He quickly dismissed Tshisekedi's government despite the unanimous support it received from HCR members. He then revived the National Assembly and packed it with handpicked loyal appointees, naming Faustin Birindwa as prime minister (March 1993 to July 1994). From that point until Mobutu's demise in 1997, there were two parallel governments. They remained locked in a stalemate that added confusion to an already volatile political situation. Tshisekedi's government retained some legitimacy, at least in legal terms. But his party lost its influence within the opposition alliance, which was broken into factions as Mobutu's successive cabinets vied for international backing.

EASTERN ZAIRE DESTABILIZED

The political confusion in Kinshasa gave way to civil strife elsewhere in the nation. In December 1992, unpaid FAZ soldiers went on a rampage in Kisangani, Goma, and Kolwezi. This brought much of the economic activity in these cities to a standstill. In January 1993, serious riots erupted in Kinshasa, leaving several hundred people dead. Later in the same year, political tension flared up in Shaba province. A full-fledged ethnic conflict arose between those who claimed to be the "native" populations of Shaba (mostly from the Lunda ethnic group) and the Kasaians (Luba, Songye, Tetela, Kanyok, and others), whom they branded as "foreigners." In all, at least 300,000 people had to leave Katanga as a result of popular xenophobic sentiments that were largely manipulated and orchestrated by Governor Kyungu. Ethnic rivalry may appear to be the underlying factor in this case. But the violence aimed at the populations of Kasai also reflected the political competition between the two leading opposition figures, Tshisekedi (a Luba from Kasai) and Nguza Karl-I-Bond (a Lunda from Shaba who broke away from the USO to form a dissident opposition group).

The most serious crisis to influence political developments in Zaire originated in Rwanda. In the summer of 1994, a conflict of unprecedented magnitude shook the Great Lakes region. Hutu militiamen in Rwanda (the Interahamwe) killed nearly 1 million Tutsis and moderate Hutus, following the plane crash of President Juvénal Habyarimana on April 6, 1994.[1] In the aftermath of the Rwandan genocide, an estimated 1.2 million Hutu refugees fled from Rwanda to the eastern part of Zaire. The Tutsi-dominated Rwandan Patriotic Front (RPF) took the offensive from its base in Uganda and closed in on the capital city of Kigali in an attempt to consolidate its position in Rwanda and dispose of the genocidal Hutu-dominated regime.

The French had backed the Hutu regime and were now intent to protect them from the RPF's counteroffensive. The French established Operation Turquoise, which aimed to provide safe conduit to Hutu militiamen. The anti-Tutsi genocide in Rwanda and the subsequent French response helped Mobutu gain the upper hand over the opposition and destroy the already lagging transition. The French connived with Mobutu to maintain instability in the region. They acted under the guise of a humanitarian operation intended to protect Hutu refugees from RPF retaliatory actions. The instability that resulted ironically provoked Mobutu's downfall. Hutu civilians took refuge in UN refugee camps set up around the town of Goma. In addition, at least 50,000 defeated Rwandan troops and many Interahamwe militiamen, still heavily armed, escaped to Zaire. They planned to reorganize their forces and launch cross-border raids against the new government of Rwanda. France and Belgium continued to offer military support to the Interahamwe militia. They hoped to wear down and eventually dislodge the Tutsi-led government of Rwanda, which was then supported by Washington.

The overwhelming waves of Hutu refugees heightened an already complicated demographic situation in eastern Zaire, where a large population of indigenous ethnic Tutsi, known as Banyamulenge, had become the target of ethnic violence fueled by the government. The Banyamulenge are the descendants of Tutsi cattle herders who settled in South Kivu, west of Lake Tanganyika, some 200 years ago, before the creation of colonial boundaries. Under Mobutu's regime, they came to be viewed as outsiders and were subsequently stripped of their Zairean citizenship in 1981. With the arrival of Hutu refugees, ethnic tensions flared up in eastern Zaire. The Hutu Interahamwe militia sided with the local population in bouts of anti-Banyamulenge violence that climaxed in a series of skirmishes in August 1996. In October, South Kivu's governor gave an ultimatum to all Tutsi, including the Banyamulenge, to leave the country within a week or face repression. Backed by the Rwandan government, the Banyamulenge organized their own armed militia and fought back with surprising effectiveness. On October 29, they captured the town of Uvira, the provincial capital, without encountering much resistance from the FAZ.

THE DOWNFALL OF MOBUTU'S REGIME

Kinshasa did not respond to the events in eastern Zaire, which seemed remote and isolated. The lack of response also reflected the fact that

Mobutu himself had vacated the capital to seek medical treatment in Europe. This power vacuum emboldened the Banyamulenge rebels, who quickly occupied key positions in Kivu. It also encouraged other groups to revive military networks. They proceeded to erode FAZ positions in eastern Zaire. An alliance of these various groups fell under the leadership of Laurent-Désiré Kabila, a man whom most Zairians had never heard of until late 1996. At this time he came forward as the spokesman for the Alliance of Democratic Forces for the Liberation of Congo-Zaire (Alliance des Forces Démocratiques pour la Libération du Congo-Zaïre— AFDL). The organization was composed of his own Marxist-oriented People's Republic Party and three other more recent anti-Mobutu groups located in both South and North Kivu. The People's Republic Party was created as a dissident movement against Mobutu's regime in 1967. The Alliance gained momentum through support from several African governments, including Rwanda, which had devised a plan for the creation of a buffer zone in eastern Zaire to prevent Hutu militiamen from carrying out military incursions across the border. Both Uganda and Angola also offered military assistance as a reprisal against Mobutu's long-standing support of opposition groups that undermined the stability of both countries. The U.S. government also backed Kabila's rebel movement. This support reflected growing competition, following the end of the Cold War, between French and American interests in sub-Saharan Africa. As François Ngolet has argued, "Kabila's victory in 1997 was not solely an African enterprise nor only the result of American-orchestrated policy, but a combination of both."[2]

But this international support was not the sole reason for the rapid success of AFDL forces. The disintegration of the Zairean army facilitated the rapid progression of Alliance troops from Kivu, where the main city of Goma fell on November 2. They continued across the country unhindered. Their process of capturing towns took on a predictable pattern. Rumors that rebels were approaching a town elicited much enthusiasm among the population. In contrast, FAZ soldiers went into hiding at this news. Before retreating, FAZ soldiers generally indulged in a final round of looting, raping, and killing. This further alienated them from the local population, which had good reason not only to welcome the AFDL as a liberating army but also to join its ranks.

Mobutu was faced with unpopularity and the collapse of the FAZ. He resorted to recruiting European mercenaries, which had played a crucial role during the civil strife of the 1960s. On December 17, he returned to Zaire with renewed purpose to hold onto the presidency, although his health had drastically declined. He elicited an audience of 7,000 supporters, who came to welcome him and promised to fight the rebels until "final victory." Mobutu enlisted white South African and Franco-Belgian mercenaries. He also called on the assistance of Serb mercenaries, Hutu soldiers from the former Rwandan government army, and a contingent of Jonas Savimbi's Angolan rebel forces. Even these foreign mercenaries were no match for Kabila's insurgent forces, which captured several cities along their unstoppable march toward the capital. The counteroffensive failed to stall the rebels' advance. Kabila refused to enforce a ceasefire mandated under a UN peace plan. On March 15, 1997, the Alliance captured the strategically important city of Kisangani. Other major cities, including Mbuji-Mayi, Kananga, and Lubumbashi, fell in early April. This suggested a strategy that aimed at putting Kabila in a strong position for negotiating with Mobutu. On May 4, the two men finally met at a face-to-face talk hosted by President Nelson Mandela on board a South African ship in the Congolese port of Pointe-Noire. Kabila had the upper hand and remained unyielding. Frail and subdued, Mobutu was nonetheless inclined to save face. His proposal called for handing over power to a third party, possibly a broad-based "national council." This third party would then negotiate with Kabila. This had a jarring effect on Kabila, who disdainfully rejected any deal that fell short of Mobutu's removal from power.

As negotiations faltered, Kabila's military forces continued to march toward Kinshasa. On May 17, less than eight months after the rebellion had started, they triumphantly entered the capital to cheers from Kinshasa's populace. The bloodbath that many had feared never occurred. Most FAZ soldiers decided to melt into the population rather than to attempt to defend the city. What happened instead was a "soft landing," masterminded by FAZ commander General Marc Mahele. General Mahele had conferred with the Clinton administration, which feared a diplomatic backlash in the event of a clash between DSP soldiers and AFDL troops. A few hours before the fall of the city, General Mahele pacified unruly elements. They had been instructed by some of Mobutu's hardline officers, including his son Kongolo Mobutu, not to surrender but to put up a fierce fight. In retaliation for what they perceived as betrayal, a group of DSP soldiers shot General Mahele to death as the first AFDL troops were making their way into the capital. By then, most of Mobutu's followers, including his immediate entourage, had already crossed the river to seek refuge in Brazzaville. A contingent of Belgian, French, and U.S. paratroops were waiting there to organize the evacuation of their respective citizens from Zaire. Mobutu himself first left Kinshasa for his presidential palace in Gbadolite, in northern Zaire. From there he fled to Togo and then to Morocco, where his longtime friend King Hassan II granted him political asylum.

Mobutu's downfall and his subsequent death in Morocco on September 7, 1997 did not immediately cause chaos as had been predicted. Nor did these changes move the country toward democracy. Kabila was determined to freeze the democratic agenda set up by the CNS. He refused to open a dialogue with the civil society or with the nonviolent opposition to Mobutu's regime. This plunged the country into a new cycle of civil strife, international conflicts, and heightened foreign interventions.

NOTES

1. The best accounts on the Rwandan crisis include: Mahmood Mandani, *When Victims Become Killers: Colonialism, Nativism and the Genocide in Rwanda* (Princeton: Princeton University Press, 2001); Gérard Prunier, *The Rwandan Crisis. History of a Genocide* (New York: Columbia University Press, 1995); David Newbury, "Understanding Genocide," *African Studies Review* 41, no. 1 (April 1998), pp. 73–97.

2. François Ngolet, "African and American Connivance in Congo-Zaire," *Africa Today* 47, no. 1, (winter 2000), p. 66.

10

The Third Republic, 1997–2001

A brief military campaign propelled AFDL forces to a position of leadership. They emerged as leaders of a country that was on the brink of disintegration. After decades of oppression and economic chaos, most Zairians wanted a change of leadership. There were critics who cautioned that Kabila did not have the ability to transform the country into a democracy. But Zairians were ready to welcome anyone who might rid the country of Mobutu. Kabila promised a new era of peace and prosperity. He officially declared the end of the Second Republic at his inaugural ceremony on May 29, 1997.

A NEW DICTATORSHIP?

From the onset, Kabila turned a deaf ear to people's aspirations for change. Apart from a few cosmetic changes, nothing was done toward social or economic reforms. The country regained its former name, the Democratic Republic of Congo (DRC). Some of the pre-Mobutu emblems, including the flag and the national anthem, were restored. Yet there were signs of a new "Mobutism without Mobutu." The sign that caused the most concern was Kabila's disinclination to share power. Revelations surfaced that implicated him in the elimination of AFDL military commander André Kikase Ngandu, killed in an ambush on January 6, 1997. He had been responsible for recruiting the "Mai Mai" combatants into the Alliance. Kabila's role within the Alliance had originally been that of spokesman. He was chosen by his comrades because he spoke French, English, Kiswahili, and Kiluba fluently. But after the death of Kikase Ngandu, Kabila tightened his grip on the AFDL and silenced those party members who opposed his methods.

After ousting Mobutu, Kabila used the same methods to exclude the "nonviolent" opposition to Mobutu from the new political system he endeavored to design. A great majority of Congolese favored a broad-based, inclusive government. They wanted a government that would work with the civil society and restore order throughout the country. But Kabila had no inclination to restart the democratization process. All political parties with the exclusion of the AFDL were banned, and their leaders were subjected to imprisonment. In February 1998, Étienne Tshisekedi was charged with subversive political activity in defiance of the government ban. He was arrested and banished to his home village.

Some semblance of order was restored in the main cities. Soldiers and policemen no longer preyed upon ordinary citizens. But Kabila's popularity quickly vanished. People did not particularly like his insistence that a "cultural revolution" was mandatory in order to eradicate all remnants of Mobutism. They rejected the regime's emphasis on an outdated Maoist ideology that supposedly reflected the realities of Congolese society. For example, the new government set up "People Committees" with the task of monitoring the activities of citizens in neighborhoods, schools, and workplaces.

The new regime's reliance on Tutsi soldiers and Tutsi cabinet members did not sit well with Kinshasa's population, which resented a government that was composed mainly of Tutsi exiles, Katangan allies, and obscure second guns with no political base of their own. This line-up was interpreted as a foreign structure imposed upon Congolese by Rwanda and Uganda. In July 1997, Rwandan president Kagame admitted that his country's involvement had been more serious than people had previously suspected. It was divulged that Rwanda had provided not only financial support but the logistics and troops that helped the Alliance capture several cities, including Kinshasa. At this point, the honeymoon between Kabila and the Congolese people turned sour.

HUMAN RIGHTS ABUSES

Flagrant human rights abuses were one of the new regime's trademarks. Displacement of populations and atrocities were reported as early as when AFDL forces advanced toward Goma. When the city fell, at least 100,000 people fled the area to seek refuge in the UN Mugunga camp, located on the southern outskirts of the city. More than 500,000 Hutu refugees had already flocked there from Rwanda to seek shelter under the protection of former Interahamwe militias. On November 14, 1996, AFDL troops attacked the camp in an attempt to dislodge the militias, killing in the process several thousand refugees and causing nearly 500,000 Hutu refugees to cross the border back to Rwanda. The massacre of Hutus in the "liberated areas" seemed to follow a clear pattern of retaliation. This may have been set in motion by the Rwandan government and executed by AFDL rebels in what humanitarian organizations characterized as vengeful genocide. In March 1997, following the rebel advance toward Kisangani, another attack targeted the camp of Tingi Tingi, to which the remaining Hutu refugees had retreated. Tens of thousands of refugees left the camp and retreated into the forests, many never to be seen again. Others were unaccounted for and may have survived despite the lack of medicine, food, shelter, and clean water. Survivors were later repatriated to Rwanda through an airlift operation organized by several UN agencies.

International organizations have estimated that approximately 200,000 refugees, mostly ethnic Hutus, disappeared on Congolese soil. Some disappeared as they attempted to flee to the west to escape the rebel advance. Others were killed as the result of a premeditated and deliberate "strategy of gradual extermination of a portion of the Rwandan population." There was mounting evidence that a planned genocide of ethnic Hutus was orchestrated during the rebel advance, even though President Kabila denied any involvement of his troops in the massacre of Hutu civilians. However, he thwarted all efforts by international organizations to conduct on-site investigations in the Kisangani area.

Political pluralism and power sharing were never Kabila's strong suits. Immediately after taking power, the new government cracked down on leaders of opposition parties, human rights advocates, and journalists. Former FAZ officers were sent to "re-education" camps. In general, any civil society activist suspected of being too outspoken or critical of the new regime was a target for repression. A general amnesty for all Congolese condemned of political crimes allowed for the release of more than 200 people in detention, but many more remained in prison. Ordinary civilians also felt the effects of the government's human rights violations. When the AFDL troops seized the capital, their top priority was restoring order and pacifying Kinshasa's vast population. Toward this end, the government relied on the Kadogos, a group of young soldiers (many of them in their early teens) who had been recruited into the Alliance army as it marched from Kivu to Kinshasa. Employed to police the capital, they were brutal with the local population. Most of them also did not speak local languages (Lingala or Kikongo). This turned Kinshasa's inhabitants and some of Kabila's local supporters against the new government.

IN THE FOOTSTEPS OF THE LEOPARD

Less than a year after toppling Mobutu, Kabila found himself under pressure from within Congo as well as from without. These pressures threatened to undermine his authority and revived the threat of civil war. Promises of a new Congo rid of Mobutism remained unfulfilled. Congolese waited for the new regime to revive the economy, but with no result. Just as Mobutu had been, Kabila was a soldier of fortune who happened to be at the right place at the right time. He was in no way prepared for the task that lay ahead of him. At the moment when he received the news that Alliance troops had entered Kinshasa, he did not have a sound economic plan of his own. The most convenient response for Kabila was to tread the same path as Mobutu. Having spent several decades in the Fizi-Baraka area in Kivu smuggling gold to East Africa before he emerged as Mobutu's most formidable opponent, Kabila had developed authoritarian methods that mirrored those that had helped Mobutu remain in power since the 1960s.

Using Mobutu's well-oiled machinery, Kabila took nepotism to new heights. Key positions in the government and the security services were filled with the president's clan members. Kabila's adopted son, Joseph, held the position of commander of land forces. General Yav Nawej, a relative by marriage, headed the army brigade based in Kinshasa. Gaëtan Kakudji, the minister of the interior and head of the country's intelligence services, was a cousin. So was the president's aide-de-camp, Colonel Eddy Kapend. Another cousin, Mwenze Kongolo, was the country's minister of justice. The chief of the national police, Célestin Kifwa, was Kabila's brother-in-law. Despite his claims to the contrary, Kabila's government was also characterized by mismanagement and corruption. Even before gaining control of the whole country, the Alliance signed agreements that gave enormous advantages to foreign companies. In April 1997, a $1 billion agreement provided the American Mineral Fields, a U.S.-based company, unrestricted access to Congolese copper, cobalt, and zinc. A week before Mobutu was ousted, the Canadian Tenke Mining Corporation shifted from a previous contract signed with the Mobutu regime to an agreement with Kabila's Alliance. These deals brought large sums of money that helped finance AFDL's military operations. Along with the Alliance's political control came new rules and new partners in the profitable business of exploiting the country's nonrenewable resources. Foreign troops from Rwanda, Burundi, and Uganda were given free reign to engage in lucrative business activities in "liberated territories." New kinds of foreign entrepreneurs, speaking only English, Swahili, or Kiniarwanda, vied for control of DRC's resources. Analysts have suggested that the financial links and transportation networks were already in place in eastern Congo during the early months of the rebellion. There are clear indications that presidents Yoweri Museveni of Uganda, Paul Kagame of Rwanda, and Laurent-Désiré Kabila had entered into an agreement to exploit Congo's resources. They had organized a plan to siphon Congo's resources through a complex network of mining companies, administrative appointees, trucking and airline companies, and financial institutions located in Kigali, Kampala, and New York. According to a report by a panel of UN experts:

> Between September 1998 and August 1999, occupied zones of the Democratic Republic of the Congo were drained of existing stockpiles, including minerals, agricultural and forest products, and livestock. Regardless of the looter, the pattern was the same: Burundian, Rwandan, Ugandan and/or RCD soldiers, commanded by an officer, visited farms, storage facilities, factories and banks, and demanded that the managers open the coffers and doors. The soldiers were then ordered to remove the relevant products and load them into vehicles.[1]

This political and financial arrangement fell apart. Kabila's partners and patrons grew increasingly dissatisfied with the way he was handling the instability on the eastern borders. Neighboring countries began to use eastern Congo as if it were an extension of their own territories. Authorities in Rwanda and Uganda helped Congolese allies secure positions as provincial governors in Ituri and Maniema. They went as far as redrawing provincial boundaries and issuing official documents to local and foreign individuals. They acted as the legal government in the respective tracts that they occupied in eastern Congo in the aftermath of the 1998 invasion. Rwanda and Uganda had masterminded Kabila's takeover of Congo. They did so to guarantee that Kinshasa would neutralize the Interahamwe militia and protect the Banyamulenge, Congo's Tutsi minority. Kabila's regime failed to deliver on its promises. Rwanda and Uganda capitalized on Kabila's inability to get the country back on its feet and increased their demands. They demanded not only safety on the borders but also the right to take control of large areas of eastern Congo, penetrating as deep as 700 miles inside Congo's eastern borders. They put their proxies in strategic niches within Congo's administrative structure, which signaled their imperialistic drive.

In June 1998, there was a falling out between Kabila and those African governments that brought him to power. Congo's leader aligned himself with the very forces that he had originally fought. Congolese Tutsis were rounded up in the capital, accompanied by vitriolic anti-Tutsi propaganda from the government. Hutu Interahamwe militias operating from their strongholds in eastern Congo, on the other hand, received unequivocal military and financial support from Kinshasa.

From this point until his demise, Kabila followed in the footsteps of Zaire's last "leopard," Mobutu, as if driven by forces he could not control. Although Kabila's rise and fall were more erratic and arbitrary than those of Mobutu, his tenure nevertheless made a huge impact on a country afflicted by chaos since its independence.

CIVIL WAR AND FOREIGN INVOLVEMENT

The second Congolese war began in August 1998. It was triggered by Kabila's decision to expel the Rwandan military officers who had helped him topple Mobutu a year before. He accused them of plotting against his regime. In retaliation, Rwandan army officers organized an airlift from Rwanda to the Kitona army base in the Lower Congo. It was there that a contingent of at least 12,000 ex-FAZ soldiers were being "re-educated." To lead this military operation, Rwanda enlisted James Kabarebe, who served in Kabila's regime as army commander. He was among a cohort of Tutsi politicians that Kabila had dismissed following his break with his Rwandan backers. The plan of the operation was to enlist these ex-FAZ soldiers to spearhead the overthrow of Kabila. Rwanda's use of Congolese troops and anti-Kabila politicians was obviously an attempt to legitimize their military campaign. However, as in 1997, this new war had less to do with Congo's internal affairs than with broader political issues concerning the entire central African region.

There followed a series of events that mirrored the 1997 campaign that had helped install Kabila in power. Rwanda and Uganda encouraged an anti-Kabila group, the Congolese Democratic Rally (Rassemblement Congolais pour la Démocratie—RCD), to take up arms against their former leader. The RCD remained a Tutsi-dominated movement. Politically it ran the gamut from former Mobutist hardliners to former AFDL leaders. It included people such as Ernest Wamba dia Wamba, a history professor from the University of Dar es Salaam in Tanzania; General Deogratias Bugera, a former AFDL secretary; Jacques Depelchin, a Marxist intellectual and long-time Mobutu detractor; and Victor Lunda Bululu, who served as prime minister under Mobutu. The movement was headed by Bizima Karaha, a Munyamulenge Tutsi who had been Kabila's foreign minister and one of the early henchmen of the regime. From the start, the rebels made it clear that their objective was to topple Kabila by military force.

In the early weeks of the rebellion, most observers predicted a quick demise for Kabila's government. This seemed especially likely when rebels captured the Inga hydroelectric dam, leaving Kinshasa without water and electricity for several weeks. The most valuable elements of the army defected to join the rebels, leaving Kabila with a beleaguered, undisciplined, and ill-equipped army. Less than a month after the rebellion began, several cities, including Matadi, Kisangani, Goma, and Bukavu, fell to the RCD. There were rumors that the rebels were closing in on the capital. Kabila retreated to Lubumbashi but remained defiant. He refused to surrender and accused the West of plotting to overthrow him.

This move was intended to elicit the support of other players, especially countries of SADC (Southern African Development Community). Angola and Zimbabwe offered military assistance. There is evidence to suggest that Kabila's ability to withstand the rebels' assault was considerably bolstered by the involvement of Angolan and Zimbabwean troops. Each country had its own reasons for intervening in the conflict. Angola resented the landing of Rwandan troops in Kitona as an encroachment on its sphere of influence. Angola may also have wanted to position itself as a regional force. Some analysts have also pointed out that Angola's intervention on behalf of Kabila's regime targeted UNITA. Since the Mobutu era, UNITA had been operating from bases in Congo against the Luanda government. With Angola's intervention, the tide rapidly turned against the rebels, who encountered strong resistance in their attempt to take Kinshasa. Zimbabwe entered the war in Congo mainly for economic reasons, although political motivations may also have played a part. President Robert Mugabe sought to divert domestic attention away from the country's devastating economic situation. He also sought to accommodate the interests of influential Zimbabwean entrepreneurs and mining ventures, which hoped to make huge profits in the DRC as a result of war and insecurity.[2] To thank Zimbabwe for its military intervention, President Kabila appointed Billy Rautenbach, a white Zimbabwean mining tycoon and a close ally of Mugabe, as chief executive of the state-owned company Gécamines.

With Angolan and Zimbabwean units fighting alongside government troops in Congo, the rebels' military advance suffered several setbacks. In addition, internal divisions within the RCD threatened to break up the movement. In early 1999, non-Tutsi Congolese members of RCD claimed that Banyamulenge held a disproportionate number of positions within the political structure of the movement. Led by professor Wamba dia Wamba, they created a rival movement, RCD/Kisangani (later identified as RCD/ML, Rassemblement Congolais pour la Démocratie/Mouvement de Libération). This was opposed to RCD/Goma, headed by Émile Ilunga. According to Kisangani Emizet, the split resulted from the inability of "doves" (led by Wamba) and "hawks" (led by Emile Ilunga and Deogratias Bugera) to coexist within the same organization. While Rwanda continued to support RCD/Goma, Uganda positioned itself behind the RCD/ML. This move signaled a falling out between the two countries and discredited the rebel movements in the eyes of many Congolese. People came to regard both RCD factions as proxies for Rwandan and Ugandan territorial and economic ambitions in eastern Congo. This impression was reinforced when evidence emerged regarding the decisions of Rwanda and Uganda to enter the conflict in August 1998. The evidence suggested that the decision was entirely influenced by top military officials who made a fortune in Congo smuggling gold and diamonds during the first war and were eager to resume their financial activities.

The rivalry between the two RCD factions and their inability to develop grassroots constituencies facilitated the emergence of a third rebel faction, the Congolese Liberation Movement (Mouvement pour la Libération du Congo—MLC). This faction operated in the Equateur province from Mobutu's former palace in Gbadolite. Although largely supported by Uganda, the MLC gained acceptance as a homegrown militia. This was partly because its main leader, Jean-Pierre Bemba, the son of Bemba Saolona, a longtime follower of Mobutu and Kabila's economy minister, originated from the northern area. The support was also partly the result of Jean-Pierre Bemba's ability to muster grassroots support.

The scission within the RCD and the lure of Congo's mineral resources sparked a falling out between Uganda and Rwanda. Rwanda's alliance with Uganda was the bedrock of its security strategy in eastern Congo in the aftermath of the Rwandan genocide. But in August 1999, there was a confrontation between the Rwandan forces (Rwandan Patriotic Army—RPA) and the Ugandan army (Ugandan People's Defence Forces—UPDF) for the control of the diamond-rich city of Kisangani. This wreaked havoc on Congo's fourth largest city. There were intermittent clashes between the RPA and UPDF between August 1999 and May 2000, which claimed the lives of several hundred Congolese civilians. The two armies finally pulled out in June 2000, leaving chaos behind.

THE LUSAKA PEACE AGREEMENT AND THE FALL OF KABILA

Military involvement by seven neighboring African countries[3] split Congo into four sections. Each section relied on its own resources and the foreign troops at its disposal. Foreign intervention helped Kabila to renew his popular image as a nationalist leader who stood up to foreign invasion. It also amplified the conflict, which threatened to engulf most of central Africa. This prompted several African leaders to broker a cease-fire as a precursor to peace talks. After several failed attempts, a cease-fire was finally signed in Lusaka, Zambia, on July 10, 1999. This was accomplished through the mediation of Zambian president Frederick Chiluba and under the aegis of the Organization of African Unity (OAU). Under the Lusaka Peace Agreement, foreign countries involved in the conflict accepted a few essential principles. These principles included the withdrawal of their troops from Congo, the respect of Congo's sovereignty within its current borders, and the deployment of a UN peacekeeping force to ensure the implementation of the Agreement. The various combatants also agreed to principles such as the release of prisoners, the arrest of those who committed genocide in Rwanda, the disarming of armed militias, and the convening of a national dialogue. A provision aimed at mollifying the rebels called for a transitional period. During this period, a government of national unity comprising all major factions would run the country. President Kabila was not interested in implementing a provision that would have created a broad-base government no longer controlled solely by him and his followers. On paper the Lusaka Agreement seemed to accommodate the demands of each party. On the ground, however, it was merely the continuation of war by other means.

That all parties failed to live up to the implementation of the Lusaka Peace Agreement is not surprising. The decline of centralized authority in Congo had allowed predatory practices by its neighbors. In theory their presence in Congo was justified by security reasons. But this justification did not conceal the fact that foreign armies were exploiting the country for its mineral resources. According to Belgian journalist Colette Braeckman, Rwanda even invoked the genocide of the Tutsis as a pretext "to play on the international community's sense of guilt and persuade the United States to look with a kindly eye on what is nothing less than a plan to conquer and control the resources of the Congo." Indeed, war was more profitable than peace. All the combatants who had signed the Lusaka Agreement plundered the country's wealth as a way of replenishing their military arsenals.

Until early 2000, the stalemate brought about by the Lusaka Agreement continued. It seemed as if all the warring parties, starting with Kabila's government, had lost credibility in the eyes of the Congolese people. It was the Congolese who continued to pay the steep price for the war being waged in their country. They suffered firsthand the human rights violations, systematic plundering, rampant corruption, lack of education, and shortage of foodstuffs and medical supplies. In several cases, troops committed the worst kinds of atrocities in retaliation against local civilians. Numerous charges of mass murder, rape, and extrajudicial executions have been leveled by human rights organizations against the Rwandan and Ugandan troops who operated in eastern Congo. One of the reported cases took place in November 1999 in the territory of Mwenga in South Kivu. Rwandan, Burundian, and Ugandan soldiers slaughtered fifteen Congolese women for refusing to become sex slaves:

> When they resisted these soldiers, they were, first, beaten, then African hot pepper was rubbed all over their bodies' wounds and inserted through every orifice of their bodies: eyes, mouths, noses, ears, anus, and vaginas, in order to make these women suffer. The women were buried alive.[4]

It was against this background that the stunning news of Kabila's assassination emerged. Exactly how and why Kabila was killed remains disputed. According to the official story, some elements within his troops held grudges against Kabila for not properly rewarding them after he seized power and for his authoritarian methods. Feeling increasingly disgruntled, they plotted to assassinate him. On January 16, 2001, one of his personal bodyguards, Rachidi Kasereka, gunned him down as he sat in the presidential palace in Kinshasa. Kasereka was then himself killed by Colonel Eddy Kapend, Kabila's aide-de-camp. Kabila's death was dubbed a "surgical removal." But this official version contains many inconsistencies. If the story was true, why were leading figures of Kabila's regime, including Kapend himself, arrested on suspicion of involvement in the assassination? It seems more plausible that Kabila's death was part of a large, well-orchestrated plan. This plan was probably masterminded by one or more of the foreign governments that still control Congo in a bid to replace him with a more amenable figurehead.

NOTES

1. "Report of the Panel of Experts on the Illegal Exploitation of Natural Resources and Other Forms of Wealth of the Democratic Republic of the Congo," United Nations Security Council (2001), p. 8.

2. Michael Nest, "Ambitions, Profits and Loss: Zimbabwean Economic Involvement in the Democratic Republic of the Congo," *African Affairs* 100 (2001).

3. Rwanda, Uganda, and Burundi have supported rebel factions while Zimbabwe, Angola, Chad, and Namibia have offered their military and logistical assistance to the Kinshasa government.

4. Cited in Ngemi (2000: 25).

Epilogue: Africa's First Continental War

As surprising as the news of Kabila's assassination was to Congolese, what followed was even more unexpected. After much stonewalling, Kabila's Katangan supporters appointed Joseph Kabila to replace his father as Congo's new leader. Little is known about the new president, not even his exact age. There is much speculation in Kinshasa about his connection with the late Kabila. The shy, approximately twenty-nine-year-old president, Africa's youngest leader, spent most his life outside the country. As a result he barely speaks French (although he is said to have attended the French School in Dar es Salaam) and no Lingala at all. He is, however, fluent in English and Swahili. Joseph Kabila appears an unassuming figure compared with his rotund, voluble, and extroverted father. During his father's presidency, he served as deputy chief of staff and commander of land forces. In the process he created a strong following within the army.

CONGO'S FORGOTTEN AGONY

Until now the new president has managed to avoid the personal foibles that alienated his late father from foreign powers and corporations. A week after his father's funeral and after being sworn in as president, Joseph Kabila took off on a diplomatic tour. He visited Western governments and corporations in Washington, Paris, and Brussels, and attempted to ingratiate himself with them. He showed clear signs that he was willing to implement some of the main components of the Lusaka Peace Agreement. He agreed to participate in an intra-Congolese dialogue under the mediation of former Botswanan president Ketimule Masire. He also agreed to facilitate the deployment of MONUC, the UN-mandated military observer mission for Congo. But the change in leadership did not bring the kind of relief Congolese had been waiting for. Most Congolese remain pessimistic about both the new government's ability to restart the democratization process and the real motives of the opposition factions.

Kabila has been blamed for Congo's desperate situation. His reluctance to implement the Lusaka Agreement has been used as a convenient rationalization for the presence of foreign troops in Congo. According to an explanation widely circulated in the Western media:

> At one level it is a conflict between two regional alliances—a 'Great Lakes' alliance of Rwanda, Uganda, and Burundi, versus one of Angola, Zimbabwe, and Namibia. On another level, it is a violent mixture of national civil wars, including those of Rwanda, Uganda, Burundi, and Angola, all of which are partly fought on Congolese soil. Finally, in the midst of this chaos, the Congo's own stew of local ethnic feuds has sparked an explosion of bloodshed in the eastern part of the country. All of these conflicts feed and reinforce one another, and together risk to transform the Congo into a patchwork of warlord's fiefdoms.[1]

As convenient as this analysis might seem, it does not take into consideration Kabila's "surgical removal" from the scene. Nor does it account for his son's willingness to comply with the Lusaka Agreement, nor the IMF "remedies" applied to Congo's economy, nor the demands of multinational corporations. These factors did not improve the situation on the ground. Competing interests over Congo's abundant mineral resources remain the prevailing reason behind Africa's First World War. It is a war of attrition, approved by Western corporations and inflicted by foreign invading armies and local militias on the Congolese people. It is being waged without receiving the kind of media attention that other conflicts have received in recent years. Herbert Weiss is right in defining the war in Congo as a "tug of war between a political culture which avoided mass violence for more than thirty years and one, more akin to many of its neighbors, where conflicts have so often turned into war and its accompanying disasters."[2]

The motivation behind this tug of war may no longer be Congo's gold, copper, and diamonds. Instead, it may be a lesser-known mineral ore that has become the centerpiece of the new economy. In processed form, columbine-tantalite, "coltan" for short, is a highly heat-resistant metal. It is vital for the manufacture of electronic components that control the flow of current inside miniature circuit boards, which are found inside almost every laptop, cell phone, VCR, pager, and hand-held video game machine. Skyrocketing demand for coltan in late 2000 created a temporary worldwide shortage of the mineral. This threatened to take the wireless world back to its pre-coltan age. The result was a tenfold increase in the price of coltan on the world market. Eighty percent of the world's coltan reserves are located in Africa, of which at least 80 percent are in Congo (See Map 4). The scramble for Congo's coltan has created a new humanitarian tragedy in the country. Illegal mines have sprouted up in Kivu, encroaching on farmlands, pristine ecosystems, protected rainforest areas, and faunal reserves that are home to endangered species, including the elusive okapi. Under military protection, local miners dig out the "black mud" wherever they can find it. The ore is bought from the miners by rebel factions and sold directly to multinational mineral companies. Rwandan, Burundian, and Ugandan occupation armies ship their share of the ore to their respective countries for export to the global market. Official statistics in Uganda, for example, show a dramatic increase in coltan exports, from 2.5 tons in 1997 to 70 tons in 1999. In exchange for Congo's coltan and other minerals, these countries acquire military equipment. According to The World Policy Institute, of the $19.5 million in arms and training that the U.S. delivered to African countries in 1999, $4.8 million went to nations militarily involved in Congo.

The economic impact of the war and the illegal extraction of mineral resources have been devastating. According to Mungbalemwe Koyame and John Clark, there have been several particularly serious effects. The production of goods such as timber and palm oil and the extraction of minerals have been largely highjacked by Congo's neighbors. There has been a steep decline in the gross domestic product and tax revenues. The government is unable to pay civil servants or to keep its programs functioning. Because of the war and the difficulty of river transportation, trade between Kinshasa and the rest of the country has come to a standstill. One result is that nearly 75 percent of the capital's child population is affected by malnutrition. There has been a decline in private business, and the savings and investment capacity of nationals is practically nonexistent. Finally, Congo is so ridden with political uncertainties that aids and grants from the international community and foreign direct investment no longer reach the country.[3]

The loss in human capital is even more staggering. The International Rescue Committee estimated in May 2001 that the war in Congo had caused 3 million deaths. Most of the victims were innocent civilians who died as a result of fighting, malnutrition, and disease. In some areas, at least 80 percent of the population has been forced to flee their homes at some point since August 1998. Many of these people (at least 100,000) are still hiding in the forest without adequate shelter, food, and medicine.

POLITICAL UNCERTAINTIES

As of January 2002, Congo's political future is still uncertain. The conflict over Congo's resources and the presence of foreign armies are clearly incompatible with enacting the Lusaka Agreement. On the contrary, these are covert strategies used by neighboring states to prevent an effective central government in Kinshasa. The situation has some Western officials, journalists,[4] and academics proclaiming that Congo is too big to be successfully governed. According to Michael Schatzberg, a well-known specialist on Congolese affairs, "the pendulum has for now swung back toward decentralization and local political control."[5] Foreign armies' presence in and balkanization of Congo, either directly or by means of rebel factions, does not indicate federalist sentiment among the Congolese population. In areas held by the rebels, lack of due process, frequent attacks on civilians, and extrajudicial punitive measures, including rape, torture, and mass murder, do not represent political or administrative alternatives favored by Congolese citizens.

A federalist solution is likely to intensify ethnic sentiments of the kind that led to atrocities perpetrated against ethnic Lendu in the Ituri area in the northeast. The war in Congo has become a means by which non–state actors achieve free reign to plunder and kill. All the recent developments on the ground and in the diplomatic arena suggest that the war is useful to many of those involved. For the Western countries that supply weapons, neighboring countries such as Rwanda, Uganda, and Zimbabwe, and rebel factions and international corporations, their interests are better served by continuing to fuel the conflict.

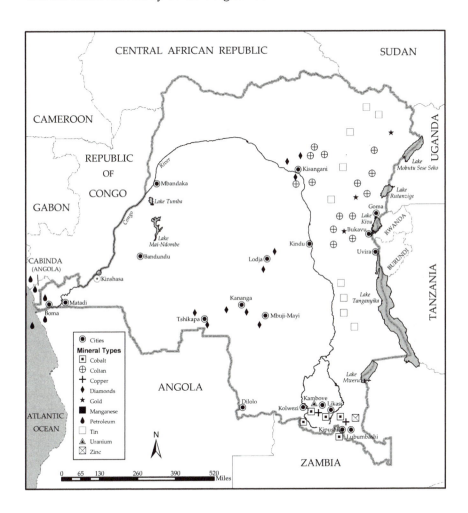

Map 4. Congo's Mineral Resources

The Lusaka Peace Agreement may never be effectively implemented. Because of this, some observers are suggesting that a solution to the conflict will only be found by upgrading the MONUC mission, which, at the time of this writing, consists of only 442 military observers with a ceasefire-monitoring mandate. This upgrade would move the mission's goals from disengagement of warring forces to withdrawal and disarmament. Most Congolese are not in favor of any far-reaching UN-sponsored initiative. The UN has proven ineffective in conflict resolution throughout most of Africa, including in the 1994 conflict that led to the mass killing of ethnic Tutsis in Rwanda. Kisangani Emizet points out that even after the Rwandan genocide, "the UN failed to provide security in the Great Lakes region and failed to stop the massacre of refugees for almost ten months."[6] Moreover, Congolese still hold the UN partly responsible for derailing Congo's independence during the early years of the First Republic. They see the UN as a potential problem rather than a solution. The notoriously feeble OAU has also failed to bring the main protagonists to the negotiating table. Congolese are further disillusioned by Western countries' purported "good will" attitude toward solving problems in Congo. Congolese people have learned the hard way that their country is far too rich to elicit anything from the West but greed.

Thirty years of Mobutu's reign precipitated Congo's economic problems and lack of political freedom. This period also forged a sense of unity that Congolese are now reclaiming. The current government controls only a fraction of the country's territory. It seems doubtful that this government has the resources or the acumen to unite Congolese behind a new political project and begin the reconstruction of the Congolese state. The new government has suggested no clear political program to replace Mobutu's corrupt system. There is no evidence to suggest that the government will develop the kind of framework that might win the support of the majority of Congolese.

Neither the government nor the rebels seem willing to put an end to the war. It is therefore essential that nonviolent political parties play a role. These parties played a crucial role in weakening Mobutu's grip on power, but they were sidelined by President Kabila and his successor. Only this might allow Congo's civil society to mobilize people's energies and restore their confidence in the state. With the collapse of the state, Congo's robust civil society continued to play a key role in providing basic economic and social services to the people. Education, banking, health, and transportation would have totally disappeared in the urban areas had it not been for family networks, church-based groups, and community organizations. The Congolese government is unlikely to regain its ability to operate unless it accommodates civil society. The government must provide ways for the people to participate in the rebirth of the Congolese nation from the ashes of chaos.

NOTES

1. ICG (International Crisis Group) Africa Report no. 26, *Scramble for the Congo: Anatomy of an Ugly War* 20 (December 2000), p. 10.

2. Herbert Weiss, *War and Peace in the Democratic Republic of the Congo*, Current African Issues 22 (Uppsala: Nordiska Afrikainstitutet, 2000), p. 1.

3. Mungbalemwe Koyame and John F. Clark, "The Economic Consequences of the Congo War," in John F. Clark, ed., *The African Stakes of the Congo War* (New York: Palgrave, 2002).

4. In 1999, the *New York Times* orchestrated a major propaganda campaign in favor of the Balkanization of Congo in particular, and Africa in general. See Ian Fisher and Norimitsu Omishi, "Congo's Struggle May Unleash Broad Strife to Redraw Africa," *New York Times*, January 12, 1999.

5. Michael G. Schatzberg, "Beyond Mobutu: Kabila and the Congo," *Journal of Democracy* 8, no. 4 (1997), p. 82.

6. Kisangani Emizet, "The Massacre of Refugees in Congo: A Case of UN Peacekeeping Failure and International Law," *The Journal of Modern African Studies* 38, no. 2 (2000), p. 183.

Notable People in the
History of Congo

Adoula, Cyrille (1921–1978), was born and educated in Kinshasa. In 1958, he was elected vice president of Lumumba's MNC party but then switched to the MNC-Kalonji after the scission. He opposed Lumumba's government and was later appointed prime minister by President Kasavubu. He devoted most of his term as premier from 1961 to 1964 to dealing with Katanga's secession. Before his retirement in 1970, he served briefly as ambassador to Belgium and to the U.S. and as Mobutu's minister of foreign affairs. He died in Lausanne, Switzerland.

Bemba Saolona, Jeannot (1941–   ), was born at Libenge in the Equateur province. During Mobutu's era he was undoubtedly the most successful businessman in Congo, with holdings in the airline company Scibe-Airlift. He also owned several agroindustrial ventures. During Kabila's brief term he was imprisoned then released to serve as minister of economy.

Bolamba, Antoine-Roger (1913–   ), was born in Boma and attended the Colonie Scolaire there. Between 1945 and 1959 he was chief editor of the native newspaper *La Voix du Congolais* but was better known for his literary works. He also briefly served in Lumumba and Adoula's cabinets as minister of information and cultural affairs and minister of information and tourism, respectively. He continued both his literary and political pursuits during Mobutu's regime.

Bolikango, Jean (1909–1982), was Congo's most veteran politician. He led the Bangala to form a powerful organization, Liboke lya Bangala, in 1954. He was among the first generation of native-born Kinshasans. After a failed bid to be elected speaker of the House of Representatives during the First Republic, he accepted an appointment in Ileo's second cabinet as vice prime minister and minister of information. Mobutu appointed him member of MPR's politburo in 1968. He died in Liege, Belgium.

Bomboko, Justin (1928–   ), served in several cabinets as minister of foreign affairs. He earned a degree in political science at the Free University of Brussels in 1959 and led the Mongo to form an ethnic organization (UNIMO) in 1960. Lumumba appointed him minister of foreign affairs in his first cabinet. Bomboko kept this post until 1969, when Mobutu named him ambassador to Washington. After a foray in business dealings, thanks to the Zaireanization policies, he came back to politics in 1977, first as member of the Politburo and minister of foreign affairs.

Diangienda, Joseph (1918–1992), Simon Kimbangu's third son, was born in Nkamba and became spiritual leader of the Kimbanguist Church after a career in the colonial administration. When Mobutu banned all religious sects unaffiliated to the Catholic or Protestant denominations, Diangienda lobbied for preferential treatment of his church in return for supporting Mobutu's regime. He died in 1992 and was buried next to his father in Nkamba.

Franco (1935–1989) was born François Luambo Makiadi in Sona Bata. He was one of the most influential and prolific African popular musicians. His career spanned nearly forty years, from 1950 to his death in 1989. His band, OK Jazz, dominated the African musical scene for at least three decades with over 150 albums produced, most of which sold over 50,000 copies each. A legend in his own lifetime, "Franco de mi amor," as he liked to be called in his early career, gained prominence and endeared himself to many of his fans not only for his acoustic feats on the guitar but also as a social satirist and commentator.

Gbenye, Christophe (1927–   ), served as minister of interior in Lumumba's and Adoula's cabinets. A staunch pro-Lumumbist, he helped organize Lumumba's ill-fated escape out of Kinshasa in November 1960. He was arrested along with Lumumba at Mweka, but he managed to escape and join the pro-Lumumbist camp in Stanleyville. In 1964, he enlisted the help of Egyptian president Nasser in setting up a formidable insurgency movement against the central government. He proclaimed himself president of a revolutionary government based in Stanleyville, People's Republic of Congo-Stanleyville. Overwhelmed by a Belgo-American military operation (Operation Dragon Rouge) aimed at liberating Belgian and American hostages held in Stanleyville, Gbenye's government quickly disintegrated. He then sought refuge in Cairo, where he lived several years before coming back from exile to participate in the Sovereign National Conference as the leader of the MNL (Mouvement National Lumumbiste).

Gizenga, Antoine (1925–   ), worked closely with Gbenye and Gaston Soumialot and was one the leaders of the eastern rebellion in the early 1960s. Before joining Lumumba, he was one of the cofounders and president of the PSA. He served as vice president until the revocation of Lumumba's government. In retaliation against Kasavubu's illegal decision, he set up a rival government in Stanleyville in September 1960 and proclaimed himself Lumumba's legitimate successor. Several African and Asian governments (including China), Cuba, all European socialist countries, and most Arab nations recognized the Gizenga government and offered military assistance. After a self-imposed exile following Mobutu's coup, he returned to Kinshasa to participate in the Sovereign National Conference as the leader of the Unified Lumumbist Party (or PALU) and has been since then a vocal opposition leader.

Ileo, Joseph (1921–1994), was one of the MNC's *caciques* that supported the scission and the creation of the MNC-Kalonji in July 1959. He served as its first secretary general. He became an important player in Congolese politics with his election in June 1960 as speaker of the Senate. In September 1960, when president Kasavubu revoked Prime Minister Lumumba, Ileo was called to form a new government. Although a proponent of an undivided yet decentralized Congo, he never succeeded to bring either Tshombe or Kalonji back into the fold. Though for most of the 1960s and 1970s he had a key role as secretary general of the MPR's Politburo, his political career during the Second Republic was less prominent.

Kabasele, Joseph Tshamala (1930–1985), was best known by fans of Congolese music as "Le Grand Kalle." Born in Matadi, Le Grand Kalle was among the founders of Congolese popular music and influenced virtually all Congolese musicians of the 1960s, including Franco. In 1953, he created the legendary African Jazz, Congo's first modern musical orchestra with a unique blend of vocals and rhythms from traditional Congo, West African Highlife music, and Cuban rumba. Although his career dipped in the 1970s, his reputation as Congo's foremost musician remained intact.

Kabila, Joseph (1971–   ), the son of late president Laurent Kabila, was born in Hewa Bora II, in South Kivu province, where his father spent some of his years in exile. Because he was born to a Tutsi mother and grew up mostly in English-speaking Uganda and Tanzania, he lacks command of French and Lingala, languages spoken in most of Congo. He was trained as a soldier in East Africa and China and held his first major position, as head of the armed forces, after the AFDL victory. Following his father's assassination in January 2001, he has been thrust into the limelight and into power without much preparation and political flair. It remains to be seen whether he will deliver on his promise to end the conflict in Congo and restart the democratic process.

Kabila, Laurent-Désiré (1939–2001), was, until the rebellion that ousted Mobutu in 1997, virtually an unknown and negligible quantity in Congo politics. Born in Moba, a Luba from the northern Katanga region, Kabila fought within the ranks of the Balubakat against the Katangan army of Tshombe. In 1963, after serving in different positions in the provincial government of northern Katanga, he joined Gbenye's Lumumbist group, CNL, to fight against Leopoldville's central government. In 1967, he created the PRP (Parti de la Révolution Populaire) with a military branch and established his base in the Fizi area in Kivu. Under the cover of an embryonic state run along Marxist lines, he engaged in lucrative diamond- and gold-smuggling activities in the Great Lakes region. In early 1996, he led the rebellion against Mobutu and proclaimed himself president on May 29, 1997. On January 16, 2001, after only two years in power he was gunned down by one his bodyguards, leaving behind him a devastated, warn-torn country.

Kalonji, Albert (1929–   ), was the leading figure of Luba nationalism. He worked closely with Lumumba within the MNC until the scission in

April 1959 that pitted those who, like Lumumba himself, advocated a strong central government against those who favored a federal solution to the Congolese crisis. Kalonji then joined the federalist camp and, together with Ileo and Ngalula, formed the MNC-Kalonji. In 1960, following Lumumba's decision not to include any representative of the MNC-Kalonji in the government, Kalonji led the Kasai region in seceding from the central government. He claimed the monarchical title of *mulopwe* and declared the creation of the "Federated Kingdom of South Kasai" in April 1961. After the collapse of the Kasai secession, he exiled to Luxembourg until 1964 when he was named minister of agriculture in Adoula's cabinet. Mobutu's second coup, in 1965, sent Kalonji to exile in Belgium, where he remained several years until Mobutu lured him back to Zaire and offered him a position at the head a few public companies. He was granted several Zaireanized properties and made a member of the Politburo of the MPR. He now lives in exile in Luxembourg.

Kamitatu Massamba, Cleophas (1931–   ), was among the group of Congolese politicians at the Independence Roundtable in Brussels in 1960. He was successively minister of interior and minister of foreign affairs during the First Republic. In 1966, he was arrested for allegedly participating in a plot to overthrow Mobutu and was jailed for eighteen months. After his liberation, he was tried and sentenced to five years in prison but fled to Brazzaville and then exiled in France where he earned a doctoral degree in political science. Upon Mobutu's announcement of a general amnesty granted to all political exiles, he returned to Zaire in November 1977 and served as minister of agriculture and then Zaire's ambassador to Japan.

Kanza, Thomas (1934–   ), was the first lay Congolese to graduate with a nonreligious degree from the University of Louvain in Belgium. A staunch supporter of Lumumba, he served in his first cabinet as Congo's ambassador to the UN and joined Gbenye's insurgent movement after Lumumba's assassination. After the defeat of the rebellion he exiled in London and then in the U.S., where he studied at Harvard and wrote novels and essays, including *The Rise and Fall of Patrice Lumumba*. In 1985, he came back to Zaire and engaged in different business ventures before resuming unsuccessfully his political career during the transitional period. In 1992, although supported by Mobutu, he was defeated by Étienne Tshisekedi for the position of prime minister of the transitional government.

Kasavubu, Joseph (1917–1969), Congo's first president, was born in Tshela, in the Bas-Congo region. After earning a theological degree, Kasavubu entered the colonial administration as a teacher and then a subaltern civil servant. In 1954, he was elected president of the newly created ABAKO and used this ethnic organization as a platform for the Bakongo people to demand independence. He was, without doubt, the principal beneficiary of Belgian reforms and Africanization policies. Following municipal elections in 1958, he was appointed mayor of one of Leopoldville's boroughs and, in 1960, was elected president. Lacking charisma and political acumen, he was overshadowed by his premier, Patrice Lumumba, when the country plunged into civil unrest. After the elimination of Lumumba he remained a weak president before being deposed by Mobutu in November 1965. After Mobutu's coup, Kasavubu remained secluded in his home village, where he died on March 24, 1969.

Kengo wa Dondo, formerly known as Léon Lobitsh (1935–   ), was born in Libenge of a Polish father and a Congolese mother. Trained as a jurist with a doctoral law degree obtained at the Free University of Brussels, he enjoyed a successful political career, starting as Mobutu's political and juridical adviser upon his return to Congo in 1968. Kengo served as attorney general, permanent member of the Politburo, ambassador to Belgium, and prime minister. During much of the 1980s, he was one of Mobutu's most powerful cabinet members and was trusted by the IMF as a competent technocrat who could help implement IMF policies in Zaire.

Kethulle, Raphaël de la (1890–1956), a Belgian Scheutist missionary, devoted most of his life to tending to the social needs of Congolese youth. He arrived in Congo in 1917 after serving during the first part of World War I as chaplain to the Belgian émigrés in London. Kethulle was responsible for setting up schools, including Kinshasa's Institute of Physical Education (created in 1954) and promoting the building of two of Kinshasa's main stadiums. He also introduced team sports, such as soccer, basketball, and volleyball, to the capital's youth. After his death in Belgium in 1956, his body was flown back to Kinshasa and buried in a mausoleum erected in front of one of the stadiums.

Kimba, Évariste (1926–1966), was the last prime minister of Congo under the First Republic. He initially sided with Tshombe's secessionist Katanga in 1960 and then became an ardent opponent of Tshombe's secessionist tendencies. In October 1965, he was appointed to the premiership by

President Kasavubu in replacement of Tshombe but failed to obtain a vote of confidence from the Parliament, thus paving the way for Mobutu's coup on November 24, 1965. In May 1966, he was sentenced to death for treason, along with three other former First Republic cabinet ministers, Jérôme Anany, Emmanuel Bamba, and Alexandre Mahamba, and publicly hanged before a crowd of more than 50,000 spectators.

Kimbangu, Simon (1889–1951), Congo's foremost evangelical figure and prophet, was born at Nkamba in Lower Congo during the construction of the Leopoldville-Matadi railroad. An avid reader of the Bible (translated into Kikongo in 1897), he was baptized in 1915 along with his wife Marie Mwilu. In 1918, he began to have visions calling him to an evangelical healing ministry. He fled to Kinshasa, where he worked for the Huileries du Congo Belge, and then, "pressed by the Holy Spirit," came back to Nkamba to start a ministry of faith healing in 1921. He performed numerous healings, advocated monogamy, and attacked traditional religion by urging people to burn their "fetishes" and abandon "pagan" rituals. He was equally vocal against colonial churches. His evangelical activity drew huge crowds to Nkamba and alarmed the colonial authorities, who feared that it might coalesce into a nationalistic rebellion. After only three months of evangelization Kimbangu was arrested, tried, and sentenced to 120 lashes and death in what even some Belgian missionaries lambasted as a travesty of justice. This opposition resulted in the royal decision to commute the sentence to life in prison. Although Kimbangu remained in captivity for thirty years, the movement he had initiated never abated until the Kimbanguist Church was finally recognized in 1959.

Liyolo Limbé M'Puanga (1943–   ) is known as Congo's foremost sculptor. Born in Bolobo, a city located on the bend of the Congo River and known for its ivory artists, Liyolo spent his youth in Brazzaville. Gifted in drawing, he continued studying art in Kinshasa before settling in Vienna, Austria, in the late 1960s and earning a degree in sculpture at the Academy of Arts of Vienna. After returning home in 1970, he became a prolific artist and produced numerous works in bronze, copper, and brass for Mobutu's presidential palaces in Kinshasa and Gbadolite and for several other public institutions.

Lumumba, Patrice (1925–1961), was Congo's foremost statesman and prime minister. Born in Katako Kombé, he studied at a Protestant mission school, wrote essays and poems, and became an accountant. He was imprisoned for embezzlement and on his release became active in politics, founding and leading the Congolese National Movement. Lumumba departed from the federalist views held by most Congolese politicians during the decolonization period by advocating national unity. When Congo became an independent republic in June 1960, he was made prime minister. Shortly after independence, the army mutinied and the Belgians flew in troops to protect their citizens and their economic interests. Almost immediately the Katanga province, the country's main mineral reservoir, seceded from the central government. Lumumba worked tirelessly to prevent the country's unity from falling apart and the Belgians from sabotaging its independence. He appealed to the United Nations and the United States government for military and diplomatic support to reestablish order only to find himself the victim of a Western-orchestrated plan to oust him from power. In September, President Kasavubu dismissed him, and although Lumumba fought back by dismissing Kasavubu in turn, his days in power were numbered. Shortly after his dismissal he was confined under house arrest by colonel Mobutu, who acted on behalf of the United States and the Belgian government. He managed to escape but was captured, detained for a few weeks in Thysville, and then flown to Elisabethville, where he was murdered in January 1961 along with his former cabinet ministers and companions, Joseph Okito and Maurice Mpolo.

Mahele Lieko Bokungu, Marc (1941–1997), was the last commander of FAZ (1996–1997) before Mobutu's overthrow. While the AFDL troops were closing in on Kinshasa, Mahele was urged by several Western governments to broker a deal with the rebels and put in place a "soft landing" in order to avoid any bloodbath in Kinshasa. He did order his troops not to put up resistance to Laurent Kabila's rebels but to keep order in Kinshasa until they arrived. This was perceived by hardliners among Mobutu's presidential guards as an act of betrayal. On the day Mobutu ceded power and fled the country, they gunned him down.

Malula, Joseph (1917–1989), was born in Kinshasa of a Luba father and a Mongo mother. Trained in theology in the Great Seminary of Kabwe alongside Congo's first president, Kasavubu, Malula was ordained as a priest in 1946. In 1959 he became Congo's third bishop and was the first Congolese religious official to campaign for independence. In 1969, he was named cardinal by Pope Paul VI following his appointment as archbishop of Kinshasa. During much of the 1970s, Malula and the government were at loggerheads over how to interpret and implement Mobutu's policies of "authenticity." As a consequence of his defiant opposition, he was forced to exile in Rome for five months. After being reinstated, he adopted a moderate attitude toward Mobutu's regime. He died in Louvain, Belgium, on June 14, 1989.

Mobutu, Joseph-Désiré (1930–1997), was born in Lisala into a modest family. His father, Albéric Gbemani, was a cook for a bush mission. In 1950, Mobutu enrolled in the Force Publique in Kinshasa as a journalist. In 1958 he joined Lumumba's party and served in Lumumba's first cabinet as secretary for administrative and political affairs before being appointed commander of the army with the task of crushing the Katanga secession. Claiming that politicians had failed to end the civil war, Mobutu staged a first coup in 1960, suspended all institutions, and installed a provisory college of commissioners (Collège des Commissaires), which proved to be mired by constant conflict, and finally relinquished power back to Kasavubu. He staged a second coup in 1965 and this time retained power. His reign was one of the longest and most authoritarian in postcolonial Africa. He was finally toppled from power in 1997 by AFDL rebels led by Laurent-Désiré Kabila. He died of prostate cancer in Morocco on September 7, 1997.

Mosengo Pasinya, Laurent (1939–   ), studied theology at the Seminary of Kabwe and at the University of Rome. He first taught theology at UNAZA before being appointed bishop of Kisangani in 1981. During the transition he served as the chairman of the Sovereign National Conference and succeeded, despite Mobutu's repeated attempts to sabotage the entire process, in preserving the credibility of the democratic transition.

Mulele, Pierre (1929–1968), was a radical firebrand who followed Lumumba's nationalistic ideology and waged a guerrilla war against Mobutu's regime in the 1960s. Participant in the Independence Roundtable, he was elected national deputy of the PSA in 1960. Lumumba appointed him minister of national education in his first cabinet. Loyal to Lumumba's ideas, Mulele vowed to resist the central government and organized an opposition movement in his home province of Kwilu starting in 1963. In 1968, lured by a promise of amnesty brokered by Congo-Brazzaville's president Marien Ngouabi, he came back to Brazzaville. Mobutu dispatched his minister of foreign affairs, Justin Bomboko, aboard the presidential yacht, to welcome Mulele as a brother and bring him back home. He was murdered immediately following his return to Kinshasa.

Nguza Karl-I-Bond, Jean (1938–   ), born at Musamba, the historical capital of the Lunda Empire, served several terms as Mobutu's minister of foreign affairs. In 1977, he was arrested and sentenced to death but was released the following year to serve another term as minister of foreign affairs. In 1981, he went on a voluntary exile in Brussels and became an ardent opponent to Mobutu's regime, but once again he ingratiated himself back to power and served as Zaire's ambassador in Washington. His political career took a downturn after the demise of Mobutu. He now lives in reclusion in South Africa.

Panda Farnana, Paul (1888–1930), was one of the first Congolese intellectuals. He went to Belgium as a child and studied agronomy and business at the universities of Vilvorde and Mons. In 1909, he returned to Congo to work for the colonial administration in the Bas-Congo region. During World War I he enrolled in the Belgian army and fought to defend the city of Namur against German invasion but was captured and imprisoned in German camps for the rest of the war. After the war, he created the Congolese Union (a mutual aid organization of Congolese living in Belgium) and participated in various Pan-Africanist conferences. He became a staunch advocate of the rights of colonial subjects and a critic of the Belgian colonial administration.

Sakombi, Dominique (1940–   ), was born in Kinshasa. During most of Mobutu's presidency he served as minister of information and propaganda and as such was responsible for engineering Mobutu's public image of a benevolent autocrat. During the transitional period he retired from politics to engage in religious activity with the Business Men of the Full Gospel, proclaiming himself a born-again Christian and minister. Many were surprised when he came back to serve in Laurent Kabila's cabinet as minister of information.

Samba, Cheri (1956–   ), Congo's foremost popular artist, was born in Kinito-Mvuila, Congo. In 1976, after his family moved from the Bas-Congo region to Kinshasa, Samba started a prolific career as a popular painter preoccupied with representing urban scenes and issues such as AIDS, polygamy, and infidelity. He remains one of the rarest African painters to be recognized by Western art dealers and connoisseurs.

Tchibamba, Lomami (1914–1985), author of several literary works, including his acclaimed *Ngando* (*The Crocodile*), which obtained a prize at the Fair of Brussels in 1948. He was born in Brazzaville from Lulua parentage and became deaf before completing his secondary studies. Before embarking on a literary career, he worked as a journalist for the newspaper *La Voix du Congolais*. In 1949, after being continually harassed for denouncing the Belgian colonial regime, he fled to Brazzaville and returned only after independence. He continued writing poems and short novels until his death.

Tshisekedi, Étienne (1932–   ), is known for his unyielding opposition to Mobutu's regime. Born in Kananga, he moved to Kinshasa to study law and, in 1963, became the first Congolese with a doctorate degree in law from Lovanium University. Before creating the most important opposition party (UDPS), Tshisekedi served in Mobutu's successive cabinets as interior minister and minister of justice. In this later capacity he helped draft the constitution of 1967. During the 1970s, he continued to be an active member of the MPR after serving as its national secretary in 1968. His opposition to Mobutu's regime started in the late 1970s. In the 1980s, he emerged as a strong voice of dissent against Mobutu's autocratic rule. He was elected and appointed prime minister several times during the democratic transitional period before being dismissed by Mobutu. With all political activities banned in Congo since 1997 and all opposition parties forced to operate underground, Tshisekedi's political career has been seriously compromised. He appears to have lost the immense popularity that had made him, in the early 1990s, the people's candidate for Mobutu's succession.

Tshombe, Moïse (1919–1969), was Congo's most controversial politician and statesman during the First Republic. Born in Musumba, Congo, he was the son-in-law of the contemporary Mwaant Yaav. He served on the Katanga Provincial Council (1951–1953) and became leader of CONAKAT, the Lunda-based party that spearheaded Katanga's secession on July 11, 1960 after it won a majority in Katanga's provincial Assembly. The UN sent troops into Katanga, and Tshombe escaped to Spain. He was recalled from exile and made premier of the united Congo (Kinshasa) Republic (1964) but was later dismissed (1965). He returned to Spain, where he was kidnapped, taken to Algeria (1967), and detained under house arrest on charges of treason. He died in custody under suspicious conditions.

Wamba dia Wamba, Ernest (1943–   ), is originally from the Bas-Congo region. Trained in the U.S., he held several academic positions there before taking a position as professor of history at the University of Dar es Salaam in Tanzania in 1980. A scholar and an activist for the cause of democracy, Professor Wamba has long been an opponent of the Mobutu regime. Since 1997, he has been at the head of several rebel movements (most recently the Congolese Democratic Movement) that aimed to topple President Laurent Kabila.

Wemba, Papa (1949–   ), is Africa's king of soukous (a popular musical form in central Africa). He was born in the Kasai region and very early on learned music and song as he accompanied his mother to wake ceremonies, where she performed as a professional singer and mourner. In 1969, he actively participated in the creation of Zaïko Langa Langa, one of the Congolese bands that forged a new musical style in the 1970s. Since 1986, Papa Wemba has been living in Paris, where he has made incursions into the world music genre, allowing him to perform in Japan, Europe, and North America.

Wendo, Antoine (1925–   ), born in Mushie, is known as the pioneer of Congolese popular music. A prodigy, Wendo taught himself music at the age of twelve and became a most accomplished musician, mixing Afro-Cuban beats with Congolese traditional rhythms and European folk songs. He created the first Congolese band of urban popular music in the 1940s and released a song, "Marie-Louise," regarded by many as the first recorded hit in the history of Congolese urban music. His career took a downturn starting in the late 1950s with the emergence of fast-paced musical styles and the success of younger talents. Wendo lived in poverty during most of Mobutu's era despite a few attempts to return to stage. But when Kabila took over in 1997, he was among the many artists that benefited from the largesse of the new regime.

Selected Bibliography

Given the profusion of literature concerning Congo, these bibliographical recommendations could only be suggestive. They are intended mostly for English speakers and as such do not include the abundant literature written in French. The best bibliographical aid in the study of Congo is Dawn Bastian Williams, Robert W. Lesh, and Andrea L. Stamm, *Zaire* (World Bibliographical Series, vol. 176; Oxford: Clio Press, 1995).

CHAPTER 1

Students who want a general approach should consult Sandra W. Meditz and Tim Merrill, eds., *Zaïre: A Country Study*. (Area Handbook Series; Washington, D.C.: The American University Press, 1994). Though slanted by colonial prejudice, George Martelli, *Leopold to Lumumba: A History of the Belgian Congo, 1877–1960* (London: Chapman & Hall Ltd., 1962), provides the first valuable overview of Congo's colonial history by an English author; while Edgar O'Ballance, *The Congo-Zaire Experience, 1960–1998* (New York: St. Martin's Press, 2000), remains an easily readable chronological review of political events since independence. Tshilemalema Mukenge's study, *Culture and Customs of the Congo* (Westport, CT: Greenwood Press, 2002), should be mentioned here as well for its readability and unique thematic approach. Congo's vast landscapes as well as its diverse peoples have attracted the interest of many European travelers as early as the sixteenth century. The vast Congo River is of course the main attraction and has generated an enormous corpus of travelogues since Joseph Conrad's classical fiction, *Heart of Darkness* (first published in 1902). Of particular interest is Peter Forbath, *The River Congo: The Discovery, Exploration and Exploitation of the World's Most Dramatic River* (New York: Harper & Row, 1977); and Helen Winternitz, *East Along the Equator: A Journey Up the Congo and Into Zaire* (New York: The Atlantic Monthly Press, 1987), an essay of political journalism that provides firsthand insights into the devastating effects of the United States' support of Mobutu's regime.

CHAPTER 2

Jan Vansina has made many important contributions to the study of Congo's precolonial polities. Among them is his pioneering *Kingdoms of the Savanna* (Madison: The University of Wisconsin Press, 1966). For an update see his *Paths in the Rainforests: Toward a History of Political Tradition in Equatorial Africa* (Madison: The University of Wisconsin Press, 1990). Of all the precolonial states Kongo is by far the most well known and studied: see George Balandier, *Daily Life in the Kingdom of the Kongo: From the Sixteenth to the Eighteenth Century* (New York: Meridian Books, 1969); Anne Hilton, *The Kongo Kingdom* (Oxford: Clarendon Press, 1985); and John Thornton, *The Kingdom of Kongo: Civil War and Transition, 1641–1718* (Madison: The University of Wisconsin Press, 1983). There are a few studies that look at the Luba-Lunda states. Among the most comprehensive is Thomas Q. Reefe, *The Rainbow and the Kings: A History of the Luba Empire to 1891* (Berkeley: University of California Press, 1981). See also Ndaywel è Nziem, "The Political System of the Luba and Lunda: Its Emergence and Expansion," in B. A. Ogot, ed., *General History of Africa V: Africa from the Sixteenth to the Eighteenth Century* (Berkeley: University of California Press; Paris: Unesco, 1992), pp. 588–607. The history of the peoples of the rainforest is probably the least documented, and further research tapping into the wealth of oral tradition is sorely needed. Nevertheless we should mention the important anthropological work of Colin M. Turnbull, *The Forest People* (New York: Simon and Schuster, 1961). See also Elikia M'Bokolo, "From the Cameroon Grasslands to the Upper Nile," in B. A. Ogot, ed., *General History of Africa V: Africa from the Sixteenth to the Eighteenth Century* (Berkeley: University of California Press; Paris: Unesco, 1992), pp. 515–545; and Jan Vansina, "The Peoples of the Forest," in David Birmingham and Phyllis Martin, eds., *History of Central Africa,* vol. 1 (London: Longman, 1983), pp. 75–117. The significance of international trade and its impact on Congo's precolonial polities is discussed in Robert W. Harms, *River of Wealth, River of Sorrow: The Central Zaire Basin in the Era of the Slave and Ivory Trade, 1500–1891* (New Haven: Yale University Press, 1981).

CHAPTER 3

Volumes devoted to the Belgian colonial conquest of Congo have not been numerous, and students interested in this period will glean much information by consulting the following works: Roger Anstey, *Britain and the Congo in the Nineteenth Century* (Oxford: Clarendon Press, 1962); W. Holman Bentley, *Pioneering on the Congo* (London: Religious Tract Society, 1900); and, of course, Henry M. Stanley, *In Darkest Africa* (New York: Scribner's, 1891), along with his second account, *Through the Dark Continent* (London: G. Newnes, 1899). Besides Stanley's own work there exist several panegyric studies of his personality and expeditions; see for example, Frank McLynn, *Stanley: The Making of an African Explorer* (London: Constable, 1989). Adam Hochschild, *King Leopold's Ghost: A Story of Greed, Terror and Heroism in Colonial Africa* (New York: Houghton Mifflin Company, 1998) provides a carefully documented and well-crafted analysis of both Stanley and Leopold's inroads into Congo.

CHAPTER 4

Leopold's brutal rule in Congo has attracted the attention of many scholars and activists. The pioneer assessment of Leopoldian Congo is Edmund D. Morel, *Red Rubber: The Story of the Rubber Slave Trade Flourishing on the Congo in the Year of Grace 1906* (New York: Nassau Print, 1906; reprinted, New York: Negro Universities Press, 1969). But one should also look at the recent work by Pagan Kennedy, *Black Livingstone: A True Tale of Adventure in the 19th-Century Congo* (New York: Viking Press, 2002), a biography of the African-American Southern Presbyterian missionary William Sheppard, who first alerted the international community to the "crime against humanity" perpetrated by Leopold's agents in Congo. Neal Ascherson, *The King Incorporated: Leopold the Second and the Congo* (London: George Allen & Unwin Ltd., 1963; reprinted, London: Granta, 1999), traces the roots of Congo's "failed state" back to the Leopoldian era and Belgian short-sighted colonialism. Two comparable studies that are less critical of Leopold's rule are Lewis H. Gann and Peter

Duignan, *Rulers of Belgian Africa, 1884–1914* (Princeton: Princeton University Press, 1979); and Ruth Slade, *King Leopold's Congo: Aspects of the Development of Race Relations in the Congo Independent State* (London, New York: Oxford University Press, 1962), which provides a good historical account from the first European explorations to the creation of Belgian Congo and looks at how Africans reacted to the presence of Europeans. For an indictment of Leopold's rule in Congo, the most insightful accounts are Mark Twain, *King Leopold's Soliloquy* (Boston: P. R. Warren, 1905; reprinted, New York: International Publishers, 1970); S. J. S. Cookey, *Britain and the Congo Question, 1885–1913* (New York: Humanities Press, 1968); and Roger Anstey, "The Congo Rubber Atrocities: A Case Study," *African Historical Studies* 4 (1971): 61–74. The best account of this period is undoubtedly Adam Hochschild's aforementioned study, *King Leopold's Ghost*.

CHAPTER 5

Of the works dealing specifically with the political and social developments in Belgian Congo before World War II, nothing compares with Bruce Fetter's two volumes, *Colonial Rule and Regional Imbalance in Central Africa* (Boulder: University of Colorado Press, 1983) and *The Creation of Elisabethville, 1910–1940* (Stanford: Stanford University Press, 1976). There are good general studies of the entire colonial period, including several that tend to extol "wise policy" in Africa. These are Roger Anstey, *King Leopold's Legacy: The Congo Under Belgian Rule, 1908–1960* (London: Oxford University Press, 1966); and Georges Brausch, *Belgian Administration in the Congo* (London: Oxford University Press, 1961). A less laudatory overview is provided in Ruth Slade, *The Belgian Congo* (London: Oxford University Press, 1961); and Maurice Hennessy, *The Congo: A Brief History and Appraisal* (New York: Frederick A. Praeger, 1961). An exhaustive examination of religious groups that challenged Belgian colonial rule is presented in Ephraim Anderson, *Messianic Popular Movements in the Lower-Congo* (Uppsala: Studia Ethnographica Uppsaliensia, 1958). Several studies of the most important of these religious revivalist movements exist: see, for example, Marie-Louise Martin, *Kimbangu: An African Prophet and His Church* (trans. D. M. Moore, Grand Rapids, MI: Eerdmans Publishing Company, 1976). Monographs of interest dealing with colonial agricultural economy include D.K. Fieldhouse, *Unilever Overseas: The Anatomy of a Multinational, 1895–1965* (London: Croom Helm, 1978); David Northrup, *Beyond the Bend in the River: African*

Labor in Eastern Zaire, 1865–1940 (Athens: Ohio University Center for International Studies, 1988); Samuel H. Nelson, *Colonialism in the Congo Basin, 1880–1940* (Athens: Ohio University Center for International Studies, 1994); and Osumaka Likaka, *Rural Society and Cotton in Colonial Zaire* (Madison: The University of Wisconsin Press, 1997).

CHAPTER 6

Of importance in understanding the factors that led the Belgians to grant independence to Congo are several works written during the first decade of independence. They are obviously tinged by the political uncertainties that beset Congo's emancipation from Belgian rule. These works include Alan P. Merriam, *Congo: Background of Conflict* (Evanston: Northwestern University Press, 1961); René Lemarchand, *Political Awakening in the Belgian Congo* (Berkeley and Los Angeles: University of California Press, 1964); Crawford Young, *Politics in the Congo: Decolonization and Independence* (Princeton: Princeton University Press, 1965); and Herbert Weiss, *Political Protest in the Congo: The Parti Solidaire Africain during the Independence Struggle* (Princeton: Princeton University Press, 1967).

CHAPTER 7

Early studies about postcolonial Congo cover only the first few years during which the country was embroiled in a long, bloody strife. As a result there is an unfortunate emphasis on political events and almost nothing concerning social and cultural developments. A clear exposition of this period is Catherine Hoskyns, *The Congo Since Independence, January 1960–December 1961* (London: Oxford University Press, 1965). The chaotic transition from colonial rule to independence is treated in Colin Legum, *Congo Disaster* (Baltimore: Penguin Books, 1961). Howard M. Epstein, ed., *Revolt in the Congo, 1960–1964* (New York: Armor Books, 1974), is an excellent collection of essays on the rebellions that threatened to dismember the country. For the U.S. involvement in the Congolese crisis, one should consult Stephen R. Weissman, *American Foreign Policy in the Congo, 1960–1964* (Ithaca and London: Cornell University Press, 1974); and David N. Gibbs, *The Political Economy of Third World Intervention: Mines, Money, and U.S. Policy in the Congo Crisis* (Chicago: The University of Chicago Press, 1991). The abundant literature about Congo's first and only democratically elected leader has been recently updated in Ludo De

Witte, *The Assassination of Lumumba* (New York: Verso, 2001), which puts forth the provocative argument that although the U.S. government acting through the CIA had repeatedly attempted to physically eliminate Lumumba, it was the Belgians that orchestrated Lumumba's murder. The French version of De Witte's work was published in 2000 and prompted the opening of a parliamentary commission that proved rather perfunctory. An examination of Lumumba's inner political circle is provided in Thomas Kanza, *The Rise and Fall of Patrice Lumumba* (Cambridge, MA: Schenkman, 1979). A unique work with numerous speeches delivered by Congo's premier is Patrice Lumumba, *Congo, My Country* (London: Pall Mall Press, 1962).

CHAPTER 8

A comprehensive text covering in detail Mobutu's Zaire is Winsome J. Leslie, *Zaire: Continuity and Political Change in an Oppressive State* (Boulder, CO: Westview Press, 1993). Crawford Young and Thomas Turner, *The Rise and Decline of the Zairian State* (Madison: The University of Wisconsin Press, 1985), is the most authoritative study on the inner mechanisms that led to the decay of Zaire's political institutions under Mobutu. Published only a few years after Mobutu's takeover, Jean-Claude Willame's study, *Patrimonialism and Political Change in the Congo* (Stanford: Stanford University Press, 1972), deals with the same issue at a time when Mobutu's system had yet to display its full arsenal of corruption and oppression. In addition to the two volumes cited above, Thomas M. Callaghy, *The State-Society Struggle: Zaire in Comparative Perspective* (New York: Columbia University Press, 1984), provides an important contribution to state formation and authoritarian drive under Mobutu. So does John F. Clark, "The Nature and Evolution of the State in Zaïre," *Studies in Comparative International Development* 32, no. 4 (winter 1998), pp. 3–23. A scathing but reliable analysis of the repressive nature of Mobutu's regime is Michael G. Schatzberg, *The Dialectics of Oppression in Zaire* (Bloomington and Indianapolis: Indiana University Press, 1988). For those interested in the role the United States has played in supporting Mobutu's plundering of his country's wealth, there are several works of similar nature, including Michael G. Schatzberg, *Mobutu or Chaos: The United States and Zaire, 1960–1990* (Lanham, MD: The University Press of America, 1991); Sean Kelly, *America's Tyrant: The CIA and Mobutu of Zaire* (Washington, D.C.: The American University Press, 1993); and Jonathan Kwitny, *Endless Enemies: The Making of an Unfriendly World* (New York:

Congdon & Weed, Inc., 1984). Although many studies have underscored the evil of Mobutu's rule, a few apologists have attempted to provide a more optimistic perspective; see, for example, Jeffrey M. Elliot and Mervyn M. Dymally, *Voices of Zaire: Rhetoric or Reality?* (Washington, D.C.: The Washington Institute Press, 1990). For a multidimensional approach to the collapse of the Zairean economy during the first two decades of Mobutu's rule, there are two similar and remarkable volumes: Guy Gran, ed., *Zaire: The Political Economy of Underdevelopment* (New York: Praeger, 1979); and Nzongola-Ntalaja, ed., *The Crisis in Zaire: Myths and Realities* (Trenton: Africa World Press, Inc., 1986). Although limited in scope to only one city, Janet MacGaffey, *Entrepreneurs and Parasites: The Struggle for Indigenous Capitalism in Zaire* (Cambridge: Cambridge University Press, 1987), provides a well-balanced analysis of the emergence of an indigenous bourgeoisie in Zaire in spite of the economic crisis. For a more recent analysis of Congo's informal sector, one should look at Kisangani N. F. Emizet, "Confronting Leaders at the Apex of the State: The Growth of the Unofficial Economy in Congo," *African Studies Review* 41, no. 1 (April 1998), pp. 99–137. In studying Mobutu's era one should not neglect firsthand accounts: Lieve Joris, *Back to the Congo* (New York: Atheneu, 1992); and Michela Wrong, *In the Footsteps of Mr. Kurtz: Living on the Brink of Disaster in Mobutu's Congo* (New York: HarperCollins Publishers, 2000), are among the most satisfactory.

CHAPTER 9

Although this and the subsequent chapter make much use of material drawn from newspapers and other media, it is also based on the few existing scholarly studies that deal with the Transition period. Leslie J. Winsome, *Zaire: Continuity and Political Change in an Oppressive State* (Boulder, CO: Westview Press, 1993), especially the last chapter, clearly delineates the political contradictions that hindered democratization. For a more detailed analysis one should read a few remarkable works: Tongele Ngbatana, *From Congo to Zaire to Congo: Challenges and Prospects for the 21st Century* (North Highland, CA: Transnational Printing Services, 1997); Kisangani Emizet's original monograph, *Zaire after Mobutu: A Case of Humanitarian Emergency* (Helsinki, Finland: United Nations University and World Institute for Development Economics Research, 1997), which provides precious economic data and analyses that shed light on Congo's recurrent humanitarian emergencies; Osita G. Afoaku, "Zaire's March Toward Democracy: Constraints and Opportunities," *The Western Journal of Black Studies* 20, no. 2 (1996), pp. 72–82; and George Nzongola-Ntalaja, *From Zaire to the Democratic Republic of the Congo* (Uppsala: Nordiska Afrikainstitutet, 1998). The involvement of the U.S. government in helping Kabila to unseat Mobutu is treated in Wayne Madsen, *Genocide and Covert Operations in Africa, 1993–1999* (New York: The Edwin Mellen Press, 1999). Jeffrey Tayler, *Facing the Congo: A Modern Journey into the Heart of Darkness* (New York: Three Rivers Press, 2000), is a gripping account of an American journalist based in Russia who embarks on a bold trip down the Congo in emulation of Henry Morton Stanley's legendary cross-continent trek. The book is filled with vivid accounts of how Congolese cope with their collapsing economy.

CHAPTER 10

A careful and exhaustive study of the war that has engulfed Congo since 1998 is sorely needed. The publication of John F. Clark's edited volume, *The African Stakes of the Congo War* (New York: Palgrave, 2002), is eagerly awaited to fill the gap of our knowledge about the international dimension of the war in Congo. Until then we should rely on Herbert Weiss, *War and Peace in the Democratic Republic of the Congo* (Uppsala: Nordiska Afrikainstitutet, 2000), which chronicles the causes and the evolution of the conflict up until the Lusaka Peace Agreement. The International Crisis Group (ICG), a private, multinational organization committed to helping the international community gather information in order to prevent and contain conflicts worldwide, has issued three reports about the ongoing war in Congo: ICG Democratic Republic of Congo Report no. 4, *Africa's Seven Nation War*, 21 May 1999; ICG Africa Report no. 26, *Scramble for the Congo: Anatomy of an Ugly War*, 20 December 2000; and ICG African Report no. 27, *From Kabila to Kabila: Prospects for Peace in the Congo*, 16 March 2001. (All are available to the general public on the ICG Web site, http://crisisweb.org.). Though prescriptive and programmatic, these reports contain stimulating, firsthand analyses about the Congolese quagmire. The horrors of Rwanda and Uganda's occupation of eastern Congo are documented in Yaa-Lengi M. Ngemi, *Genocide in the Congo (Zaire): In the Name of Bill Clinton, and of the Paris Club, and of the Mining Conglomerates, So It Is!* (New York: Writers Club Press, 2000).

Index

About the Author

CH. DIDIER GONDOLA is Assistant Professor of History at Indiana University–Purdue University at Indianapolis (IUPUI). A specialist of urban colonial history and popular cultures, he has published numerous articles on youth cultures, music, fashion, and memory. His first book, *Villes Miroirs: migrations et identités urbaines à Kinshasa et Brazzaville, 1930–1970* (Paris, 1997), explores the use of popular cultures by African migrants in Kinshasa and Brazzaville. His current research deals with the production of cultural spaces of resistance and African anti-colonial discourses in Congo-Brazzaville.